SOCIOLOGY Made Simple

The Made Simple Series
has been created
especially for self-education
but can equally well
be used as
an aid to group study.
However complex the subject,
the reader is taken
step by step,
clearly and methodically,
through the course. Each volume
has been prepared by experts,
taking account of
modern educational requirements,
to ensure the most
effective way of
acquiring knowledge.

In the same series

SOCIOLOGY   Made Simple

Jane L. Thompson, BA

MADE SIMPLE
BOOKS

Made Simple Books
An imprint of Heinemann Professional Publishing Ltd
Halley Court, Jordan Hill, Oxford OX2 8EJ

OXFORD   LONDON   MELBOURNE   AUCKLAND   SINGAPORE
IBADAN   NAIROBI   GABORONE   KINGSTON

First edition, 1982
Reprinted 1985
Reprinted 1987
Reprinted 1989

ISBN 0 434 98508 2

Made and printed in Great Britain by
Richard Clay Ltd, Bungay, Suffolk

Preface

The theories and practice of sociology as a legitimate way of examining society, social relationships and social behaviour date back well into the last century, but it is only recently—in the last twenty years or so—that sociology has become a popular subject for study in schools, colleges and universities.

The questions asked by sociologists and the kinds of evidence they identify to support their studies have become a powerful influence on policy-making, and the social issues raised by sociologists are now commonplace in political discussions and in the media.

The content of contemporary sociology is something which the general reader may well feel familiar with—family life, education, social class, employment, crime, politics and welfare, for example—but familiarity is only one form of knowledge. What is familiar, and indeed 'common sense', to one individual or social group is frequently outside the experience or understanding of another. Patriarchy is a good example: different groups—if you were to question them about it—would have very different definitions of patriarchy and very different explanations for its existence and experiences of its implications.

Sociology attempts to provide a systematic and profound examination of social organisation and behaviour, and by the generation and application of various theories about society, describe and interpret the complexities and significance of human social relationships. It is an exciting area of study and often a challenging one. Many who come to sociology for the first time are provoked into asking questions about the significance of the familiar which they had long 'taken for granted', and often the answers lead to a thorough re-examination of their own attitudes, values and opinions.

In this book I have tried to introduce you to some of the issues being discussed in contemporary sociology in a way which I hope will raise interesting questions in your mind and point the way to further reading and study should you want it. The book should not only be of interest to the general reader but of positive assistance to students engaged in an A level sociology course or an introductory college or university course. There is a revision section at the end of each chapter in which you can check your understanding and practise essay writing, and guidance is given to further reading. A full glossary explains in simple language the kind of technical terms you are likely to come across in both this book and other introductory readers.

JANE L. THOMPSON
University of Southampton
August 1981

For Sidney and Helen Thompson

Contents

1

WHAT IS SOCIOLOGY?

In today's world most people have probably heard of sociology. If you regularly watch television documentaries or discussion programmes you will have noticed sociologists introduced as special experts who are supposed to know about 'social problems' and 'other people's behaviour'. They often appear to be rather earnest, radical types with a dishevelled appearance and left-wing political ideas. They either use terms few people understand, like referring to the family as an 'ideological state apparatus', or terms that sound very political like 'bourgeois' and 'capitalist'. Sometimes they appear to be talking in everyday language—about 'culture' and 'social class', for example—except that the meanings they give to these words seem to be different somehow.

It is only fairly recently that sociology and sociologists have become familiar to people generally in this way. When I left school in 1965 and applied to study sociology at university, I had little idea what it was about, or what I was letting myself in for. I can remember the interview with horror. When asked why I wanted to study sociology by the fearful, elderly professor with thick glasses and a pronounced mid-European accent, I announced bravely, 'Because I want to help people.' 'Then why don't you become a bus conductress?' he replied. Since the early sixties there has been a considerable growth in the popularity of sociology, so that today most people know of its existence. I am not sure they are much better informed about what it all means than I was in 1965, however.

Sociology and the Social Sciences

Sociology is about **social behaviour**, why people behave as they do, what factors in society affect their behaviour, how groups of people in society organise themselves and come to be as they are. Of course, an interest in 'people' could be claimed by almost every academic discipline in one way or another. Even nuclear scientists cannot fail to take account of the behaviour and expectations of the people in the society in which they work. But sociology is about more than an 'awareness of' or 'an interest' in people. It is an attempt to study, in as scientific and systematic a way as possible, **how societies operate**. This means trying to 'stand back' from society a little—watching, recording, measuring, evaluating and interpreting what is going on, and

1

trying to explain how and why so many of the things we all take for granted about society come to be as they are.

Of course, societies are made up of countless individuals, all different from each other in many respects. The idiosyncracies of individual behaviour, which in part cause different people to think and react differently, are of interest to sociologists, but are probably more the concern of psychologists. Both disciplines are closely related, but whereas the psychologist tends to start from the individual, the sociologist usually concentrates on the **social group** he or she belongs to. Sociologists look more for similarities and patterns that can be detected in the behaviour of numbers of individuals who maybe share the same environment or social class or nationality. They try to make **accurate generalisations** about the characteristics of human behaviour and social organisation, to identify what causes them and to suggest what their implications might be. It is probably this kind of concern that has in the minds of many laymen earned the sociologist the reputation of being 'nosey'.

The interests of social historians, economists and political scientists are often confused with those of sociologists too. Like psychology, their areas of work are closely related. In fact, together they comprise the main group of subjects usually referred to as the **social sciences**. Because each discipline sets out to study some aspect of social behaviour there is a good deal of overlap between them in terms of subject matter and they are certainly dependent on each other's expertise. But there are differences of emphasis which are crucial. The historian is concerned principally with recording what has happened in the past, the economist with the financial business and trading arrangements made by societies, and the political scientist with the ways in which societies govern themselves and distribute political power and responsibility. Each has developed its own theories, methods of study, frames of reference and terminology. Together it is not surprising that they reflect a range of different interpretations and points of view, as well as encouraging more than a little professional rivalry. But equally, together they make a fuller understanding of the complexities of human behaviour possible.

Sociology and Science

Because the attention of sociologists is focused on all of these areas—social change, the distribution of wealth, political power and many others—critics often ask, 'So what is special about sociology? Is it just a mixture of everything else?' As the work of contemporary sociologists has become more familiar to people, however, their distinctive contribution has become more obvious. Increasingly, people are coming to appreciate that to study social behaviour properly, a knowledge of different theories, specialist skills and carefully collected evidence are all essential. There is a good deal of disagreement about which theories, what skills and whose evidence, however, as we shall see later.

In addition, because sociologists have tended to concentrate their studies on what society usually regards as 'problems' such as poverty, delinquency and racial tensions, their findings have always been closely related to the absence or imposition of social policies and have been widely debated in the media. It is this connection which has contributed to the belief that sociologists 'help' people or 'hinder' them, depending on your particular viewpoint. And since most of what they say about society seems to be critical, they are also regarded as politically radical. Both of these are beliefs which sociologists like my 'fearful professor' would reject. Sociologists like him see themselves as neutral scientists who investigate and analyse different kinds of behaviour with reference to relevant theories and supported by evidence which has been systematically collected. Their aim is accurately to **describe, explain** and **understand**. They would probably argue that it is not the responsibility of sociologists to say what should or should not be done about the phenomena they describe. That should be the job of governments, policy makers and other professionals of various kinds.

This sense of 'scientific detachment' has done a great deal to establish the reputation of sociology as a responsible academic discipline founded on ideals of scientific objectivity and value-free analysis. It has also been the characteristic of sociology which has come under the most persistent attack from within the ranks of sociologists themselves. Many would reject the approach completely and argue that human behaviour is much more difficult to measure scientifically than are natural phenomena. There are so many different social forces affecting behaviour and their interaction and influence is shifting and changing all the time. The intricacies and complexities of human society working on so many different levels and with so many different twists and turns of relationship, demand inspiration, insight and even imagination to make sense of it all—not something that can easily happen in tightly controlled laboratory conditions. Also it is very difficult, and some would say impossible, to be neutral about what is being studied. Because sociologists are also human with human values, prejudices and traditions they cannot help but be affected by these when they decide what to study, how best to study it and what conclusions to draw from their investigations.

Because society is the subject of their study they must also have a view of how society might be improved or changed by what they discover and recommend. Inevitably this will mean disagreement, conflicting theories and controversial interpretations. Present-day social scientists are far less confident about claiming to have dis-

covered 'absolute truths' than their forebears would have been and
talk much more about the 'probabilities' and 'likelihood' of things—
and increasingly about how it all appears to the people who are being
studied. What is *their* interpretation?

But whilst sociology may not be a science in the same way as we
think of laboratory-based experimental physics or chemistry or biology, that is not to say that it cannot be 'scientific'. The tradition of
collecting evidence with which to test and refine theories, and the use
of this evidence, as distinct from opinion or speculation, on which to
base interpretation, are key features of both scientific and sociological
enquiry. Interpretations may in the end vary, and different people
may draw different conclusions from their scrutiny of the evidence,
but they will all have approached it in as systematic and objective a
way as they can. Otherwise they will not have been pursuing sociology.

Early Sociology

Sociology today is a very different discipline from the one which
emerged at the end of the eighteenth century in Europe, faced the
challenges of nineteenth-century social and economic changes, grew in
popularity in Britain after the Second World War and which has been
reviewing and refining itself ever since. It is ironic that at a time
when the name of sociology has never been more commonplace in
everyday language, its composition has never been more complex. To
understand a little of why this is we must look back briefly to its
origins and more recent developments.

The emergence of sociology as a new from of knowledge is usually
reckoned to have been at the end of the eighteenth century when
social philosophers of the time developed very wide-ranging theories
to explain the development of different kinds of societies throughout
human history. But important things happened to the intellectual climate in Europe in the nineteenth century which affected the direction
in which sociology developed and made it much more concerned with
the contemporary world in which the sociologists were living.

As a direct result of the French and Industrial Revolutions a rather
different kind of society emerged in Europe—an industrial capitalist
society. The old social and political relationships based on agriculture,
feudalism, religion and small workshop employment gradually gave
way to a new order based on industry, urbanisation, new forms of
communication and international trade. It was not an overnight
change by any means, and it has since developed and changed yet
further, but in nineteenth-century Europe it had a startling effect on
those who reflected on its implications. Political and social power no
longer depended so much on inherited landed wealth as the emphasis
shifted to industrial production and power to those who controlled it.

At a time when such an arrangement was not so taken for granted as it is today, because it was new, it was an ideal opportunity to devise theories to explain what was happening.

Some feared that social upheavals of such magnitude would lead to the 'breakdown of society' and the loss of the 'community' and 'tradition' they associated with the feudal order. They saw individualism and isolation as the characteristics of the new age which would together destroy what had gone before. Others welcomed the challenge to feudal power and traditional authority and saw the emergence of a new society based on industrial labour as a significant step in the direction of socialist revolution.

The other main influence on sociological thought at the time was the legacy of the Enlightenment. From this intellectual tradition came the fascination with science and the respect for rational systematic study as distinct from philosophising and speculation.

The important sociologists of the time—and the most famous were **Emile Durkheim, Max Weber** and **Karl Marx**—were much influenced by the world in which they lived. But this does not mean that they have nothing to say to us today. Most contemporary sociologists still refer back to the writings of these 'founding fathers' to seek inspiration from their theories and methods of study. Their influence, either directly or indirectly, informs most of what is written today.

Emile Durkheim (1858–1917)

Durkheim's most famous work did a great deal to establish sociology as a science of social life and something separate and distinct from other studies of human behaviour like psychology and biology. His work was **empirical**, which means he relied on observation and the collection of evidence with which to test theories and make predictions about behaviour.

Set against the background of a changing French society he was preoccupied by the relationships between society and the human beings who depended on it. He questioned how society held together and how common values and beliefs and patterns of behaviour came to be.

For Durkheim society was almost like a living body, all its separate organs were linked together and dependent on each other and all had to function properly for the general health and well-being of the whole. When this analogy was applied to society he never questioned whether or not society *should* be preserved as a well-functioning, healthy organism. He assumed that this was something that could be taken for granted, just as he seemed to think that there was a recognisable thing called 'society' which had some kind of existence separate from the individuals who comprised it. The function of institutions like religion, law and education was to provide the common rules, laws, customs, obligations, attitudes, values and climates of opinion which would exercise control over individuals and groups and ensure that they lived cohesively together. His view was of forces external to individuals which had considerable control over them.

One of his most famous studies was that of suicide: not whether it was a good or a bad thing, but an attempt to link the personal act of committing suicide with the social forces in operation which might encourage it. He collected all the available statistics and analysed them in terms of categories like age, sex, religion and family relationships. At the end of his study he was able to show that certain people in certain situations are more likely to commit suicide than others. His method of investigation provided an example to others about how they should conduct investigations empirically, and has been debated, refined and disagreed with ever since. By revealing, for example, that a married, Catholic woman, with several children, was less likely to kill herself than an unmarried, childless, Protestant male, he claimed to have produced scientific generalisations about human behaviour which were not based on individual idiosyncrasies, and which were social facts quite different from what the expertise of biology or psychology could account for.

But although he claimed to be scientific in his approach, Durkheim was obviously very influenced by his own reactions to the society around him, particularly what he took to be the breakdown of social relationships by the forces of industrial capitalism. He described **anomie** as a state of social isolation and rootlessness brought about by the collapse of common values and social order so that people could no longer relate properly to each other or to society.

Max Weber (1864–1920)

Like Durkheim, Weber was also very influenced by the social climate of his times. He believed that other German sociologists, especially those who agreed with Marx' analysis of society, over-exaggerated the influence of economics and did not take enough account of the influence of ideas and the impact of significant individuals on developments like the growth of capitalism. In reaction to what he considered the political bias of some of his colleagues and contemporaries, he championed the ideals of value-free sociology and the need to 'understand' and explain, rather than merely describe, human behaviour.

For Weber one of the main characteristics of industrialisation and social change was the growth of bureaucratic organisation which he saw as a serious threat to individual freedom. The Marxist view that capitalism would ultimately be replaced by socialism caused Weber to predict even stricter bureaucratic controls under socialist organisations.

Weber always made the starting point for his analysis the behaviour of individuals rather than the large-scale and external institutions and forces which sociologists like Durkheim concentrated upon. Whereas Durkheim seemed almost to attribute society with an existence and an identity of its own, as something 'out there', and somehow separate from the individuals who comprised it, Weber was adamant that it was only an abstraction. For Weber society was really only the sum total of lots of individuals interacting together. And in the process of interaction, he believed, they exercised a good deal of mutual influence upon each other's behaviour.

Weber's emphasis on the 'actions' of individuals has had a big influence on the approaches of other sociologists since his death and his own writings are best remembered for his studies of Protestantism in relation to the rise of capitalism, bureaucracy, religion, music and industry.

Karl Marx (1818–1883)

It is not only sociologists but also economists, philosophers, political scientists and even historians who claim Karl Marx as an important contributor to the theory and argument of their particular disciplines. Perhaps it is safest not to label Marx but to refer to him as an analyst of economic, social and political life. Although he was provoked by the industrial and political changes he witnessed in nineteenth-century Europe, and did most of his major writing in Britain, he was not confined to the events of one period of history or the social characteristics of one society. In fact, he was more concerned with 'changing' society than merely trying to 'explain' it. His method of analysis was not to divide politics or economics or history from society, but to try to unite them in theory and practice.

In showing how the capitalist system of industrial production, and the relationship between its owners and workers, had come to be, he always took a historical perspective. He was also concerned to reveal the links between industrial capitalism in one country and economic developments and social relationships in other societies, particularly the 'third-world' empires of the industrial nations.

A third characteristic which demonstrated his refusal to be bound by the present, and underlined his enthusiasm for 'changing society' rather than merely recording it, was the 'predictive' emphasis in his writings. The logic of his historical, comparative and contemporary analysis of society, culminating in the development of capitalism as an economic, social and political means of organisation and control, enabled him to predict how this in turn would give way to something else. Capitalism as a means of organisation and a concentration of power would, he argued, be replaced by socialism.

The political implications of Marx' writings are obvious, and though

claiming to be scientific and systematic, he never adhered to the philosophy of neutrality. He considered the capitalist system to be unjust
and oppressive to the workers who had to provide the labour power
for it to become established. And he predicted, and indeed advocated,
a time in which the control of the wealth and social power produced
by the achievements of industrialisation would be taken over by
workers, so that a different type of society, based on social equality,
could be established.

Whether or not people agree with Marx' economic analysis of
society, and particularly his political sentiments, it is undoubtedly the
case that his writings have had more influence, both directly and indirectly, on subsequent social scientists than those of almost any other
theorist. Modern sociology comprises many who base their analysis
and their work very much on Marxist ideas and frames of reference.
There are others who are not Marxists in outlook or sentiment but
who have none the less incorporated much of his methodology and
many of his concepts into their approach. For these reasons his writings have to be taken seriously.

Marx' view of man was of one who was both 'created' by the social
forces around him, but also a 'creator' of those forces. The tension
between the two, being 'determined by' but also 'seeking to determine',
was for Marx the dynamic which made society always changing. By
far the most important relationship in this process was that between
man and labour. Through work man can become either 'fully human',
in the sense of being fulfilled, creative, autonomous; or stunted. A
man's labour can also keep him unfree, powerless and exploited. The
key for Marx was the conditions under which labour is created and
work is carried out. Under capitalism the worker does not have an
equal relationship with the owner of capital. He must work for the
owner in return for the wages he needs to survive. And his survival
depends on that work and those wages always being available to him.
He does not own the tools he uses, or the machines and factories he
works in. He does not own what he produces, he has little control
over what is produced or how it is produced, and no control over
what becomes of it. In all these respects, the owner is at an advantage.
He owns capital and plant, he has the power to hire and fire workers,
he decides what will be produced, where it will be sold and how much
it will cost. Once he has paid his workers' wages and invested in new
machines and factories to keep production going well, all the remaining profits are his. Both workers and owners are almost automatically
in conflict therefore.

It is in the owner's interest to keep production as high as possible
and wage costs as low as possible to get the maximum amount of
profits for himself. It is in the worker's interests to make sure that he
does not become a 'slave to production' at the expense of his health,

leisure and family life, and that the wages he earns to support himself and his family are as high as possible. It is this conflict of interests between those who own and those who labour which Marx saw as crucial in the explanation of social organisation and social change. It explains why both sides 'organise to outdo each other'.

Important Marxist concepts that you will come across time and again in contemporary sociology are to be found in his explanation of the relationships between men and labour. For example, the notion that because of the unequal relationships of capitalism, workers cannot achieve their full potential and autonomy, is a condition referred to by Marx as **alienation**. The fact that in industry a worker must do more work than is necessary to satisfy his own needs, produces **surplus value** for the capitalist. The inherent conflict of interests between the different elements in social relationships provides the **dialectic**, the growth of one thing out of another, that brings about social change. All of these ideas and more are to be found first in Marx' writing and now in sociological analysis today.

One of the other most important legacies has been to explain the significance of **social class**. Not merely the difference between 'capitalists' and 'workers' or to provide definitions of Marx' use of 'bourgeoisie' and 'proletariat', but a systematic explanation of the links between people's economic circumstances and the ideologies, or sets of ideas, which sustain them. But all of this is quite complicated and we shall look at it again in more detail in Chapter 2.

Different Approaches

You will already have realised that sociology is not one simple, mutually-agreed way of studying society. There are a variety of different approaches within sociology which are based on different theories of society and different methods of investigation. New developments are happening all the time. Many experts still refer to sociology as a 'new' discipline and argue that a lot of the groundwork, which more established subjects take for granted because they have been around for longer, still has to be done in sociology. Perhaps it is more accurate to say that sociologists are continually re-examining their own approaches and their own assumptions about what they study and how they study it. As more aspects of social behaviour come under the scrutiny of sociological enquiry the discipline inevitably splits up and areas like religion, education, industrial relations, deviance, communications, law, family life, etc., have all become specialist concerns. But the important distinctions in sociology today are not these. What is more important is the way in which different sociologists approach their work.

In simple terms, the main distinction is between those who see the patterns and characteristics that can be detected in social behaviour, as things into which people fit or are fitted, and those who see the characteristic patterns as the consequences—both intended and unintended—of the actions and interactions of individuals. In the first, social behaviour is seen as created by forces and institutions outside the control of individuals, which mould them into shape. In the second, human beings, as individuals and members of social groups relating together, produce the impetus for creating the characteristics of the social organisation of their groups and their societies. In the end it is probably most useful to see both of these as different sides of the same coin. But before going on to explain why this might be so, let's look at the two sides in more detail and see how different approaches to sociology fit into them.

One is usually referred to as emphasising **systems** and the other **action**, and their main differences are as shown opposite:

Positivism

Positivism is an approach in sociology which likens it to the natural and physical sciences. In just the same way as the chemist or the physicist collects evidence, tests hypotheses, formulates theories and arrives at general laws about the phenomena they are examining, it is argued that a sociologist must base his explanations on **empirical investigations** not on philosophy or intuition and that he must eliminate all value judgements from his analysis. The main criticisms about the positivist approach and the question of scientific detachment are explained on p. 3.

Functionalism

Functionalism has been one of the most influential approaches in sociology, particularly among twentieth-century British and American sociologists. Its origins go back a long way in the philosophical tradition of considering social institutions in relation to the contribution they make to the overall functioning of society. I referred earlier to the notion of society as an organism, a body whose separate parts had to function properly and in harmony if the whole was to be kept healthy. The English sociologist **Herbert Spencer** (1820–1903) first applied this analogy to society and much of Durkheim's work assumes this kind of relationship.

Contemporary sociologists refer to society as a system rather than an organism but the interest in how various parts of the system relate together is much the same. Functionalist sociology is concerned, therefore, to **analyse the functions** of different parts of the system, to question how they relate to each other and to the whole. In practice this usually means an examination of social subsystems like politics, economics and culture, or institutions like the family, marriage, education, law and religion, among others, to identify the

Systems Approach	Action Approach
1. Emphasis on **social systems**, structures and institutions in society.	1. Emphasis on **social action** and interaction of human beings.
2. A **macro** (global) view of society in which systems and institutions are 'out there' and 'outside' the individual.	2. A **micro** (particularised) study of social action in which what happens is 'in here', 'inside' the heads of individuals.
3. Emphasises **society** in relation to man.	3. Emphasises **man** in relation to society.
4. Stress on **common value** systems and shared norms in society.	4. Interest in the ways in which men **vary** in their interpretations of and reactions to society.
5. Concern about the problems of how society holds together and maintains social order.	5. Interest in how men manage and get control over social institutions.
6. Stress on value freedom, neutrality and objectivity in approach.	6. Recognition of subjectivity in analysis and that the subjective interpretations of reality made by human beings are likely to be different. An interest in the interaction between different subjective realities.
7. A view of social order as something which is **given** or **inherited** from the past and which men passively receive.	7. A view of men actively and continually making and re-making the social order around them.
8. Empirical collection of evidence and data by surveys, questionnaires, statistical analysis, standardised tests and structured interviews. Emphasis on objective facts and figures.	8. Collection of data from participant-observation and open-ended interviews and discussions. Recognition of different subjectives and emphasis on the 'meanings' and 'interpretations' made by men in the process of social action.
9. Sociological theories which involve a **systems analysis** of society include 'functionalism', 'positivism' and some varieties of Marxist sociology.	9. Sociological theories which involve an **action analysis** of society include 'symbolic interactionism', 'phenomenology', 'ethnomethodology' and some varieties of Marxist sociology.
10. The 'founding father' most associated with a Systems Approach was **Emile Durkheim**.	10. The 'founding father' most associated with an Action Approach was **Max Weber**.

links between them and to enumerate the functions they fulfil for society.

There has been quite a reaction against this kind of approach in recent years, however, particularly the **'structural-functionalist'** variety associated with the American sociologists **Talcott Parsons** and **Robert Merton**. The main criticisms concentrate on the implicit assumption in functionalist analysis that there are 'common values' in society and 'common interests' which are best served by the preservation of society. In practice this usually means a rather conservative attitude to social order and social control. This kind of perspective, it is argued, disguises the conflicts and contradictions which exist in every society and underestimates the significance of social change.

There is also the tendency to attribute a kind of 'existence in their own right' to social institutions, as if morality or education, for example, were something you could see, keep in a box or hold in your hand. The danger of seeming to make 'things' out of abstractions is called **reification** and is criticised by those who believe that it ignores the active participation of individuals in creating, re-defining and changing society by their behaviour and interaction.

Even when it is accepted that social institutions exist, and do serve particular functions for society, it does not explain how those institutions came to be in the first place, and what causes them to change over time. The causes of both these phenomena, it is often felt, are inadequately explained by functionalist sociology.

Symbolic Interactionism

The origins of symbolic interactionism are in the writings of **Charles Cooley** (1864–1929) and **George Herbert Mead** (1863–1931), two American sociologists who were greatly influenced by Weber's emphasis on social action but who tended to concentrate on the interaction between individuals and small groups rather than relate the behaviour of individuals to larger social, economic and political structures, as Weber did.

The starting point for an examination of behaviour in this approach is the individual and how the individual is made into the kind of person he becomes by his interaction with others. It is the view of symbolic interactionists, and indeed sociologists generally, that whilst some physical and biological characteristics are inherited by human beings, most of their behaviour is learned and considerably influenced by the social environment they grow up in.

The human infant first begins to learn his identity in the family and, according to Mead, his learning is very dependent on the symbols that mediate between himself and others who are important to him. (In Mead's words, 'significant others'). The growing child learns to attach meanings to symbols such as language, facial expressions, dress, gestures and skin colour in response to the behaviour and reactions of others. Whether it is the difference between a frown or a smile, the knowledge of what gives pleasure or pain, words which indicate whether he's a boy or she's a girl and what's expected of people in these roles, the learning is endless, and is 'internalised' or taken into the consciousness of the young child as he gradually comes to know who he is and to develop a sense of his own identity. Other relationships will continue this process throughout his life as his behaviour responds to the interaction between his own thoughts, feelings and reactions, and those of others he comes into contact with. And, of course, it is not a one-way process. Just as the one is forming and modifying and adapting his behaviour in response to the reactions and expectations of others, they in turn are being affected in their behaviour by their reactions to him.

The 'meanings' that people give to situations and the 'interpretations' they make of actions and events are a crucial feature of this approach. An incident like a fight, for example, might be interpreted quite differently by different people. Some might see it as an act of aggression or deviance, others as an act of self-preservation or frustration. For some it may seem the most logical and normal way to react to emotional disturbance, for others it may be an indication of weakness or lack of self-control. According to this perspective there is no such thing as only one social reality. There are many realities and each is different and dependent upon the context in which they occur and the past experiences and present identities of the different observers.

Equally, people attribute different 'meanings' to what might seem to be the same experience. An enquiry into someone's personal life may 'mean' a gesture of friendship or a nosey intrusion. Some people may mean a lot when they offer friendship. Others may mean very little. The same words, looks and gestures exchanged between two people may mean totally different things to each of them. But in each case, their behaviour is affected by what they believe those words, looks and gestures to mean. And in such circumstances 'the truth of the matter', whatever it might be, is hardly relevant. The truth about whether God exists or not is of little interest to sociologists. But the ways in which people's behaviour is affected by the belief that God exists is of considerable interest.

This insight has been developed by symbolic interactionists to discuss the significance of 'labelling' people. As soon as a school teacher applies the label 'trouble-maker' to a pupil, for example, after perhaps one or two 'naughty pranks', it often encourages the pupil to 'live up to' the label, and all that it implies. Equally, the teacher may well come to expect 'nothing but trouble' from the pupil in the future. Whether or not the label was true or justified in the first place becomes forgotten, as both the teacher and the pupil behave as if it were. And the label becomes a symbol, which considerably influences the expectations each has of the other, and the behaviour that results from those expectations.

Phenomenology and Ethnomethodology

Phenomenology is a relatively new term in sociology, but again its origins go back to earlier times and other disciplines. Its perspectives derive from the emphasis placed on 'interpretation' and 'understanding' by Weber and the phenomenological philosophy of **Edmund Husserl** (1859–1938). The two branches came together in the writing of **Alfred Schutz** (1899–1959) and the outcome, phenomenological sociology, has since been developed by both symbolic interactionists like **Berger** and **Luckmann** and the more unusual (in terms of conventional sociology) ethnomethodology of **Harold Garfinkel**.

The emphasis in these approaches is on small-scale investigations, or micro-sociology, and the subject matter is 'everyday life'. One of the main criticisms of functionalism and social interactionism, as we have seen, is based on the unacknowledged assumptions which influence the sociologists' work. Whole areas, categories and attitudes are left unexamined, 'taken for granted' or distorted by reification. The approach of phenomenology and ethnomethodology has been to try to supply these 'missing elements'. The starting point is to take nothing for granted, to question the commonplace and the ordinary, to treat even the most simple things as 'problematic'. For example, functionalist sociology has been able to relate 'educational success and failure' to 'social class origins and characteristics'. Phenomenologists would be unhappy about 'taking for granted' notions like 'success', 'failure' and 'social class' without recognising that many people mean different things by these terms. 'Whose definitions of success and failure are being applied?', they would ask. 'Where did these definitions come from?' 'Does everyone accept them?' 'What do they mean?'

But phenomenology is not merely a close examination of 'meanings' and commonplace assumptions, it is also concerned to discover how people arrive at those meanings and assumptions in the first place. How do people, as they go about their everyday life, come to construct the meanings, attitudes and responses to society that they then take so much for granted? And what is the significance of other people's perceptions in this process?

Phenomenological sociology has obviously presented a challenge to other forms of sociology because its inspiration has been based so much on a criticism of other approaches and has forced a re-examination of many old ideas. In some cases it has led to exciting developments—in the sociology of knowledge, for example—and encouraged important breakthroughs in the investigation of individual and small-group behaviour. Taken to extremes, the denunciation of conventional sociology by ethnomethologists like Garfinkel has been devastating.

One of the main reactions of ethnomethodology has been against the mystification of 'expertise' and the apparent insight of 'professional sociologists'. The emphasis of ethnomethodology is on the ways in which 'ordinary people' make sense of their everyday lives, and apply meanings and make interpretations which, it is claimed, are equivalent in significance to those made by sociologists. They are often not in agreement with the definitions made by sociologists either, a factor which is significant enough to make Garfinkel question the credibility of 'so-called' experts. Ethnomethodologists claim that sociologists are merely using complicated language and an exaggerated view of their own professional knowledge to do much the same kind of thing as ordinary people do all the time. If this is true, sociology as such is pointless and all can be explained by common sense.

Needless to say, not many sociologists would subscribe to this extreme view. The main criticism of ethnomethodology is that in claiming that understanding society is common sense, and by assuming that all definitions are equally valid, no account is taken of the existence of power and inequality in society. It is not that experts 'know better' than ordinary people, it is that some groups are given the status of experts, and the power and authority that go with it, and others are not. Why this is the case and how it comes to be is the important question, and ethnomethodological approaches provide no way of answering it. Neither do they provide a way of moving from an understanding of the particular and the specific towards an explanation of social organisation and patterns of behaviour at a societal level. The fact that there are economic, political and social differences in society between different groups which keep some powerful and some powerless cannot be accounted for by a preoccupation with the particular.

Marxist Sociology

The influence of Marx on contemporary sociology is immense and the distinction made between a Systems and an Action approach is not altogether helpful because both find inspiration in his ideas and methodology. The work of **Structuralists** like Althusser and Poulantzas, and the American 'political-economists' Samuel Bowles and Herb Gintis, for example, tends to reflect the Systems Approach in that they see social behaviour as determined by economic forces which are largely independent of the will of individual men. The Action emphasis is reflected in the 'critical philosophy' of sociologists like Adorno, Habermas and Marcuse (often referred to as the Frankfurt School) who employ a kind of phenomenological Marxism to stress the creative and re-creative capacities of men and their ability to intervene consciously and deliberately to change the course of social life.

The difficulty of classifying Marxist sociology is further frustrated by the wealth and diversity of his writings and the fact that his ideas have been taken on board by many other disciplines. Some regard Marxism as almost a 'world view'—a total explanation of the development and characteristics of human society, whose myriad elements from political life to industrial relations and from medicine to literature can all be examined, explained and understood from the perspective of Marxist ideas. Also, the stress laid by Marx on 'changing the world', as distinct from merely describing and understanding it, and his linking of theory and practice, have provided a practical, political recipe for action, as well as a philosophical theory, so that some societies—in Eastern Europe and the third world, for example—have been organised according to what are thought to be Marxist principles. Also, different and sometimes opposing branches of sociology are influenced by his ideas. Marxist concepts of, for example, class, social conflict and ideology have been incorporated, though often in a modified form, by all kinds of approaches, and controversy over the meaning and interpretation of his 'early' and 'later' writings still flourishes.

After taking all these difficulties into consideration, however, the following characteristics are probably the ones which best describe what is distinctive and most valuable in Marx' contribution to sociology:

1. The primary significance given to the **economic structure** and the relationship between labour and production in the analysis of society. Of all the factors which influence what society is like and how people behave, economic considerations are seen by Marxists to be most significant.

2. The concern to place the society, relationship or social phenomenon being studied into a **historical economic** context, to see where it came from, how it developed, what caused it to change.

3. The view that society does not merely evolve gradually, but that social development is frequently brought about by **revolutionary breaks** in continuity as society changes from one form to another. The emphasis on 'conflicting interests' and 'contradictions' within structures as the key to the 'dialectic' which produces revolutionary change is central to a Marxist analysis of society.

4. The link between theory and practice which is usually referred to as **praxis**, the view that action must first be reflected upon intellectually and then carried out consciously. Marx' great achievement was to devise a social theory which could be used to analyse society, and at the same time provide a guide to action, in that men were encouraged to 'make their own history'.

This last characteristic has produced perhaps the most criticism, especially in its commitment to socialism, and it has sometimes been difficult to differentiate between theory, analysis and dogma in the writings of those influenced by Marx' ideas. Similarly, the prediction Marx made about the destruction of capitalism and the characteristics of the socialist and communist societies which would replace it have not happened quite as he imagined. But as the criticisms and controversies continue to rage, the effect is to force contemporary sociologists continually to re-examine their assumptions and their approaches and to produce a stimulating and fruitful climate in which the perceptions and authority of sociology as a way of understanding society is continually being extended.

Two Sides of the Same Coin?

No doubt there will continue to be differences of emphasis and of interpretation so long as sociology survives and sociologists continue to be human! And in the last analysis students and audiences must make up their own minds about which perspectives are most useful. In fact, both approaches, Systems and Action, are probably best seen as two sides of the same coin. Society, its institutions and organisation are 'man-made' as the Action Approach suggests, and yet the human being's experience of society is one in which his freedom is constrained by social arrangements and forces which have a tremendous influence over his life, his behaviour and his thought processes, as the Systems Approach suggests. Both sides have to be taken into account in order to understand society properly and to recognise that the nature of man is to be both a 'created' and a 'creative' being.

The current trend in sociology seems to be one in which the values of different perspectives are gradually becoming integrated into a more unified approach (see, for example, the argument in *New Rules of Sociological Method*, by Anthony Giddens). And some agreement has at last emerged on the Marxist view that 'man makes his own history', although with the qualification that it is probably not always as he pleases!

The caricature of British sociology which was popular in the sixties, as 'the ammunition' for radical students to establish a new kind of society, has also shifted. The emphasis in recent years has been on enabling students of sociology to understand better the things they take for granted in the societies they study, and in which they also live, to uncover the hidden arrangements which influence social behaviour, the power structures, the ideas, patterns of belief and the contradictions, so that they can be more critical about their own assumptions and more perceptive about the complex nature of human society.

Where's the Evidence?

All kinds of sociologists, whatever their differences might be, agree on the need to base their interpretations of social behaviour on the systematic collection of evidence, though different approaches have developed different methods of collecting evidence, as you might expect.

The information necessary to be able to explain and understand social behaviour is perhaps more difficult to obtain than the data collected by physical scientists, in that human beings are the 'raw material' and not inanimate objects. They have dignity and a sense of privacy which must be respected, public opinion would be loath to condone the kind of experiments on people which natural scientists are allowed to carry out on chemicals and animal life, and of course the 'involvement' of the 'human' researcher in the investigation of 'human' activities can produce problems of bias or distortion. The most that can be expected is that a researcher must be as 'scientific' as possible. He must consider as many aspects of the phenomenon he is studying as he can and make all the evidence he collects and the methods he uses available for scrutiny by others. He must be sensitive to his own assumptions and the effects they are likely to have on his conclusions and he must recognise the fact that his 'doing research' into a particular phenomenon is likely to affect the phenomenon he is studying to some extent. Research, like all social relationships, is a two-way affair, a process of interaction between different people, and the behaviour of each of them will obviously be linked to that of the others. Put simply, a sociologist cannot expect to question a group of people, for example, without recognising that their responses will be influenced by their perception of him as a researcher. And if, as a group, they happen to be 'battered wives', 'homosexuals', 'drug addicts' or 'army officers', it would be unusual for the researcher not to have some preformed opinions about them as particular 'types' of people. So the business of collecting 'human evidence' is fraught with difficulties. But these are all problems which the methods of investigation used by different sociologists try to take into account.

When sociologists set out to investigate some aspect of social behaviour, they obviously have available the kind of background information that is generally accessible to any commentator on social life—official records, government statistics, previous reports, newspaper articles, etc. They may treat them with a fair degree of scepticism, but they provide a starting point. They will probably set the subject being studied into some kind of historical perspective, and possibly make comparisons with the behaviour of other groups in other societies, if it seems relevant. They will certainly be conscious of whether they are investigating something in an urban or a rural setting and in an industrial or a pre-industrial society. And they will probably make some kind of assessment of the political, economic and social characteristics of the group they are studying or the environment in which they are at work.

After establishing this general background, the sociologist has to build up a more detailed picture using a variety of methods. In an effort to simplify these a little, we can divide them into three broad types: **positivist, interpretive** and **ethnographic**. To fix them in your mind right away it might be helpful to note that positivist research is usually linked to a Systems Approach, interpretive research is usually linked to an Action Approach, and ethnography, inspired by symbolic interactionism, has an eye to incorporating 'the best of all the rest' into a more integrated perspective.

Positivist Research

Surveys, Questionnaires and Interviews

The main characteristics of positivism, as we have seen, are that sociology is regarded as being equivalent to the natural sciences, and social facts are capable of being measured objectively, in the same way as natural facts. The methods most frequently used, therefore, are surveys, questionnaires, structured interviews, attitude scales, controlled clinical experiments and statistical analysis.

Surveys and questionnaires are the techniques most often associated with sociology. They provide the possibility for large numbers of people to be questioned, either in person, according to a previously determined schedule of questions, or by leaving a questionnaire to be filled in by the respondent, returned by post, or collected later by the researcher. The responses are then 'analysed' and turned into statistics, often with the help of a computer, so that sociologists are able to say, '57 per cent of our sample were . . .' or '49 per cent of the women questioned agreed that . . .'. Sometimes this approach is used with relatively small samples of people, to compare their experiences of marriage, for example, or their views on religion, and is usually followed up by personal interviews. But it is a technique which best lends itself to large-scale investigations in which the researcher wants to contact as many as several thousand people.

Obviously the ways in which the questionnaires are compiled and the surveys are conducted are quite central to the credibility and the success of this method. Postal questionnaires are relatively cheap, but they risk the failure of respondents neglecting or forgetting to return them. A personal collection of the forms, and even the presence of the researcher whilst the questionnaire is being filled in, is often more efficient, but it is also more time-consuming, costly and perhaps more intimidating for the respondent. He may well choose to put down what he thinks the researcher wants to know, or will approve of, rather than what he really believes.

Interviewing respondents personally is usually thought to be the most reliable way of getting questionnaires completed, and making sure the respondent knows what he is expected to do. Interviewers are trained by sociologists to be as neutral and objective as possible, but, as symbolic interactionists are swift to point out, this is a virtually impossible ideal.

The questions themselves have to be simple enough to be understood by the respondents, they have to be phrased in as unambiguous a way as possible, and they have to be capable of being analysed and turned into statistical presentations. A question which is badly worded, like 'Do you read books very often?', may produce the response 'Yes' or 'No' but give no indication of what the respondent means by 'often' or how different individuals' understanding of 'often' varies. It may also disguise the fact that individuals may mean different things by 'books'. Some may mean hardback or paperback novels, others magazines.

Questions which are so simple and unambiguous that there can be no mistake about them are usually only capable of providing the most simple and obvious information. If sociologists want to find out about feelings, opinions or patterns of behaviour, they must frame their questions in a more 'open-ended' way and encourage their respondents to reply at length. But again, if the sociologist wants to put people at ease and get them talking naturally about what they really believe, it is unlikely that an interviewer with a clip-board and a set of inflexible questions or a bureaucratic-looking form will remove the barriers between them.

Another problem is deciding who to question. Since it is obviously impossible to interview *all* divorced women or *all* juvenile delinquents, for example, the sociologist has to draw up a representative **sample** which he assumes is a fairly typical cross-section of the group he is studying. In some cases sociologists prefer to take a 'random sample' on a kind of 'first-come-first-served' basis as being as good a way as any of getting a cross-section of the population. Others try to balance their sample in terms of age, sex, social class and other characteristics that might be important. If you were doing a study of marriage, for example, and you questioned only men, it is likely that your findings would be rather one-sided!

Sociologists try to get over some of these problems, before they begin their main research, by carrying out a small **pilot study** first. This means drawing up a questionnaire, selecting a small sample of people and trying out the questions on them first. If, as a result, any of the questions are proved to be ambiguous, or the results seem unduly biased, or the method of giving out and getting back the forms does not work, the sociologist can make modifications and changes before undertaking his main survey.

Clearly this approach does have a number of advantages, especially if sociologists want to contact a lot of people, but it also presents many problems. And of course the biggest criticism made by sociologists from opposing camps is that 'it's just not a good way of understanding the complexities and idiosyncracies of human behaviour'.

Attitude Scales and Clinical Tests

If surveys, questionnaires and interviews are regarded sceptically by many people, attitude scales, clinical experiments and statistical analysis present even more problems. Again the aim is to be as scientific as possible and to apply the best tried methods of natural science to social science. All of them are ways of 'measuring' human behaviour in an effort to relate 'individual' reactions to 'general' categories.

A sociologist investigating racial prejudice, for example, might present a subject with a list of statements about black people, to agree or disagree with. He would then give their replies a rating on a scale which ranged from 'extremely prejudiced' to 'totally unprejudiced'. Another sociologist may set up an experiment, under controlled laboratory conditions, to test the reaction of 'sexual deviants', for example, to photographs of the naked human body. Both of these methods owe much to the influence of clinical psychology and are used most by sociologists who have a commitment to psychological explanations of human behaviour.

The problems involved in the two methods are probably clear to you. What is meant by 'prejudice' and 'sexual deviance' first of all? Surely these can mean different things to different people. They are not terms which can be 'taken for granted' as 'commonly agreed upon' categories. So whose definitions are being used in experiments like these? Equally, there are so many different social, emotional, personal, historical and economic factors influencing people's prejudices and their definitions of 'normal' and 'deviant' sex, that they cannot easily be measured in clinical or laboratory conditions which are shut off from the rest of social interaction. The success of scientifically-controlled and laboratory-based experiments relies on the exclusion of 'confusing outside influences', but in social science it is likely that these extraneous 'confusing influences' are the very ones which provide the important insights into the phenomena being studied.

Statistics

Statistical analysis always gets a bad press. The notion that you can 'make statistics prove anything you like' dies hard. But ironically, a great deal of emphasis is placed on official statistics when recommendations are being made and new policies introduced. You are more likely to be allowed to build 10,000 new council houses if you can show that 20 per cent of a city's population is living in substandard housing, than if you provide five or six detailed, but personal, accounts of living in damp and decaying conditions.

Official statistics drawn up by government departments, trade unions, the Census Office and other organisations are obviously a useful source of information for sociologists, but they need to be used carefully. One problem is that official categories are not always the ones sociologists would use. Sociologists are interested in the *social* causes of crime or suicide, for example, but these are not the sort of things which are recorded on police records or death certificates.

Equally, some kinds of statistical information which would be useful just are not recorded. We no longer have any accurate records about the numbers of children from racial minorities in British schools, for example. The reasons why such information is not kept are open to speculation, but its absence enables all kinds of conflicting beliefs about 'the numbers involved' and 'the problems posed' to be both magnified and underestimated.

A third difficulty is that statistics are not always available in a way which is useful to sociologists. Figures may be presented separately from each other. For example, the number of people owning the largest amounts of wealth in Britain, and the numbers of people involved in different occupations. It might be the relationship between these two circumstances which is of interest to sociologists, but the link is not made in the original collection of statistics.

In providing their own statistics from the findings of surveys and questionnaires sociologists are on surer ground, because they can cross-reference and inter-relate different categories, to fit in with what they are trying to find out, or to prove. But so long as popular cynicism about the authenticity of statistics continues, they must ensure that their sources and procedures are as sound as possible.

Interpretive Research

The Action Approach, as we have seen, is sceptical about claiming any allegience to the natural sciences, and sees people not as 'things' to be studied like objects, but as individuals capable of thinking, interpreting and attaching meanings to everyday existence in a complex and varied way. It is these 'subjective meanings' which the social action sociologist is keen to highlight. To do this he must 'get into a relationship' with the individuals and groups he is studying, a relationship that is not 'cluttered' or 'distorted' by the paraphernalia of questionnaires and tightly structured interviews. His aim is to be more informal, to meet people on their own territory, rather than in a university or a special interview room, for example, to 'observe' things as they happen, and to allow enough time to enable confidence and trust to be built up between the researcher and his subjects. Interviews are most likely to be 'unstructured', 'open-ended' and 'in-depth' discussions, in which subjects are encouraged to expand at length, and in their own words, about their experiences. A tape-recorder is often used so that the sociologist has an accurate record of what they say without having to remember or note down specific responses.

Meanwhile, the sociologist's interpretation of what is happening has to pass through three phases. He must first try to identify the subjective meanings which influence the behaviour of those he is studying, and, with empathy, try to 'see things from their point of view'. The second stage is to observe, analyse and interpret what they say and do, in an attempt to find the reasons for and the causes of their behaviour. The third phase is to recognise that the sociologist's participation in the discussion, and observation of the action, in some senses changes it, as he in turn is changed by it. So there can be no question of the 'objectivity' of his findings in the positivist sense. If his conclusions are to be credible, therefore, he must ensure that the stages in his analysis are rigorous, logical and consistent. If his procedures are seen to be sound and his deductions convincing, the results will speak for themselves.

Ethnography

Ethnography is a term that means quite literally 'a picture' of the way of life of a social group interacting together, and comes originally from anthropology. A group's 'total way of life' or culture is considered to be 'on-going' and 'ever-changing' and the methods of ethnography aim to capture this as thoroughly as possible, in all its various shades and nuances, in as much detail, and with full recognition of the 'many levels' at which relationships function. The ethnographer tries to begin with no preconceived ideas about people's roles or positions or what he expects to be happening but waits for these to become revealed to him over time.

The main method of ethnography is 'participant observation', which clearly puts the researcher right into the middle of the action. The starting point for the study of a family group, for example, would not be to assume that 'two happily married adults were looking after and bringing up a number of dependent children in a more-or-less successful kind of way'. The researcher would begin by asking rather different questions like, 'What's going on here?' or 'What are these people doing to each other?' and he would try to 'build up a picture' of the family group by building in what each of them say about it. Now obviously there are problems here. The individuals' accounts may differ, they may not know why they do things, they may not be able to put into words what they feel without being misleading. And how is the sociologist to make sense of it all? Ethnographers take the view that the sociologist gains insight which an outsider or a positivist would not, from 'participation'—not merely 'sitting in on' an unstructured group discussion, but actually 'taking on a role' within the group or the institution and making some contribution to its day-to-day functioning. Some sociologists have actually joined street-corner gangs, spent time in prison, become 'hippies' or taught in classrooms. As a member of the group, with a role to play, they can gradually begin to analyse their own behaviour and feelings and their interaction with others.

Here again the problems are obvious. If you join a gang, for example, do you reveal to the members that you are a sociologist? And what if you develop loyalties to the gang which prevent you being detached enough to see clearly what is happening? You may find yourself 'defending' their behaviour rather than 'studying' it. Being a teacher may present fewer problems, except that to gain the confidence of colleagues to get their views may prevent the researcher getting close enough to the pupils to be trusted by them. Alternatively, a researcher who is not 'identified' with the teachers by the pupils, may be mistrusted by the staff.

In the last resort a great deal will depend on whether or not members of groups believe in the researcher. If his motives and his behaviour are in any way suspect, he will have difficulty in continuing with his work, and his access to information will be blocked. Often the most revealing information is not disclosed because the researcher feels it would be a betrayal of the trust he has built up.

Ethnographers claim that this 'deep involvement in the action' over a considerable period of time is the best way of building up a picture of social behaviour in a given group. But it is obviously not the only way. Social relationships exist on a variety of levels and are influenced by many innerconnected factors. It makes sense therefore to 'cross-check', to get as many different accounts of the 'same' experience as possible, and to recognise that in any situation there will be not only one, but many realities.

Part of the picture might include more structured interviews, a review of 'official' sources of information, a detailed analysis of the legal factors involved, or a reference to what has been learned from similar studies elsewhere. To understand fully the behaviour of the family group mentioned earlier, it may also mean an analysis of their economic circumstances, an account of the jobs they do, their educational experience, the social characteristics of the environment they live in and the links between all of these and the wider society. In all of these respects the ethnographer has much to learn from other sociological methods, but whereas other sociologists may take a macro view of society as a starting point, and formulate hypotheses about the families' behaviour from an analysis of wider structural arrangements, the ethnographer is more likely to let these links be revealed in the process of working closely with the group over a period.

Some sociologists feel that ethnographic case studies are merely 'high-class reporting', and at best are only a very detailed 'description' of behaviour, without providing scientific analysis of the 'causes' of behaviour. This is largely because the ethnographer does not begin in the usual empirical way of starting with accepted theories, formulating hypotheses and working out categories in advance. Ethnographers argue that the danger of this is to predetermine the outcome before you start, and risk the possibility of missing potentially crucial features and subjective meanings, which are not available to the outside observer until they become revealed in the process of interaction. Being too hidebound by established theories and well-tried methods may actually *prevent* the generation of new insight, new methods and new theories. In other words, sociologists should 'make sense of what's going on as they go along' and utilise methods and 'discover' theoretical perspectives from the situation itself.

Of course a lot depends on what is being studied. It may be that the sociologist who is preoccupied with the 'elusive nuances of small-scale interaction between individuals in groups' is blind to the structural constraints of the wider society. Social action does not take place in a vacuum. Alternatively, the sociologist concerned 'to relate economic forces to power and control in society' may ignore the effects on small groups, as people experience these constraints at a personal level.

In Conclusion

In practice methods of investigation are decided both by what is being studied, as well as the theories of different schools of thought. It would be wrong to assume that one method is always right, or that another is always wrong. In some circumstances surveys and questionnaires will be more appropriate than participant observation. In others unstructured interviews and the personal involvement of the researcher will be more revealing. They are all, to some extent, versions of the same practice—the attempt by sociologists to make their studies as scientific as possible, and to provide the evidence which will allow them to make an interpretation of the complex social causes and characteristics of human behaviour.

Revision

1. Refresh Your Memory

Make sure you know the meaning of the terms: empirical, anomie, alienation, surplus value, dialectic, social system, reification, significant others, praxis, survey, questionnaire, sample, pilot study, attitude scale, statistics, ethnography, participant observation.

2. Check Your Understanding

Be able to explain in your own words:

(*a*) The difference between sociology, psychology, history, economics and political science.

(*b*) The differences between the social sciences and the natural sciences.

(*c*) The main differences in emphasis between a Systems and Action Approach to studying society.

(*d*) The difference between a macro and a micro view of social behaviour.

(*e*) The main characteristics of positivism, functionalism, phenomenology and ethnomethodology.

(*f*) The main characteristics of Marxist sociology.

(*g*) The difference between structured and unstructured interviews.

(*h*) The difference between a balanced and a random sample.

(*i*) The main differences between positivistic and interpretative research methods.

3. Essay Questions to Try

(*a*) Some claim sociology to be a science while others refute this. Discuss this controversy.

(*b*) How do sociologists study society? How does their approach differ from that of other social scientists or historians?

(*c*) Outline briefly any major perspective in sociological theory (such as functionalism, symbolic interactionism or phenomenology) and show how it has been used.

(*d*) What are the main factors to consider in constructing and using a questionnaire?

(*e*) 'Sociologists claim scientific status for prestige reasons only. Scientific analysis of social phenomena is both impossible and undesirable.' Discuss.

(*f*) Discuss the ways in which the theoretical perspective embraced by a particular sociologist influences his writings.

(*g*) In what ways is it helpful to view society as analogous to a machine or a biological organism? What drawbacks do these approaches have?

(*h*) Compare the usefulness of survey work and participant observation to sociologists, giving appropriate examples.

(*i*) 'Sociologists have values and therefore an objective social science is not possible.' Do you agree?

(*j*) 'When we use official statistics we must assume that such statistics all refer to the same thing ... but ... if we look at how these statistics are actually constructed, we find that we are compiling additions of different things.' (Valliamy, *New Perspectives in Sociology*, ATSS Monograph No. 2.) What problems does this present for sociologists?

(*k*) Men have purposes and motives; it is not possible, therefore, to be scientific about human behaviour. Discuss.

(*l*) Some would claim that social behaviour is merely the sum of individual acts and that it is possible therefore to explain human behaviour solely in psychological terms. Do you agree?

(*m*) 'We can be certain about the trivial or unsure about the important, such is the dilemma which inevitably confronts the sociologist.' Discuss.

(*n*) 'So in capitalist countries, many think of sociology as a kind of academic synonym for socialism, whilst in communist countries it was banned for decades as "bourgeois" ideology.' (Worsley (ed.), *Introducing Sociology*.) Discuss.

Further Reading

Introducing Sociology, Peter Worsley (ed.), Penguin, London, 1970.
Sociology: A Guide to Problems and Literature, Tom Bottomore, Unwin University Books, Allen & Unwin, London, 1962.

2

SOCIAL CLASS IN BRITAIN

One of the first things a sociologist wants to know about a person is 'What social class do they belong to?' Terms like upper class, middle class and working class are ones we all use. But what do we mean by them? Do sociologists mean the same thing? And why does it matter anyway? Before trying to answer some of these questions, stop for a moment and ask yourself what you mean by social class. Here are a few questions to help you.

Test Your Class-Consciousness

1. What social class do you think you belong to? Make a note of your main reasons for putting yourself in one social class rather than another. (If you do not think you belong to any social class, jot down the main reasons for your opinion.)

2. Think of one or two people you know very well and imagine you had to decide upon their social class. These are some of the things you might take into account. Rearrange the list into an order of importance, putting the most important consideration at the top and the least important consideration at the bottom.

What kind of education they have had.
What kind of house they live in.
What kind of job their mother did.
The amount of respect and admiration they get from others.
How much money they have.
Their dress and general appearance.
Their general attitudes to life.
Their general behaviour and relationships with others.
What kind of job they do.
What kind of neighbourhood they live in.
How much they earn.
What kind of job their father did.

3. Do you think that class differences are very important in Britain today? Do people look up to some, or look down on others, because of their social class? Jot down as many illustrations as you can to support your point of view.

As soon as anyone mentions social class there is likely to be a full-scale argument about whether or not social class exists or matters these days. Your own answers to the questions above are probably just the sort of thing to get any group of adults agreeing or disagreeing with your point of view. Try it out when you are next in the pub with some friends! Social class is certainly a subject which can stir up a lot of emotions, especially if people associate it with 'too much money', 'too much power', 'rowdy behaviour', 'snobbish' or 'irresponsible' attitudes. The stereotypes we all have about what is 'typical' of upper-class, middle-class and working-class people are many, and like all stereotypes, they often contradict each other.

In this kind of atmosphere the sociologist's job is a difficult one: how to make generalisations about social class that are meaningful, as objective as possible and yet sensitive to different people's emotional reactions to the issues involved. Sociologists start from the conviction that, not only does social class definitely exist in our society, but also its influence, in all kinds of organisational and personal ways, is very important. Whilst a lot of the different characteristics have changed over the years, as society has changed, and the divisions between social classes are maybe not as clear-cut as they used to be, membership of one social class rather than another still has a tremendous influence on people's lifestyles, behaviour, opportunities and attitudes.

Before considering some of these, let's return to your thoughts on the matter.

Subjective and Objective Definitions of Social Class

Whatever social class you put yourself into, the first thing to notice is that people's views of themselves do not always correspond with the description a sociologist would make. The distinction is often referred to as the difference between subjective definitions of class and objective definitions of class.

Some people, for example, consider themselves to be 'middle-class' if they think of their occupation as a respectable white-collar job or if they associate 'owning their own house' with middle-class status. Others may feel that 'everyone who works' is working class, or they may still feel a part of the working-class family environment they grew up in, even though education and occupation has changed their social circumstances considerably.

Whatever people's personal or subjective feelings might be, sociologists have rather different criteria for deciding their social class. They use a number of categories like occupation, income, wealth, education, lifestyle and behavioural characteristics to put people into different social class groupings. In general, most importance is given to the kind of job a person does and how much money he has. The type of house he lives in, where his children go to school, what he does in his spare time, how he dresses and what he expects from life usually follow on from the first two—though of course the relationship between them is often a lot more complicated than this. Usually seven categories are used. The edges may be a little blurred, and obviously there are exceptions to every rule, but in general they are accepted as the most accurate way of distinguishing between different groups in the social class structure. These are the seven categories:

Upper class	Aristocracy and large property owners.
Upper middle class	Professional occupations, e.g. lawyers and architects.
Middle class	Managerial and technical jobs, e.g. shop managers and computer operators.
Lower middle class	Non-manual, white-collar and clerical jobs, e.g. office workers and supervisors.
Upper working class	Skilled manual jobs, e.g. electricians and vehicle mechanics.
Working class	Semi-skilled manual jobs, e.g. machine operators and trawler men.
Lower working class	Unskilled manual jobs, e.g. road sweepers and canteen assistants.

In some cases you will find only five categories used and the divisions referred to as Social classes 1 to 5 in the Registrar General's scale. These are the occupational groups used for census purposes and for other statistical returns. They are also widely used by sociologists. Ronald Davie and his colleagues used a five-point scale in their child development study report 'From Birth to Seven'. Here is how they describe the categories they used:

'Social class I consists of occupations which require the highest professional qualifications, usually a university degree or its equivalent. Occupations in social class II also often demand a professional qualification and, for example, schoolteachers and many higher civil servants are in this group; it also includes managers and others of similar position in industry or commerce even if they are "unqualified". Virtually all the occupations in these two groups are of a non-manual nature.

'Social class III, by far the largest single group, is usually subdivided into a manual and a non-manual section. In the former are placed almost all the remaining non-manual occupations, such as foremen in industry, shop assistants and clerical workers. The occupations in the other sections are all regarded as skilled manual. Social class IV consists almost exclusively of semi-skilled manual occupations and social class V contains the unskilled manual occupations. The classification is summarised in Table 1 together with the proportion who fall into each group. If there is no father or male head of the household the members of the family are not classified.'

Table 1. Classification of occupations

Social class	Proportion of the population
I	5
II	14
III (non-manual)	10
III (manual)	44
IV	17
V	7
Not classified	3

(Source: *From Birth to Seven: A Report of the National Child Development Study*, Ronald Davie, Neville Butler and Harvey Goldstein)

The Middle Class and the Working Class

In practice Davie's classification and the Registrar General's Scale on which it is based tend to get collapsed into a distinction between middle class and working-class occupations. You may think that a class structure with a bottom and a middle but no top makes little sense, and indeed the omission of an upper class from Davie's definition, and a good many other studies which use this form of occupational classification, is a significant one.

Doug Holly makes this point in his article 'The Invisible Ruling Class':* 'The notion put about by many sociologists is that we live in a two-class society. How strange we hear so much of the middle class and the working class whilst we hear almost nothing about any upper class.' The working class is easy enough to identify. In size and significance it is much bigger than people think. In a society like ours in which few people own very much wealth and property most of us have to sell whatever labour power we have in return for wages. In this sense we are all workers. But whilst most people are involved in doing the actual work which produces the manufactured goods and services, there are others who do the organising and whose status and way of life is sufficiently different from the workers to make them into a distinct group. These are the 'managers' who make the day-to-day decisions, who organise the necessary technology, who look after government, administration, health, culture, finance, business, education and legal matters. These are the people who hold 'professional jobs'—the well known middle class. But what about those at the top? Who are they?

The Upper Class

Ideas of aristocracy may seem to be a bit old-fashioned in today's Britain although people with titles do still exist. They are still extremely

* 'The Invisible Ruling Class', by Doug Holly, in *Education or Domination*, Arrow (Hutchinson), London, 1974.

wealthy compared to most other people, many of them live in large country houses on vast rural estates as their fathers and forefathers did before them.

In more recent times they have been joined by a slightly different group. They may not have inherited titles but they do have enormous amounts of wealth. Their money comes from industry, either from the profits made by industries which they own directly, or income from investments in the stocks and shares of large profit-making companies at home and abroad. This 1 per cent of the adult population owns one quarter of all the wealth in Britain. The richest 10 per cent own two thirds of it.

Income and Wealth

Accurate information about income and wealth is quite difficult to obtain. In practice we know who the rich people are but it is very difficult to find out just how wealthy they are. This is because there is a distinction made between income and wealth. **Income** is defined as the money earned from paid employment and the dividends received from investments. Incomes have to be declared to the Inland Revenue and income tax has to be paid. But there are all kinds of perfectly legal ways in which people can get tax relief on things like mortgages, life assurance, schools fees and business expenses.

Wealth refers to people's other financial assets like land, property, stocks and shares. The assessment of liability for tax on these is much more difficult to determine and consequently easy to avoid. For example, there are legal ways of transferring wealth before death to avoid paying death duties. Since rich people do not have to divulge the extent of their wealth to anyone, it is almost impossible to find out just how much they own.

What is known is that the majority of income and wealth is concentrated in the hands of a relatively small section of the population, as Figs. 1–4 illustrate. And things have not altered very much, despite the apparent changes in British society over the last hundred years.

Economic and Cultural Definitions of Social Class

So far most of our discussion has been about occupation, income and wealth. This kind of definition of social class relies very much on an analysis of the distribution of economic resources in society. In your answer to question 2 on page 28, did you place job, money and earnings at the top of your list or choose some other criteria?

Some people would argue that you can tell a person's social class by how they talk and how they dress, where they live and how they behave. People from different social classes tend to do different things in their leisure time, read different newspapers, watch different programmes on the television, feel differently about education, politics

total incomes

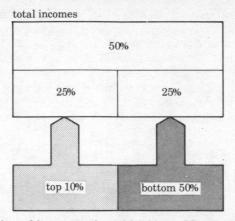

Fig. 1. Distribution of income and wealth. About 25 per cent of all income earned goes to the top 10 per cent of wage earners; another 25 per cent goes to the bottom 50 per cent of wage earners.

(*Source:* Royal Commission on the Distribution of Income and Wealth, 1975. Reproduced by permission of the Hutchinson Publishing Group.)

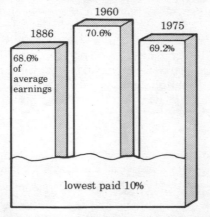

Fig. 2. No progress. The lowest paid 10 per cent of men doing manual jobs earned 69.2 per cent of the average earnings in 1975. Not much progress since 1886.

(*Source:* PIB Report on New Earnings Survey, 1975. Reproduced by permission of the Hutchinson Publishing Group.)

and the jobs they do. Or so the arguments go. In other words, the general behaviour, attitudes and lifestyles of people are different in different social classes. When sociologists emphasise these kind of criteria they are using a 'cultural definition'* of social class.

---

* When sociologists use the term 'culture' they mean an individual's, a group's or a society's *whole way of life*, everything from dress and behaviour to beliefs and attitudes. It is important not to confuse this with the more familiar use of the term culture in everyday language to refer to 'high-quality' art, literature and music (see p. 110).

Sociology

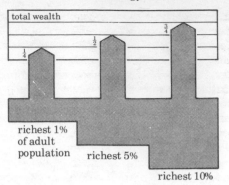

Fig. 3. Who is rich? The richest 1 per cent of the population owns about one quarter of all wealth. The richest 5 per cent own one half. The richest 10 per cent own two thirds.

(*Source:* Royal Commission on the Distribution of Income and Wealth, 1975. Reproduced by permission of the Hutchinson Publishing Group.)

Fig. 4. Who owns shares? Those with a total wealth of more than £10,000 own 95 per cent of all personally held shares.

(*Source:* TGWU evidence to the Royal Commission on the Distribution of Income and Wealth, 1975. Reproduced by permission of the Hutchinson Publishing Group.)

But cultural definitions can produce problems if they are not applied carefully. The main danger is one of 'putting the cart before the horse'. It is certainly the case that people in the same social class have many things in common—the same monopoly or lack of access to scarce resources, for example; the same good or bad standards of housing; the same access to, or restrictions on, educational opportunity; the same shared experiences of comfort, travel, hardship or enjoyment. But all of these cultural characteristics are the *consequences* of social class rather than the *causes* of it. People's lifestyles are a reflection of their economic condition in society, not the reason for their position.

A second problem with cultural definitions of class is that of stereotyping and 'labelling'. In making generalisations about the behaviour and attitudes of people in different social classes, there is a tendency to assume that *all* working-class people or *all* middle-class people are much the same. And so often these generalisations are accompanied by implicit judgements about the behaviour being described. The fact that the children of working-class parents are less likely to be successful in school than the children of middle-class parents, for example, has focused a good deal of attention on their family background and upbringing. Doug Holly captures the flavour of much of it in this extract from *The Invisible Ruling Class*:

'The working class show only a limited interest in education and aren't much good at it. The parents fail to encourage the children at school or provide the right setting at home for educational successes. They don't read many books and they watch the wrong sort of television. Their language too, we are told, is all wrong. The working class, except for a small group trying to get their children a better start in life, are, in fact, born educational failures.'

The kind of labelling which Holly is paraphrasing here has the effect of stigmatising all working-class backgrounds. By sleight-of-hand 'cultural definitions' of working class are translated into judgements about 'cultural deficiencies' which, as we shall see in chapter 4, can become self-fulfilling prophecies.

By comparison, middle-class parents are said to 'take more interest in their children's progress at school than the manual working-class parents do, and they become relatively more interested as their children grow older. They visit the school more frequently to find out how their children are getting on with their work. They are also outstanding in the use they make of the available medical services. Their children benefit not only from the support and encouragement they get in their school work but from the excellent personal and medical care they get at home.' In this extract from the influential study *The Home and the School*, by J. W. B. Douglas and his colleagues, you can begin to see how the label of 'good' applied to middle-class parents came to be established. The effect of sociological research like this has been to stereotype the repercussions of social class divisions in society and to contribute to social prejudices about the supposed cultural superiority of some in comparison to others. But more of this later.

What About Women?

How did you rate 'the kind of job their mother did' in your answer to question 2 on page 28? You may have noticed by now that definitions of social class are very sexist! Occupational classifications always rely on the employment of the 'male head of the household'. Whether or not a woman earns more than her husband or is employed when he is unemployed, she is assumed for census purposes and in the majority of statistical returns to be dependent on a man for her economic and social status. The social class of children, until they are old enough to be self-sufficient, is decided by the position of their parents. The social class of women is decided first by the position of their fathers and then by that of their husbands. Even widows and divorcees are classified according to previous relationships. The only exception is economically independent single women. Few classifications take this group seriously, however, because they are assumed to be 'untypical' and in most cases are regarded as 'temporarily in transition' from one 'male-dependent' relationship to another.

Does Class Count?

How many of you in your answer to question 3 on page 28 felt that social class does not really matter very much? We are often reluctant to admit that social class differences still exist, or to accept the view of Britain as a class society. Sometimes this is because we do not like the idea of 'looking up to' or 'looking down on' people and because our ideas about social class are often related to notions of 'inferiority' and 'superiority'.

Sometimes it's because the old differences of income and wealth do not seem to apply these days. The Conservative Government's message of the 1950s and early 1960s was 'You've never had it so good' and 'We're all middle class now', and public opinion was encouraged to believe that low income and poverty were things of the past. The popular view today is somewhat different. We know that poverty still exists and that more people are out of work than at any time since the Second World War, but we have also witnessed a sharp increase in the influence and prominence of trade unions, in public life. The industrial strife of the early 1970s, accompanied by one or two large pay awards to certain industries, have created the impression of workers 'never having it so good' *at the expense* of the middle class. Even the unemployed have been depicted in the press as essentially 'workshy scroungers' who live 'a parasitic existence on the misplaced charity' of the welfare state. A good deal of popular belief is consequently contradictory. On the one hand there is a reluctance to admit that social class exists, in the sense that some people have more prestige and privileges than others, but equally there is a tendency to believe that some sections of society have more power and privileges than is good for them.

The Embourgeoisement Debate

The notion of a classless Britain—or at least a Britain in which the economic position and lifestyles of middle-class and working-class people become indistinguishable—has been the subject of sociological investigation. In the course of the 1950s statistics became available which suggested that a significant increase in the incomes of manual workers had taken place, and that many of them were now earning wages which were directly comparable with those of white-collar workers and supervisory staff. Information about consumption patterns also indicated a big increase in consumer spending among manual workers who, in addition to material goods like televisions, vacuum cleaners, and washing machines, also began to buy the motorcars and houses, which were formerly the exclusive preserve of middle-class buyers.

Using this information, it was argued that the working-class characteristics of inferior economic resources and consumer power were no longer applicable. The age of the 'have-nots' was written off as a passing phase of industrialisation. The stage of development now being attained was one in which the bulk of the population enjoyed middle-class living standards.

Arguments about increased economic parity led to claims that cultural differences would also be removed. As manual workers achieved middle-class incomes, they would also take on middle-class lifestyles. In terms of speech, dress, eating habits, styles of décor, entertainments, leisure activities, child-rearing practices and parental aspirations, they would become indistinguishable from their middle-class neighbours.

Sociologists describing this phenomenon talked in terms of the 'embourgeoisement' of the working class, by which they meant manual workers taking on bourgeois or middle-class lifestyles and joining the ranks of the middle class. The increase in home ownership was seen as particularly significant, in that manual workers would now be able to live physically much closer to their middle-class neighbours. In taking on middle-class lifestyles, it was also assumed that they would take on middle-class attitudes—attitudes which would radically alter their traditional allegiance to the Labour Party, for example, and the trade unions. Rather than regarding their work relationship with the employers and their social relationship with the middle class as an 'us and them' situation, they would rapidly forgo their class loyalties and increasingly identify with their middle-class counterparts.

It was these arguments which John Goldthorpe and David Lockwood, together with Frank Beckhofer and Jennifer Platt, set out to investigate in 1962: the extent to which affluent workers in the car industry had become 'middle class' in their behaviour and attitudes as a consequence of earning more money and increasing their spending power.

Their research produced three major studies of affluent workers in relation to industrial attitudes and behaviour, political attitudes and behaviour and in relation to the class structure. Their findings are well documented and worth following up in more detail, but in essence they combine to refute the notion of embourgeoisement. They show how social class differences were changing in their surface characteristics, and possibly even 'converging' in terms of values and aspirations. But they could find no evidence of any radical reshaping of the class structure or alteration in the relationships between different status groups within it.

Developments during the 1970s to some extent confirmed their findings. The enhanced power of the trade unions and the close allegiance between the labour movement and the Labour Government was based on the increasingly vociferous demands of the working class to enjoy economic and material prosperity in line with middle-class standards of living. The fact that they were not altogether successful in achieving these expectations and were forced to moderate their claims in defence of a Labour Government, highlights the conflict of interests which still exists in British society—the conflict between different class interests and their political expression in the Labour and Conservative parties. But more of this in Chapter 10.

The point to note here is that the embourgeoisement idea, as it was argued in the 1950s and 60s, was largely discredited by Goldthorpe and Lockwood's studies and replaced by notions of **'class convergence'**. Seen in their historical context, the arguments used to support theories of embourgeoisement seem out of date. Even the findings of Goldthorpe and Lockwood have been overcome by events. Times change and the balance of conflicting interests has shifted with the impact of new developments. Differences in the class structure have taken on different characteristics but the essential divisions remain because they are inevitable.

Social Stratification

In practice there is no known society in which social divisions of one kind or another do not exist. Sociologists use the general term 'social stratification' to describe the ways in which people can be grouped horizontally in terms of their wealth, power, prestige and influence, rather like the different strata in rock. In most cases the arrangement of strata is 'pyramid-shaped' with more people at the bottom than in the middle and at the top. The higher up you go the fewer are the people but the greater is their share of wealth, power and prestige.

But the business of 'social stratification' is not merely a question of putting people into categories which sociologists have invented. Certainly the terms that are used like 'social class', 'scale' and 'structure' have been coined by them, but only to describe what is already existing. Social class is the version of social stratification which our society uses to distribute valued resources between different groups of people. In other societies different forms of distribution occur with different degrees of permanence. The resources might be wealth in capitalist societies, political power in communist societies, inherited titles, land and obligations in feudal societies or prestige and respect in some pre-industrial societies. But in no society are these resources distributed equally or coincidentally. In every known society some people have more than others, and are ranked differently from others. And in all of them patterns of belief and types of organisation can be identified which ensure that the division remains.

Distributing Resources

Perhaps the easiest way to see how social stratification occurs is to list the resources which a given society values. Let's take Britain as an example. Britain is an industrial, capitalist society in which resources such as property, wealth and specialist skills are highly valued. The distribution of these resources—the extent to which they are monopolised or shared out equally—is both decided by and reflected in the distribution of power in our society. In other words, those who have most power are in a better position to decide on how the resources will be distributed. But their possession of power is also a reflection of having obtained a good proportion of these resources in the first place.*

Inevitably the competition for resources and power breeds conflict between contending groups. The other characteristic of social stratification in societies like Britain, therefore, is that it is not an absolute or static arrangement. Different groups are in competition with each other to further their own interests, and to attract unto themselves as big a proportion of the available resources as they can. Sometimes one group wins, but on other occasions they may be less successful. In theory at least, nothing is fixed and there can be a continual readjustment in the distribution and balance of power as a result of their achievements. In practice, however, the competition between conflicting interests is not always 'an open affair' in which each side is capable of being equally energetic or equally familiar with what is going on. The exercise of power in British society is relatively sophisticated and is usually most effective when it operates covertly. Think of the power of the media to mould public opinion, for example (see p. 140), or the ways in which ideologies operate (see p. 269).

In such circumstances access to education, the decision-making process and the kind of influential appointments which shape financial, social and legal policies, give the group which secures them the opportunity to reflect and reinforce their own economic interests more effectively. In practice, the extent to which these opportunities are

---

* Power, in terms of British society, does not mean 'brute strength' or 'armed force' but the power that is amassed by owning and controlling wealth, by being close to where influential decisions are made, and by being well educated (see Chapter 10).

'equally available to everyone', regardless of their economic position in society, is a matter of debate. Some argue that 'ability and application' are the criteria which count in 'getting in' and 'getting on'. Others see them as being in direct relationship to the absence or ownership of wealth.

This kind of analysis which defines social stratification in relation to economic resources, the inherent conflict between contending interests and the interdependence of economic and social power owes much to the theories of Karl Marx and others who have been influenced by his ideas.

The intricacies and implications of this relationship are much more difficult to sort out than the relatively more straightforward definitions of social class outlined above, which rely principally on occupational categories and cultural characteristics. Before reading on, you might find it useful to re-read pages 15–17 to remind yourself of some of the main characteristics of Marx' approach.

Marx' Theory of Class

You will remember from Chapter 1 that Marx' central concern was with the economic structure of society and the generation of conflict created by the relationships of work. It was also the relationship between men, labour and production which was the basis of Marx' definition of social class.

Marx defined classes as groups of people who share the same relationship to the means and organisation of production. And in any system of production the key feature for Marx was the identification of owners and controllers. Capitalism as a system simplified the struggle between contending groups into two mutually opposed camps whose interests were irreconcilably different and diametrically opposed. The two groups, according to Marx, were the **bourgeoisie**, or the owners and controllers of the means of production, and the **proletariat**, who own nothing but their labour power, and sell it to the bourgeoisie in return for wages.

Marx regarded the relationship between the two as one-sided and based on the exploitation of the one by the other. So long as the majority of wealth, property and profit was concentrated in the hands of the bourgeoisie, and so long as they continued to regard the proletariat merely as their source of labour power, to be bought and set to work as efficiently as possible, for as little as possible, their treatment of the proletariat was bound to be exploitative. Consequently they formed the 'superior' and more powerful class.

The proletariat, who as a group had non-ownership of wealth and the mutual experience of exploitation in common, made up the other great class in capitalist society. Marx saw the conflict of interests between the two as the relationship which would ultimately lead to the destruction of capitalism, the overthrow of the bourgeoisie, and their replacement, first by a society organised on behalf of the proletariat, in which property and power would be transferred to their control, and then by the establishment of an egalitarian and genuinely classless society.

In considering the bourgeoisie and the proletariat Marx made a distinction between capitalists and petit-bourgeoisie, and between the proletariat as 'a class *in* itself' and 'a class *for* itself'. The capitalists among the bourgeoisie were those who were most wealthy and most powerful and who derived their wealth and power from their owner-ship and control of property. The petit, or lesser, bourgeoisie were the 'managers' and organisers who, at a lower level, manage pro-duction and its various support systems like administration, educa-tion, law, technology, finance, etc., on behalf of the owners and controllers.

The proletariat represented 'a class *in* itself' so long as they shared the condition of selling their labour to the bourgeoisie. They did not act in their own interests as 'a class *for* itself' until they recognised the significance of their shared condition. To become aware of their common interests and to act collectively as a class meant they had to develop 'class-consciousness', and to overcome what Marx called 'false consciousness'. False consciousness existed so long as members of the proletariat saw their problems, struggles and relationships at work as essentially 'personal problems' as distinct from 'problems which they shared' with other members of the proletariat. False consciousness also existed when members of the proletariat were persuaded by force, social and ideological conditioning or sophisticated propaganda, to think and behave in a way which was detrimental to their class inter-ests. To take a modern example, Marx would probably describe the tendency of large sections of the working class to vote Conservative as a reflection of their false consciousness, since the Conservative party in Britain is the traditional political expression of the interests and concerns of the bourgeoisie.

Marx blamed the continuation of 'false consciousness' among the proletariat on what he identified as the bourgeois control of the 'superstructure' in society. The distinction Marx made between the 'base' or 'substructure' and the 'superstructure' can probably best be illustrated as shown in Fig. 5.

The 'substructure' in society was depicted by Marx quite simply as the prevailing economic system, its characteristic means and rela-tionships of production. The 'superstructure', on the other hand, was made up of those subsystems and institutions in society which were developed by men to encourage the political, social and ideological circumstances in which the needs of the economic system, and in par-

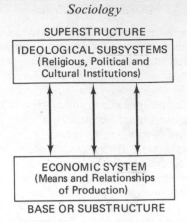

Fig. 5. Base and superstructure.

ticular its owners and controllers, could best be supported and rein-forced.

The ideological characteristics and the concentration of power in both the substructure and the superstructure were not regarded as absolute or static by Marx but the product of conflict and contradic-tion in the relationships of labour. This is not to suggest a 'pluralistic' arrangement in which contending groups have a roughly equal op-portunity to promote their interests and ideas. As we have already seen, the bourgeoisie, according to Marx, constitute the most powerful class. As the 'ruling class' they can generate, through their control of the superstructure, the kind of beliefs, values and explanations which serve to justify the status quo. Notions of 'common interests *between* classes', the encouragement of attitudes of materialism and free enter-prise, together with the message that 'the way things are' is more or less 'the way they *have* to be', conspire to keep the proletariat in a state of 'false consciousness' about their true class interests, and is much to the advantage of the bourgeoisie.

The entrenched power of the ruling class, reinforced by the ideolo-gical and organisational support of the superstructure, is conse-quently fairly invincible, and quite resistant to significant change of a revolutionary kind. But the circumstances for revolutionary change are not impossible. They exist, according to Marx, in the inevitability of 'the dialectic' and in man's capacity to 'make his own history'.

Marx also regarded the bourgeoisie as being ultimately 'their own worst enemies' in that they were already contributing to their inevit-able destruction. He gave two simple examples. In order to increase efficiency in production, and by implication profit, it was necessary to concentrate workers in factories and to arrange for them to live close together and near to their work. One of the main characteristics of industrialisation in the nineteenth century, when Marx was writing, was the growth of factory-based production and the growth of towns. But in bringing disparate members of the proletariat together, rather than allowing them to remain isolated geographically, or scattered in small workshops, the opportunity was provided for them to recognise their common condition and common interests, and to begin to develop the class-consciousness Marx spoke about as the necessary prerequisite for releasing themselves from exploitation.

Another example he gave of the way in which the bourgeoisie were 'sowing the seeds of their own destruction' was in the provision of education. The nineteenth century also witnessed the beginnings and general development of educational provision by the state for the proletariat. The reasons and the justifications for moving towards the full-scale provision of state education were many and varied, but some of the first steps and earliest arrangements operated with the intention of educating the workers. So far as the bourgeoisie were concerned, there were two main justifications. One was that the process of industrialisation needed a more educated workforce. The other was provoked by the fear of revolution. Throughout Europe political upheavals had challenged the authority, property and power of ruling groups. It is interesting to speculate why Britain avoided the kind of revolutionary outbursts which spread throughout Europe but the provision of education certainly provides part of the answer. Contemporary advocates of introducing and extending educational opportunities talked in terms of 'gentling the masses' and providing the kind of instruction in religion, respect for property, law and order, and the sense of duty which would, it was hoped, turn potential revolutionaries into responsible citizens, who had learned to identify with the values and interests of the bourgeoisie.

Whatever the original intentions were for beginning to educate the masses, the seeds were sown and, according to Marx, the opportunity was provided to learn the skills necessary to reason, to develop arguments, and to make the intellectual connections between 'experience' and 'its implications', which could be used, not to learn efficiency and obedience, as the bourgeoisie had intended, but to develop an awareness of 'class-consciousness'. Once you have taught someone to think, to read and to write, you can soon lose control of what they think and read and write. And Marx saw in this development a potentially valuable weapon in the process of social change. He also saw the struggle for the control of this tool 'education' as a significant feature of the more general 'class struggle'.

In a nutshell, the bringing together of more and more workers, into larger and larger units, and identifying their need to be educated for whatever reasons, created the circumstances in which they could become aware of their shared economic and political interests, and develop the class-consciousness and strength necessary to begin to challenge the power of the bourgeoisie.

Criticisms of Marx' Theory of Class

It is often said that Marx' view of class was a biased one, and that he allowed his political beliefs to influence his sociological analysis. This is undoubtedly true, but it should not automatically invalidate his theories. To accuse Marx of political bias assumes that there is another way of analysing the class structure in society which is 'value free'. The extent to which another analysis could be totally objective in this way is doubtful, however. Even the classification of occupations and the cultural definitions of class described earlier are based on assumptions about rank, worth and quality which are far from neutral.

Another criticism of Marx is his oversimplification of the class structure into two camps, and his failure to anticipate how the conflict between them would be reduced by the increase in middle-class occupations, the development of the welfare state, and working-class affluence. No doubt Marx would have explained the gentling and disguise of conflict as the effectiveness of the superstructure in its preservation of false consciousness. But neither has the destruction of the bourgeoisie and the replacement of capitalism by socialism happened quite as he predicted either.

Perhaps it is fairest to say that Marx was not really trying to describe a particular social class system, in a specific society, at a particular time. His definitions of class were rather an attempt to offer *a way of analysing* societies and systems, and to provide terms of reference. It is not really surprising that changes have happened which he did not foresee, and which provide complications for the simple application of his theories to present class circumstances. Subsequent theorists have tried to develop and refine his arguments to take account of social change, and the extent to which his analysis is still held to be one of the most important insights into the nature of social class in capitalist society is some indication of the strength and scale of his arguments. Also the way in which conflict operates and is yet somehow justified and disguised by the effectiveness of the superstructure has been immensely useful to sociologists, economists and political scientists alike in their various studies of industrial society. Charges of personal bias and wrong predictions therefore have to be set against the recognition that Marx' analysis is still thought to be relevant to our social class system today.

Max Weber's Theories of Stratification

Max Weber was also an early contributor to the discussion on social stratification. Like Marx he defined people's social class in relation to their economic power, but unlike Marx he made a distinction between different aspects of social stratification. Weber's major criticism of Marx was that he over-generalised from what is 'sometimes the situation' to what is 'always the situation'. Neither did he believe that class conflict and class-consciousness were the inevitable product of the class situation as Marx suggested, but that a variety of different actions could result, depending on the circumstances, from such a relationship. He wrote in *Class, Status and Party*, 'the direction in which the individual worker is likely to pursue his interests may vary widely' and 'the rise of societal or even communal action from a common class situation is by no means a universal phenomenon'. Weber took a more pragmatic and empirical line than Marx in this respect and concentrated rather on recording and comparing the different types of action that came from different groups in the class system.

He also drew attention to other dimensions of stratification which Marx tended to assume were all part and parcel of the same thing. Weber believed that not just their economic position but people's social standing was a significant feature of the way in which they were regarded by society. He referred to this as **status**. Usually people's status is a reflection of their job and economic position but the link is not always a direct one. Some groups receive more respect and prestige than others, and whilst the criteria change over time, they are usually based on social judgements about occupation, lifestyle, birth, culture and education. The ways in which such 'qualities' are defined and come to be agreed upon make an interesting debate. There seems to be a remarkable consensus in society at any one time about what is thought to be worthy of respect. The questions for sociologists to ask are of course, 'Who says that one kind of lifestyle, education or cultural behaviour is better than another?', 'Who makes these judgements in the first place?' And 'How do they become so widely accepted?' The ways in which ruling groups in society tend to promote and reinforce their own culture as the superior kind, and conspire through their control of key economic and social institutions to restrict entry to it, whilst at the same time setting it as the goal for other groups to aspire to, is a discussion provoked by Marx and Weber's debate and taken up again recently by sociologists like Bourdieu and Althusser and the arguments which contribute to the sociology of knowledge and control.

Whilst Marx tended to regard class and status as synonymous, Weber believed that status considerations often cut through and overlapped class divisions. For example, the distinction made between the 'respectable', 'hard working' and 'aspiring' working class and the 'rough', 'feckless' and 'unreliable' lower orders. Or the high status attached to individual craftsmen and the sense of vocation attributed to occupations like nursing and social work, neither of which is reflected in the economic rewards and social power of their holders.

The other dimension in Weber's view of social stratification besides class and status was **party**. Parties for Weber were groups of people who organised themselves to attract and exert power. They might be political parties, but also trade unions, pressure groups of various kinds, professional associations, or indeed any kind of group acting together in some form of collective action. In Marx' terms, political action in groups like these would be a direct reflection of their class position and class interests. But Weber conceded that such groups could well overlap class and status distinctions. A good example would be the present-day Labour Party, which is often identified as 'the party of the working class' but which, in fact, attracts votes and membership from different classes and various status groups.

In Conclusion

As you will appreciate by now, discussions about social class and social stratification among sociologists are not merely arguments about definitions and numbers, as the earlier sections in this chapter might have suggested. They are also theoretical discussions about the nature of society, the distribution of power and the conditions which provoke social change. In such circumstances it is very difficult to find a single definition of social class which is satisfactory, because it either becomes so general as to include all opposing views, or else seems biased by a concentration on one theoretical analysis rather than another.

You may also have wondered what the debate between Marx and Weber has to do with contemporary social class patterns in Britain. But as was pointed out in Chapter 1, a good deal of current sociology still engages in 'conversations with the founding fathers'. And though the characteristics and, to some extent, the terminology have changed, the terms of reference they identified, like conflict, power and status, are still the most useful ways of measuring and assessing social divisions today and asking important questions about their implications for the kind of society we are. Some of the implications of being a member of one social class rather than another, in relationship to educational opportunity, work experience and political behaviour, for example, will be taken up again in subsequent chapters.

Revision

1. Refresh Your Memory

Make sure you know the meaning of the terms: culture, stereotype, labelling, proletariat, bourgeoisie, embourgeoisement, affluent worker, social stratification, conflict, substructure, superstructure, power, status, party.

2. Check Your Understanding

Be able to explain in your own words:

(*a*) The difference between 'subjective' and 'objective' definitions of social class.

(*b*) The criteria used by sociologists to determine people's social class.

(*c*) The difference between the sociologist's seven-point scale and the Registrar General's Scale.

(*d*) The difference in definition between 'income' and 'wealth'.

(*e*) The difference between economic and cultural definitions of social class.

(*f*) The difference between 'embourgeoisement' and 'class convergence'.

(*g*) The difference between 'class-consciousness' and 'false consciousness'.

(*h*) The difference between the 'substructure' and the 'superstructure' of society.

(*i*) Weber's distinction between 'class', 'status' and 'party'.

(*j*) The main differences between Marx and Weber's theories of class.

3. Essay Questions to Try

(*a*) Does the concept 'embourgeoisement' adequately characterise post-war changes in the class structure of Britain?

(*b*) Examine the class position of either white-collar employees or affluent workers.

(*c*) 'We are all middle class now.' Discuss this slogan in relation to the class structure in Britain.

(*d*) Is a system of social stratification inevitable?

(*e*) Assess the view that Britain is ruled by an Establishment.

(*f*) What light can sociological theories throw on definitions of social class in contemporary Britain?

(*g*) Examine the view that social stratification is both universal and functional for social systems.

(*h*) The 'fact' and the 'consciousness' of class do not always coincide. What problems does this produce for sociologists?

(*i*) Is the social structure of Britain becoming more egalitarian?

(*j*) Examine the relationship between class-consciousness and social change.

(*k*) 'An affluent worker is still that; he is still a worker.' Discuss.

(*l*) 'Although in the nineteenth century the capitalists were a ruling class they have been replaced by party officials in the East and by the "Captains of Industry" in the West.' Discuss.

(*m*) Consider the implications of the growth of white-collar occupations for theories of social stratification.

Further Reading

Class and Class Conflict in an Industrial Society, Ralph Dahrendorf, Routledge and Kegan Paul, London, 1959.

Class Status and Power, R. Bendix and S. M. Lipset, Free Press (Collier Macmillan, West Drayton), 1953.

Classes in Modern Society, Tom Bottomore, Allen and Unwin, London, 1968.

Social Stratification: An Introduction, James Littlejohn, Allen and Unwin, London.

The Affluent Worker in the Class Structure, J. H. Goldthorpe, D. Lockwood, F. Bechhoffer and J. Platt, Cambridge University Press, Cambridge and London, 1969.

The Communist Manifesto, Karl Marx and Frederick Engels, Foreign Language Publishing House, Moscow.

The Making of the English Working Class, E. P. Thompson, Penguin, London.

3

THE FAMILY

It is a well-known truism that 'you can pick your friends but not your family'. Families are the organisations which, for good or ill, infants get born into, and for the most part are dependent upon until they are old enough to fend for themselves. The simple definition of a family is a social unit made up of people related to each other by blood, birth or marriage. Of course this relationship can take many different forms and embrace a wide variety of behaviour.

The examination of different family organisations in different societies has been a popular source of study for sociologists and anthropologists during the last fifty years or so. As a result a number of generalisations can be made about family life—but as with all generalisations and all 'established' bodies of knowledge, it is important to re-examine continually their accuracy and relevance in a world of rapidly changing circumstances. The significance of this will probably be most obvious when we come to an examination of family life in contemporary Britain.

Human Nature or Social Convenience?

One of the most important observations that can be made about the family is that it appears to be a universal phenomenon. In all human societies it has been found that some form of family arrangement exists and flourishes. The 'man or woman in the street' would probably explain this as being because of human nature—some instinctive, natural, biological drive that makes human beings cluster together in family groups. Certainly human beings are social animals who need to relate to other human beings for their survival. An infant, for example, takes a number of years of physical growth and human learning before it becomes self-sufficient and able to fend for itself. And of course if there was not some arrangement like a family, society would have to find another way of organising the reproduction of the next generation.

But if the reason why the family is a universal phenomenon is attributed to 'natural' or 'instinctive' behaviour and the need to be continually reproducing life, then you would expect family life in different societies to be more or less the same. If people had no control over their behaviour and it merely happened as a consequence of biological or physical forces in their make-up, then it would surely produce the same outcomes in any circumstances.

But this is not the case. Studies of family life in different societies and at different periods of time reveal a bewildering variety of behaviour, attitudes and organisational characteristics. In some societies the typical family unit is made up of one man and one woman and their dependent children. In others, two or three generations of the same family live together with their relations by marriage in an independent and almost self-sufficient community. In some societies a man may have several wives, or more rarely, a wife may have several husbands. These kind of polygamous relationships contrast markedly with contemporary British society in which monogamy—or the marriage of one man to one woman at a time—is the only legally permitted matrimonial relationship.

In some societies a far amount of free choice in the selection of marital partners is permitted, although in ostensibly 'free choice' situations like Britain cupid's bow seems to send its arrows in a remarkably predictable direction. In general, people tend to marry others of the same social class and background who they have come into contact with at school or college, at work or whilst involved in the same leisure activities. The age at which people decide to marry each other is also remarkably similar for most couples and the sequence of meeting, 'going out together', engagement and marriage follows a pattern which might cause a cynical outsider to doubt that there is any freedom of choice in the proceedings whatsoever.

In other societies more deliberately arranged marriages are the norm. Economics, religion, culture and tradition all play their part in encouraging the belief that parents within families are the best able to decide who their offspring should marry. The considerations are usually financial. In some cases the couple are allowed to meet and to say whether they accept their parents' choice, but among the Manus people of the Admiralty Islands, for example, when they were studied by the American anthropologist Margaret Mead in the 1920s, marriages were arranged in childhood or adolescence and the couple were not allowed to see or speak to each other until their wedding day.

Arranged marriages may seem a strange custom to those who have been brought up in Britain but in fact it is little more than a century ago that those with money and economic assets to offer were fully committed to the practice of making lucrative marital arrangements for their offspring.

The permanence or impermanence of marriage also varies in different societies. Traditional Christian teaching depicts it as a relationship which should endure until death, although current trends in the West have brought about some modification of this view. In Eire the constitution does not recognise the right of couples to get divorced and in other countries, in which catholicism has a strong hold, divorce, adultery, contraception and abortion are either illegal or shrouded in guilt and condemnation. In some American states couples can get divorced and married again very easily and quickly and the so-called 'tolerance of the permissive society' has encouraged a number of alternatives to conventional marriage to become accepted. In Britain divorce is possible, and since new divorce legislation came into effect in 1971 it is much easier now than once was the case. But complex separation and maintenance arrangements and a legacy of social and moral censorship are preserved to prevent the dissolution of marriage becoming 'too easy'.

In some Asian communities the man may divorce his wife but she is not allowed to divorce her husband. In other societies the remarriage of a widow is compulsory on her husband's death.

Relationships between parents and children also vary. In some, child-rearing is seen to be a woman's responsibility, in others fathers play a more equal role. In yet others, children are looked after in a much more communal way by relatives and kinfolk. In British society high priority is given to what are considered to be important childhood needs. The first few years of life are generally considered to be crucial in deciding what kind of adults children will become. A good deal of importance is attributed by experts to the kind and quality of relationships which a child enjoys at home. However accurate this contention might be, it lends a good deal of support to the idea that a woman's main responsibility is to care for her children, and to the claim that any kind of unorthodox behaviour in this respect is likely to result in 'maternal deprivation'.

The 'child-centredness' of British society also contributes to the consumer value of children. In such a climate parents can be persuaded to buy a vast range of material goods, special foodstuffs and services to enable them to be 'better parents' and 'to do the best' for their children. It also means that childcare and child-rearing can be concentrated in the family and women who seek work outside the home can be penalised by lack of state support and made to feel guilty for neglecting their children when the economy does not need their labour.

In other societies too, children are precious commodities. The Arapesh treat a baby as a 'soft, precious, vulnerable little object, to be protected, fed and cherished'. In some societies children, like wives, are a measure of a man's virility and status. But not all societies are so 'child-centred'. The Mundugumor women of New Guinea actively dislike child-bearing and they dislike children. In traditional Samoa, children were handed over, almost as soon as they were weaned, to the care of relatives and other young girls in the household. In many tribal and pre-industrial societies it is not uncommon for children to be reared by adults other than the child's parents. Children learn the customs and traditions of their tribe by emulating others and in societies in which authority and esteem are given to the elders they soon learn their place in the social order.

All of these illustrations, and there are many others, merely serve to show that family organisation and behaviour are immensely flexible. Society's need to make sure that continuing reproduction ensures its own survival is organised in different places in a variety of ways. The variety is dictated by social factors like economic conditions, law, religion, custom and tradition. As economic circumstances change so too do the social conditions which give rise to particular family organisation and behaviour. Thus the family, far from being a natural and instinctive relationship, is more accurately seen as a social and economic arrangement which is considerably determined by the prevailing economic and social characteristics of the society in which it operates.

The Functions of the Family

Those who take a functionalist view of social behaviour (see Chapter 1) have tended to monopolise the discussion about the social characteristics of families in contemporary society. According to their analysis families serve a number of important functions for their members and for society and thereby assist in both the preservation and recreation of social life. The functions performed by the family are said to include:

1. The organisation and regulation of sexual behaviour in a way which is legitimised by reproduction.
2. The care of children until they are capable of caring for themselves.
3. The socialisation, or 'informal training', of children to exhibit the kind of behaviour, values and attitudes which are expected of them by their society.
4. The organisation of a 'division of labour' between man and wife in terms of breadwinning, household maintenance, child-rearing and so on, so that the family group can operate as an efficient and interdependent unit.
5. The definition of roles like wife and mother, husband and father, grandparent, son, daughter, etc.—all of which enables family members to develop appropriate expectations of each other and to learn in turn what is expected of them.
6. The provision of love, care, emotional security and shelter for all members of the family which, unlike other groups they might belong to, ensures an intimate, enduring and responsible base in an otherwise impersonal and often alienating society.
7. The provision of leisure and recreation for family members and a unit within which to share celebrations and significant occasions like births, marriages and deaths.

This kind of analysis is no longer so popular among sociologists as it once was, however, largely because it begs a lot of important questions about the unacknowledged assumptions and values underpinning the analysis. It paints a picture of 'normal' family life as a happy, secure, enduring and mutually advantageous arrangement, which when functioning properly clearly provides an efficient unit for the procreation and rearing of children and the ongoing support of its members. In practice, however, many people's experience of family life is very different from this. For them the family is a source of struggle, pain, guilt and unhappiness—even when it is functioning 'normally'. The number of families which are split apart by broken marriages, unfulfilled expectations, resentment and even violence, is too common an occurrence to be dismissed as aberrations.

Another criticism of this kind of analysis is the ease with which it accepts the propriety of defining roles and dividing labour in exactly the kind of terms which best suit the prevailing economic system and the preservation of social stability, rather than recognising that there might be other kinds of arrangements and better kinds of arrangements which better suit the individuals involved. In defining certain kinds of behaviour as 'normal', then by implication, other varieties are abnormal. By setting yardsticks against which certain family behaviour is measured, it also implies what other behaviour can be said to lack. Built into these measurements is a whole range of unacknowledged assumptions about what is normal, proper and right, without any recognition of the social origins of these categories and the interests they might be said to reflect.

The major criticism of this analysis is its failure to take account of the economic characteristics of society, the implications these have for family structure and behaviour and of the interplay between economic needs, family organisation and change and the assumptions which different people have about family life.

The Family and the Economic System

We have already commented in Chapters 1 and 2 upon the significance of the economic system in society in determining relationships between different groups and influencing in turn the distribution of wealth, power and influence in society.

When sociologists refer to the economic system they mean quite simply 'the system by which goods (e.g. manufactured goods, foodstuffs, services, etc.) are produced and consumed'. Different societies have different economic systems.

Subsistence Economies

The Kgatla tribe live in parts of what is now Botswana in Southern Africa. Although life has changed there in recent years, the economic system described by Isaac Schapera in his book *Married Life in an African Tribe* is still a good example of family arrangements in pre-

industrial societies in which members of the same family and their
relatives are closely dependent upon each other for their economic
survival.

In communities which have not yet experienced much industrialisation or planned government intervention in the production of goods
and services, family and relatives are more dependent upon each other
than they might otherwise be. In the Kgatla tribe a family was defined
as a man and his wives, their dependent children and other kinfolk.
They not only lived, ate and played together, helped each other out
with personal problems and shared in each other's good fortune—but
as a unit they had to produce almost all their own food and other
material needs. They built their own huts and granaries, prepared the
food, fetched the water, wood and earth, collected wild plants, hunted,
reared cattle and collected timber for building. Such families attempted, by sharing the work and dividing the labour between men and
women, old and young, to be self-sufficient. If they could not rely on
each other they had to swap services and barter goods with other
households.

This kind of economic system which provides only enough for bare
survival, plus a little left over with which to barter and trade with
others, is known as a **subsistence economy**. People dependent upon
subsistence economies are very vulnerable to the vagaries of the climate, pests and natural disasters and it is important to remember that
millions of people all over the world still eke out an impoverished
existence at a subsistence level. Their poverty is perhaps even more
acute today in comparison to the relative opulence of the industrialised
world.

Socialist Economies

In the majority of modern industrialised societies the production of
goods and services is a much more complex business. Some societies
which call themselves socialist favour economic systems in which
capital in the form of factories, farms and industrial plants, for example, is owned by the state. The state employs workers to help produce the various goods and services in return for wages. In theory, if
any additional profit is made, over and above what is required to pay
out wages, it is used to expand and develop the economy on behalf of
everyone. Wages are not particularly high in state-owned and state-run
economies, and individual workers may find themselves with less freedom of choice about where they will live and work than people have
come to expect in our society. But there is less of a wage differential
between those who earn the most and those who earn the least and
the opportunity to do different kinds of work is less influenced by sex
and social class factors than in societies like ours.

Services like housing, cheap transport and heating, free education and medicine are generally regarded as the prerequisites of a just and equal society and are, therefore, subsidised by the state and made available on a more equal basis than in many other societies. Costly and less essential consumer goods like expensive household gadgets, cosmetics, pre-packaged and convenience foods and luxury items are less evident in socialist economies. The emphasis has tended to be on the *general* improvement of the *general* level of production and consumption for *all* people, rather than on creating a visible distinction between the consumption patterns of the wealthy and the less wealthy.

Of course, like all industrial societies, socialist societies are also dependent upon trade with other countries. They cannot produce all they need for their own consumption and the profits made from goods sold abroad are needed to expand their economies and to offset the cost of importing goods. International trade not only puts them in competition with other societies trying to increase their economic assets but also brings them into contact with economic systems based on rather different ideas. The major problem facing socialist economic systems in the world today is that of maintaining the ideal of an egalitarian distribution of wealth within their own societies when they are faced with competition from economic systems which do not hold to this criterion.

The Family in Socialist Societies

So far as family life is concerned in socialist societies, as in all societies, it plays a complementary role to the needs of the economic system. In Russia before the socialist revolution of 1917 the Church, the Mosque and the Synagogue dominated family life. Under the rule of the Tsar religious laws of various kinds governed marriage, divorce and family responsibilities, and they were used to transmit the traditions of the past from generation to generation. The power of religion was closely aligned to the social and economic interests of the Tsars and was used to terrify and dominate the vast majority of the population in an extremely unequal society. One of the first actions of the Bolsheviks after the revolution was to try to curtail the power of the various religions which were seen as counter-revolutionary forces supporting bourgeois interests.

In 1918 civil marriage was substituted for religious marriage and divorce was made easily obtainable. A wife was not bound to live with her husband, or to take his name, and legal discrimination against illegitimate children was abolished. The attempts to liberalise the relationships of marriage and divorce were in line with the Marxist view that under capitalism the form of the family creates inequality between the sexes, so that men are encouraged to 'dominate' women and to regard them and their children as an extension of their property. Old traditional ideas perpetuated within the family were seen by the new régime to be a hindrance to their attempts to establish a socialist state and a socialist economy.

But it took more than change in the law to alter relationships within the family and a variety of developments in the 1920s, partly stimulated by political ideals and partly by political expediency, produced a very confusing period in which family relationships and responsibilities appeared to be in chaos. According to most Western observers, the results of new sexual freedoms were disastrous. The Soviet press of the thirties reported that promiscuity flourished and that juvenile deliquency was on the increase as a result of irresponsible parents and broken homes. It became clear that whilst the bourgeois and religious domination of family life under Tsarist rule had supported the economic and social exploitation of the vast majority of the population, the answer was not to undermine the family but rather to encourage it to reflect more socialist and egalitarian ideals. It was still the most efficient unit for organising reproduction and child-rearing. What needed to be prevented was injustices between men and women within the family.

In contemporary socialist/communist societies like Russia and those of Eastern Europe, civil arrangements as distinct from religious ceremonies are still encouraged as the basis of family organisation, divorce is relatively easy and women are encouraged to play an equal role in work outside the home. Comprehensive nursery and childcare provision is made by the state to ensure that this is possible.

In China the pre-revolutionary practice of arranged marriages and the repressive authority of elderly relatives has now been removed. Up until 1949 the ideas of Confucius, a philosopher who lived almost 500 years before the birth of Christ, were still used to keep people in their place. Women had to abide by the three obediences and the four virtues laid down by Confucius. The three obediences demanded that women should obey their fathers and elder brothers when young, their husbands when married and their sons when widowed. The four virtues demanded that a woman should know her place, hold her tongue, take care to look attractive and do the housework willingly. In practice this meant that Chinese women were amongst the most oppressed in the world. Poverty forced them into marriage at an early age and they had no choice of whom they could marry. Weddings were arranged for them by their parents and were more like business deals than love affairs. Child marriages were usual, although young girls were bought and sold into prostitution as an alternative to marriage. They had no say in the matter. It was quite common for a wealthy man to have a number of wives and several mistresses. Their main duty was to produce children and from an early age their feet were bound to restrict their movement and to be a sign of their slave-like existence. They were not allowed to divorce their husbands and if their husbands died they could not remarry. But husbands could get rid of them any time they liked, leaving them penniless, ridiculed and despised. Old Chinese sayings like 'noodles are not rice and women are not human beings' and 'a wife married is like a pony bought, I'll ride her and whip her as I like' vividly describe the attitude to women in old China. They were not allowed to work in the fields because it was believed that potatoes planted by a woman would not sprout and melons planted by a woman would be bitter. It was thought improper for them to expose any part of their bodies except their face and hands and even in an emergency, like a drought or a flood, they were not allowed to help the men save the crops.

The Chinese look back to the period before 1949 as 'the bitter past'. In October of that year came liberation. After a tough war with Japan and a civil war at home the People's Republic of China was set up under the leadership of the communist party and its Chairman, Mao Tse-tung. Since then many things, including family life, have changed dramatically.

One of the first things the new communist government did after liberation was to introduce new marriage laws which did away with the buying and selling of young girls, arranged marriages and prostitution. There was to be no discrimination against illegitimate children and divorce, though frowned upon, was to be granted if both partners wanted it. By law women could not marry until 18 and men had to wait until 22. But today late marriages are encouraged—25 for women and 28 for men is usual. The Chinese believe that the early twenties are the years in which a young person should study and work hard and that marriage should not be allowed to interfere.

Marriage is a simple affair. No vows, no reception, no honeymoon—just a quick visit to the local government offices to say that the couple love each other and want to marry. Families often share facilities like bathrooms and kitchens with other families and elderly parents often take responsibility for childcare and domestic arrangements to allow the younger parents to work. In China the state has taken positive steps to help working parents. Nurseries, public dining, washing and sewing facilities have greatly reduced the domestic burden that women previously carried. Family planning, abortion and sterilisation are all easily available and do not carry any of the stigma or restrictions which are imposed on people in some other societies. In schools children are brought up to consider themselves as equal, and taught that as workers they will have an equally important contribution to make in the establishing of a socialist society.

Capitalist Economies

The economic system characteristic of the majority of Western industrialised societies is that of capitalism. In a capitalist economic system the means of production—the factories, industrial plants, farms and machinery and so on—are owned not by the state but by private individuals and shareholders who make up a relatively small percentage of the population (see Chapter 2). The majority of the population sell their labour power to the owners of capital in return for wages. The simple relationship between those who own capital and those who work for the capitalist class has become more complex, of course, since Marx and Engels first described it more than a hundred years ago. As capitalism has developed and expanded, it has taken on national and international proportions (see Chapter 7). Now multi-national labour forces often cooperate, but frequently compete, to make their companies' goods as cheaply and efficiently as possible.

In the competition between workers to protect their jobs, and in turn their standards of living, high productivity and low wages are the two variables which employers are anxious to exploit, because both of them imply profitability. The principal motivation of capitalism—the aim to increase wealth and to amass profit for the owners of capital—is not, as in socialist economies, based on egalitarian ideals. Capitalist societies are essentially unequal in their distribution of wealth, income, opportunities and influence. Individual workers may benefit from a thriving and expanding economy. Their wages might well increase and their ability to buy material goods and services will rise proportionately. But in periods of economic decline, or when new technologies make their labour obsolete, or when the owners of capital close down specific plants and redirect their resources to more lucrative areas, then workers are extremely vulnerable. Unemployment, low pay and bad working conditions are as much a feature of capitalism for many workers as relative affluence and improved standards of living are for others.

In such circumstances, the visible poverty of some, compared to the relative affluence of others, obviously provides a basis for conflict in capitalist societies—especially if the discrepancies between the two become a source of grievance among the less affluent. Those who profit from a capitalist economy need to ensure that no serious threats to their interests are allowed to develop, otherwise they may find their wealth and privileges removed or reduced. They must ensure that workers accept their financial and social inequality as a matter of course and learn to accept the assumptions and values on which they are based. The capitalist economic system needs not only a labour force which is efficient, healthy and capable of working hard, but one which in terms of attitudes and values is attuned to the ideas and sentiments which encourage capitalism to flourish.

The Family in Capitalist Societies

In describing family patterns in societies like Britain sociologists usually make a distinction between **nuclear families** and **extended**

families. The nuclear family is usually depicted as a modern phenomenon which has come about because industrialisation and the factory system, geographic mobility by people in search of work, birth control and the emancipation of women from the home have all encouraged smaller families which are not dependent on social relationships and support from other relatives. The nuclear family therefore refers to a unit made up of husband, wife and their dependent children. 'Extended family', on the other hand, is a term frequently used to describe the family arrangements of working-class people in traditional working-class communities. Just as in many pre-industrial societies, like the Kgatla mentioned on page 53, extended family life means two or even three generations of the same family living in close proximity to each other, sharing in each other's social, emotional and economic lives on a fairly regular, day-to-day basis.

Although historians have shown by their investigations into town records and parish registers that nuclear families existed in the sixteenth and seventeenth centuries in Britain, long before the Industrial Revolution, and recent studies have shown how extended families have survived well into the twentieth century in long-established working-class areas, it is true to say that the small, mobile and relatively isolated nuclear family is the one which, looked at from the point of view of society, best reflects the needs of an industrial, capitalist economy like ours.

As we have seen, one of the main requirements of a capitalist economic system is a healthy, responsible and docile labour force: healthy in that it is well fed, clothed and cared for; responsible in that it has others dependent upon its capacity to earn wages; and docile in that any serious challenge to the prevailing organisation of production may result in a reduction of the wealth and power of the owners of capital.

All these characteristics are facilitated by the division of labour in the family and the distinction made between **wage labour** and **domestic labour.** In order that the major breadwinner in a family, most often the man, can be enabled to go out to work, the other partner, in most cases the woman, must take on related domestic responsibilities.

Within the family the future labour force is born, reared and encouraged to prepare itself for future wage or domestic labour. The learning of sex roles appropriate to the inequalities of opportunity experienced by men and women in capitalist societies is well established by the differing socialisation experiences of boys and girls in their early years of family life—experiences which are later reinforced by education, the mass media, legislation and patterns of employment. Within the family the primary labour force is provided with the domestic services necessary to enable it to work, and with the various 'home comforts'—sexual, spiritual and material—which appear to make it all worthwhile. As a focus of responsibility, the nuclear family provides an ideal support system for capitalism and as a unit of consumption it provides a lucrative market. Single people or those living in communal groups which pool resources like cars, labour-saving devices and household gadgets do not spend as much on material goods as separate family units can be persuaded to do.

In her book *Wedlocked Women*, Lee Comer argues that, so far as capitalism is concerned, the very best arrangements people can make is to preserve the distinction between wage labour and domestic labour in the nuclear family. Thus a man will:

1. Take a wife who will care for him and see to all his needs and bear his children.
2. Live with them in a small isolated group and preferably away from his first family with whom his links must be only nominal (aged parents are a liability).
3. Be intent upon improving his standard of living, thereby committing himself to overtime or professional ladder-climbing, both of which require long hours away from home and a patient uncomplaining wife.
4. Be prepared to move house and town from time to time, but not to strike.
5. Support a wife and growing family.

To support the requirements of a capitalist economy the best arrangements a woman can make are to accept the priority of her domestic role as a means of servicing her 'breadwinner' and to provide the childcare and emotional security which the state under capitalism divests to the family.

The economy, of course, frequently has need of female labour to act as a 'reserve army' in the unusual, but critical circumstances of, for example, war and as a source of cheap secondary labour. The expansion in women's work outside the home since the war has been in the service industries, in which women frequently perform an extension of their 'caring' and 'domestic' roles in return for wages which are consequently low in relationship to the jobs usually done by men. The other main growth area in female employment has been in unskilled factor work and part-time employment, which for the various reasons outlined in Chapter 8 has also been rewarded with significantly low wages. Despite the increasing need for many women to work, to supplement the nuclear family income in a time of rapid inflation, and frequently as sole breadwinners in single-parent families, women are dissuaded from being too attached to their work roles. Low wages, lack of training and job opportunities, and the meagre provision by the state of nurseries and childcare facilities all conspire to reinforce the secondary and casual nature with which women's labour outside the home is regarded.

Competition between workers and the 'freedom' to acquire skills, promotion and even jobs in the present economic circumstances, require a workforce which is prepared to go wherever its skills are in demand. It could not do this if it was tied emotionally or by obligation to the wider family group. Where small pockets of close-knit family groups still survive in Britain they do so in the most depressed and economically deprived areas of our country like Glasgow, South Wales and the South West. The classic studies of working-class extended family life in Bethnal Green in London, in Nottingham and in Hull were all carried out in the fifties and sixties before slum clearance, redevelopment and increasing unemployment forced family members to separate and to live in strange and often unwelcoming new towns where they moved to find work.

The main examples of extended family relationships in Britain today are to be found among Asian communities who have transferred the forms of family organisation which made sense in India, East Africa, Pakistan and Bangladesh, to their new homelands. In a potentially hostile society, in which all non-white immigrants face varying degrees of prejudice and discrimination, it may be that the extended family helps to provide a source of collective comfort and strength for those who face common problems. Their concentration in the older areas of industrial and commercial centres like Bradford, Leicester and the East End of London, reflects the types of work they were first recruited, and later compelled, to undertake. Areas of cheap and frequently inadequate housing are often the only alternative in a society in which council housing is constrained by long waiting lists and private housing is increasingly expensive.

For Asian youngsters, born and brought up in a totally different cultural and economic environment from that of their parents, however, the obligations and expectations of the extended family can provide a number of conflicts. Arranged marriages and the particularly authoritarian subjection of women are just two examples of traditional behaviour which many of the younger generation of Asians now find oppressive. For those who wish to challenge these limitations and escape from the obligations to their elders, it is likely that they, like many aspiring workers before them, will find themselves susceptible to the attractions of 'getting on' and 'moving up the social scale' as an alternative, and in the process come to adopt the values and characteristics of nuclear family life.

Not only does capitalism expect families to be geographically mobile but also socially mobile. To maintain a non-egalitarian distribution of wealth and resources, educational competitiveness, notions of individualised self-improvement and materialism need to be fostered to keep people in competition with each other. Max Weber's association of 'the Protestant ethic' of hard work and thrift as a philosophy particularly sympathetic to the early rise of capitalism provides an interesting parallel to contemporary capitalism's creation and reliance upon assumptions about 'meritocracy' as a way of justifying its non-egalitarian practices. On the basis of these assumptions, the unequal distribution of power and influence, wealth and material resources and the absence of equality of opportunity, can be explained in terms of 'inequality of ability and application', rather than as the result of economic, social and cultural control exercised by those who own capital and whose interests dominate society. In practice these assumptions support the belief that through hard work, application at school, deferred gratification and a willingness to move about, people can rise out of their 'lower station' and come to enjoy the rewards of better jobs, more money and increased status—even if, and largely because, it is at the expense of rejecting the class they came from, in order to identify with the class they are aspiring to. And in the process 'conspicuous consumption' is clearly an important indication of having been seen to make this transition.

Of course not everyone is prepared to behave in the ways which best suit capitalist society. The conditioning which society exerts upon us all to conform to certain 'norms' is exceedingly powerful and remarkably effective but it is not always successful. We noted in Chapter 1 that people are 'determining' as well as 'determined' beings. Individuals do not always do what is expected of them. In the majority of instances their idiosyncracy is not the result of conscious decisions to oppose the values and expectations of a philosophy and system of economic arrangements which they reject. Many of the alternatives, which if they were allowed to take hold would seriously challenge the power of those who benefit from a capitalist economy, are more frequently regarded by the powerful and the powerless alike as 'aberrations' or 'signs of failure'. In the event, society is prepared to tolerate a lot of individual differences in family living arrangements, but is always careful to ensure that not too many people 'rock the boat' by trying to be different. Divorced people, for example, are pressured by the difficulties of living on their own in a family-centred society, the romantic view of love and marriage encouraged by the mass media, and the social assumptions that 'normal' people are happily married, to remarry as soon as they can. As Lee Comer points out in *Wedlocked Women*, we tend to find uncomplimentary categories for those who, whether or not by choice, live 'outside the nuclear family'—spinsters, divorced people, single parents, lesbians, homosexuals, childless couples, middle-aged bachelors and aging widows and widowers: 'Whatever their personal circumstances, these people are daily reminded, with everything from the ideal happy family type advertisements to banter from their work mates, that they don't fit into society's straight jacket. ("Waiting for Mr Right are you?", "We'd prefer a family man for this job", "This one'll get you to the altar. You can't hold out much longer.") They are the curiosities and casualties of a family centred society.

'Single and divorced people are supposed to be lonely and bitter and if they're not then there must be something wrong with them. Homosexuals' and lesbians' only usefulness is as a subject for dirty jokes and ridicule. Not only are they "outside the family", but because they threaten it, they were until recently outside the law. Childless couples are pitied or badgered with questions, and suffer endless innuendoes about "the patter of tiny feet". One-child families are always considered incomplete (Don't you think it's cruel/selfish/niggardly to have an "only" child?).'

In attempting to explain why, for example, unmarried mothers are considered to be serious social problems in Britain, illegitimate children are discriminated against, homosexuals have to engage in furtive secrecy and women still lack free and easy access to contraception, abortion and sterilisation, Lee Comer concludes that 'the thread which links all these things is the fact that each one poses a threat which, if it was allowed free rein and social acceptability, would seriously erode the inflexibility of family life' and in turn the services it performs for our economic system.

Family Problems

Divorce

In societies like ours we tend to react to all forms of behaviour which do not support the 'happy family ideal' as problematical. Divorce is a case in point. Until very recently divorce in Britain was both difficult to obtain and characterised by a sense of shame and stigma.

The difficulties have been partly to do with a religious heritage in which both Protestant and Catholic Churches were influential and powerful enough to condemn divorce and help to make it a rare and expensive occurrence.

The difficulties have also been exacerbated by the legal system which has supported both the moral imperatives of the Church and the economic division of labour in the family, which assumes that a man is financially responsible for his wife and children, and that in return for economic dependency, a wife must provide domestic and sexual services. These assumptions made it impossible, for example, for married women to own property in their own right until 1882; to vote on equal terms with men until 1928; to have an equal right to matrimonial property on the dissolution of marriage until 1969; and to be able to secure possession of the matrimonial home in the event of a husband's brutality until the Domestic Violence and Matrimonial Property Act of 1976.

The legal position has also contributed to the preservation of a double standard about acceptable male and female sexual behaviour in marriage. A man can still not be convicted of raping his wife, since sexual intercourse is considered to be part of his conjugal rights. A woman separated from her husband was unable to claim maintenance in the Magistrates' Court until 1978 if it could be proved that she had committed adultery. The extent to which her husband had committed adultery was not an issue. Still in the matters of sexual behaviour, adultery, rape and domestic violence, a woman must be able to provide the law with corroborating evidence if the offence is being contested. The law is still bound to take a man's word in preference to a woman's if there are no witnesses, and to remind the jury that women, like children, are notoriously unreliable in what they say.

Divorce in Britain was actually illegal until 1670 and until the middle of the nineteenth century it was necessary to have a private Act of Parliament passed to get a divorce. Clearly the difficulty and the expense of obtaining a private Act of Parliament meant that in practice only wealthy men had access to the rights of legal divorce.

In 1857 the Matrimonial Causes Act set up the first court to deal with divorce proceedings, but whilst a man could be awarded a divorce on grounds of adultery only, a woman had to prove both adultery and either desertion, cruelty, incest, rape, sodomy or bestiality against her husband. By making divorce easier for men than women, the new law helped confirm the inequality between men and women in society. And although the Act made divorce more widely available, it still remained the prerogative of those who could pay the high legal costs involved—in practice, wealthy men. By this Act divorce was firmly related to 'guilt' and 'matrimonial offences'. Divorce by mutual agreement and consent was not permitted. In fact, any suggestion of collusion between man and wife in the presentation of a case was enough to prevent the divorce being granted.

In 1878 another Matrimonial Causes Act gave Magistrates' Courts the power to grant Separation Orders. This entitled an aggrieved wife to maintenance and the custody of any children under the age of 10. She was not entitled to maintenance if she had committed adultery and she had little power to force a separated husband to pay his maintenance if he chose not to. Although Separation Orders in the Magistrates' Court were the only legal option available to the majority of people who could not afford High Court proceedings, unlike divorce they did not entitle people to remarry.

In 1923 the grounds for divorce on the basis of 'simple adultery' became equal for men and women. In 1937 the grounds on which a divorce could be obtained were extended to include incurable insanity, desertion for three years or more, and cruelty, but until 1969 the notion of matrimonial offences which had to be corroborated by evidence, all served to perpetuate the shame and stigma associated with divorce.

The 1969 changes in divorce legislation came into effect in 1971. It was then possible for couples who had been married for at least three years to get a divorce if their marriage was 'irretrievably broken down'—after two years with mutual consent, and after five years without mutual consent. Matrimonial offences could still be cited to accelerate the proceedings but it now meant that divorce could be a much less acrimonious and painful affair if couples were prepared to use the new grounds.

Although when it was introduced it was heralded as the 'Casanova's Charter', which would encourage irresponsible and promiscuous behaviour especially among men, the new legislation has, in fact, taken a lot of the shame, misery and guilt out of divorce. It has enabled many people who were living in unsatisfactory marriages or with partners who refused to give them a divorce, to have new grounds to free themselves. In practice this has meant an incredible rise in the divorce rate since 1971. This can be explained partly by changing attitudes to marriage, especially among the young, and the increasing emancipation of women from social and economic dependency on unsatisfactory husbands, but it is also because divorces which were impossible to obtain before 1971 are now legally permitted.

Changes in the law have encouraged changes in social attitudes and divorce no longer carries the kind of stigma which it once did, but it would be wrong to assume that it is now a relatively automatic and painless operation. When most people get married, they do so expecting the marriage to last, and few break-ups occur without a good deal of unhappiness on the part of the people involved. Whilst moral and legal attitudes might present fewer problems these days, there are still very real practical problems to be faced for those left caring for children on their own. There are something like one million single-parent families in Britain today, not all of them the result of divorce, but they are among the poorest sections of society, especially when the sole breadwinner is a woman.

Also society, as was suggested earlier, has a vested interest in favouring the family unit. Although the Courts negotiate complicated custody and maintenance arrangements and make special arrangements for the legal and financial protection of children after divorce, maintenance frequently goes unpaid and special Court action is needed to chase up recalcitrant husbands. So far as state benefits are concerned, women are still considered to be financially dependent on men and a single woman's rights to social security, supplementary benefits and family income supplement are withdrawn as soon as she begins co-habiting, however temporarily, with a man.

The difficulties of living as a single parent or without the custody of children in a family-centred society encourages 75 per cent of divorced people to remarry fairly soon. And so long as romantic love as a basis for marriage is encouraged, and social and media pressures are exerted to romanticise the family ideal, then people will be highly susceptible to the idea of trying again. For men, perhaps more than women, who have not been quite so well prepared for the domestic side of life, remarriage may represent a purely practical response to the disadvantages of living alone. For women who by force of circumstances are not economically self-reliant, life without a man can be a financially difficult experience. For them remarriage may also represent a purely practical response to the disadvantages of poverty. For all of these reasons, the economic benefit to capitalism guaranteed by a family-centred society is not seriously challenged by divorce so long, as we have seen, remarriage can be made more or less a matter of course.

Illegitimacy

Illegitimacy does not seem to have presented much of a problem to our ancestors until the strict morality of Puritanism held the government and social order in its grip. Until the sixteenth century the upper classes passed their titles on to illegitimate children in the same way as to their legitimate heirs. Among the peasantry marriage was a relatively casual affair by all accounts, and the promise to marry sometime in the future rather than the marriage itself was usually considered to be the most important declaration between couples in the lower classes.

The growth of cottage industries in the late seventeenth and early eighteenth centuries meant that a young couple did not need to fear pregnancy. They could both stay at home, work and look after the child. A woman would not be blamed for premarital intercourse and the birth of illegitimate children unless the father left her. In such circumstances she became dependent upon the Poor Law. In law an illegitimate child was regarded as 'the child of no one' since he or she had no legal parents. The fact that the child had a mother who might be looking after it was considered to be irrelevant, since children were regarded as belonging only to the father. (Mothers only received equal rights with fathers in all matters to do with children in 1973.) Since an illegitimate child belonged to no one, no one could legally be held responsible for supporting it.

In 1731 the Poor Law was changed to force a woman to name the father as a condition of receiving any assistance. Midwives had to take an oath promising to refuse help to an unmarried mother during the birth of her child unless she named the father. Sometimes women, during the agony of birth, named the local landowner rather than be forced to marry the child's natural father. Once named, magistrates could issue a warrant for the father's arrest, pay for the marriage licence, and take him by force if necessary to the nearest church. The shame was not so much in having illegitimate children but in being unable to support them. At the same time as these 'shot-gun weddings' were being forced on the poor, George IV was living openly with his nine children, all of them illegitimate.

In the nineteenth century the government tried to stamp out illegitimacy among the poor by making poor relief lower and the conditions even harsher. As with other characteristics of Victorian life, women suffered most by the double standard in moral behaviour. Women in domestic service seduced by their employers and other servants were the ones who lost their jobs if they became pregnant. Many of them killed their babies or paid exorbitant amounts of money to have them looked after by 'baby farmers', who generally exploited the mothers and neglected the children.

In almost all respects illegitimate children were at greater risk than legitimate children from premature birth and premature death, child abuse and exploitation, but successive governments sought to tackle the problem by penalising mothers rather than by preventing their social exploitation by others. Even during the First World War the sharp increase in the number of 'war babies', whose fathers were subsequently killed before they could marry their mothers, brought no changes in the laws relating to illegitimacy. It was not until 1926 that an illegitimate child was given legitimate status by the marriage of his or her parents and only in 1926 could childless couples adopt illegitimate children.

The Victorians, like the Puritans before them, made a significant contribution to the stigmatisation of illegitimate children and their mothers. Before contraception was freely available and at a time when the 'immorality' of men was regarded as less significant than the 'immorality' of women, it was felt that the mothers of illegitimate children were at best unwise and at worst immoral—both undesirable characteristics which contemporary ignorance assumed would be automatically inherited by their children. Legal and social discrimination against these 'unpredictable' and 'dubious' people was consequently regarded as perfectly logical.

In the thirty years after the Second World War the 'problem' of illegitimacy was given prominence again as one of the 'disturbing side-effects of an increasingly permissive society'. Social commentators and churchmen prophesied the 'end of family life as we know it' and pointed to high levels of premarital intercourse and illegitimacy to substantiate their fears. Attempts to make contraception more widely available, to make divorce easier and to provide legal abortions were all achieved against a 'prohibition' lobby determined to associate such reforms with declining moral standards, a threat to family life, and practices directly contrary to the teachings of the bible.

In fact, the illegitimacy rate has doubled in the years between 1950 and 1980. In 1977 it stood at 9.7 per cent compared to 4 per cent in 1901 and 5 per cent in 1950. The number of girls who are pregnant when they get married has also risen since the war. In 1973, for example, out of every 100 live births, 56 were conceived before marriage and 8 were illegitimate. Of the 55,000 or so illegitimate births in 1977, 11,000 were subsequently legitimised by the marriage of the parents, 7,000 children were adopted, 27,000 lived with their unmarried parents in a stable relationship, almost 2,000 were brought up by mothers on their own, and the rest lived with mothers who married other men.

As in the past, the stigma of illegitimacy has tended to be unequally applied to the middle class and the working class. Middle-class women in the more sexually permissive atmosphere of the sixties and seventies have been more inclined to make use of oral contraceptives and to be able to afford private abortions to avoid illegitimacy. For working-class women, less easy access to contraception and abortion has made them more likely than middle-class women to have illegitimate children, but not more likely to have premarital sexual intercourse. Because of their greater economic independence, a significant number of the unmarried middle-class women who became pregnant in the sixties and seventies chose to support their children on their own. Such women were frequently admired for 'keeping their children' and not succumbing to hasty and potentially unhappy marriages. The options were less easy for working-class women, however, because of their limited earning power and the traditional stigma of illegitimacy still applied to the behaviour of 'the lower classes'.

On July 5th, 1979, the Law Commission published a Working Paper on Illegitimacy as a prelude to changes in the law, which made as its main recommendation 'the abolition of the status of illegitimacy ... to ensure that the legal relationship between father and child can be the same as that between legitimate children and their fathers'. On the face of it the recommendations seem eminently enlightened. By removing the status of illegitimacy it should help to create the climate of opinion which will cease to regard illegitimacy as a social stigma. And anything which can improve the lot of illegitimate children is to be welcomed. Even in 1979 the perinatal mortality rate (i.e. children who die shortly after birth) is still higher among illegitimate children than legitimate children and illegitimate children with single parents are more likely to experience social and economic hardships than children brought up in a stable family union. The Law Commission, in suggesting that the father of an illegitimate child should have the same rights and responsibilities to that child as the mother, is no doubt hoping that he will in turn be more likely to maintain the child properly.

There is a fair amount of opposition to the Commission's proposals, however. The feminist lawyers group 'Rights of Women' argue that the law, and indeed society, has increasingly ceased to discriminate against illegitimate children. With some minor reforms in the maintenance and inheritance laws, and in the rules relating to nationality, there would be almost no legal discrimination at all. They see the Law Commission's recommendations as being not about 'children's rights' as they claim, and not about 'mothers' rights' which they totally disregard, but about 'fathers' rights'. They point out that if the father of an illegitimate child wants to take an interest in the child and provide for its welfare he will be doing this by either marrying, living with, or helping to maintain the mother. They argue that fathers who have not shown this concern should not be given automatic and equal rights to the child if they have no responsibility for bringing it up. Their interference and harassment at a later date could cause serious pain and suffering to the mothers and children concerned. They object to the legal assumption that only a father can legitimise a child, give it a name and an acceptable place in society. They ask why it should be considered such a disgrace for the child to take the mother's name and nationality. By giving all fathers—good, bad and indifferent and those who have had only fleeting associations with the mother—automatic and equal rights to their illegitimate children, the Law Commission will restore to men important controls over women, at a time when women are increasingly demanding their independence and their right to choose to look after their children themselves, rather than marry unsatisfactory husbands. According to this group a better reform would be to do something about low wages, inadequate housing and poor childcare facilities that many women bringing up children alone are forced to endure.

Domestic Violence

It is only recently that 'the problem of domestic violence' has been examined. This is not to say that 'wife beating' is a new phenomenon or that the problem is well documented. We have seen already how English law has historically supported the notion that women and children are an extension of man's property. These kinds of assumptions have supported his right to treat them as he likes and have long discouraged the intervention of the law in matters relating to 'domestic arguments'. The historic inequalities between men and women in British society have contributed to marital and other sexual/social relationships in which men have traditionally been in control of women and in which women have learned to tolerate the less acceptable varieties of male behaviour as natural or inevitable.

Concern about the plight of battered women first came to the attention of the public and the authorities almost by accident in the early seventies when a small group of women, campaigning against rising prices in Chiswick High Street, encountered lots of young mothers complaining about isolation. They decided to open a community centre of some kind where women and their children could escape from their loneliness for a time. This was the beginning of Chiswick Women's Aid, which rapidly became famous both as 'a haven for battered women and their children' and infamous for the overcrowded and even squalid conditions in which the women fleeing from domestic violence were forced to live.

In 1974 the government set up a Select Committee to investigate Violence in Marriage and by 1975 approximately one hundred voluntary and charitable refuges for battered women and their children had been set up in different parts of the country. In 1975 they came together to form the National Women's Aid Federation (NWAF). In a relatively short time the battering of women became a public issue. The media sensationalised it and the government called for research to explain why it happened.

Small-scale research projects designed to investigate the causes of domestic violence have been established over the last ten years or so in America and Britain but their value and accuracy have still to be substantiated. R. J. Gelles (*The Violent Home*, 1972) says that the 'categorization of intra-family violence depends on whose norms and whose perspectives one takes', and as Elizabeth Wilson points out (*The Existing Research into Battered Women*, 1976) a good deal of the evidence submitted to the government's Select Committee relied on value judgements which were 'nothing more than a repetition of old stereotypes and prejudices'. For example, the Northumberland and Tyneside Council for Social Services attributed domestic violence in their area to the special attitudes to marriage in the North East of England in which women could expect to be beaten and too much Newcastle Brown Ale led 'men to boast of their prowess' and beat up their women.

In an article in the *Welfare Officer* (January 1976) Dr Jasper Gayford divided battered women into nine 'types', to which he then gave names like 'Tortured Tina', 'Violent Violet', 'Fanny the Flirt' and 'Go-Go Gloria'. 'Fanny the Flirt . . . early in life learned to manipulate people and found the glory of being the centre of attraction. With puberty she found new toys to play with, but unfortunately she did not learn the consequences of their action. Pregnancy did not force her to marry, for even while pregnant she found another man, more exciting than the father of her child . . . If she manages to get away she soon hurries back and once more is not slow in finding another man. It is quite possible she finds him where she found the others—in the pub—and as Fanny advances in years, she has a long list of relationships and children, some still with her but others abandoned en route.'

Gayford's research, on which this article was based, was carried out at Chiswick Women's Aid and has since come in for a good deal of criticism for its 'peculiar assumptions' about domestic violence. His questionnaire, for example, lays considerable emphasis on the woman's previous sexual experience and on the masochistic and sadistic elements in her sexual behaviour.

Elizabeth Wilson comments, 'The vulgarity of this way of writing about what is a serious and tragic problem for many women and their children needs no comment. It once again throws the problem back onto the women—this way of discussing battering somehow implies that it is the shortcoming of their personalities that are really at the root of it all'.

She emphasises instead the importance of discussing domestic violence within the context of the organisation of families as social institutions, and others have agreed with her. W. J. Goode (*Explorations in Social Theory*, 1973) describes the family as a power system based on force in which the authority of the male results from his greater economic power and prestige outside the family. It is argued that in this context husbands often resort to violence as a way of regaining dominance when they feel their authority is threatened. Jalna Hanmer (*Women's Aid and the Women's Liberation Movement in Britain*, 1976) points out the extent to which battering occurs as a consequence of the unequal relationships between men and women both in the family and in society generally and expressed in terms of income, access to housing, and the degree of protection guaranteed by the law.

As Jan Pahl makes clear, however, 'no reliable evidence is available about the amount of violence within marriage *in general*' (*A Refuge for Battered Women*, 1978). All the work that has been done relies on unrepresentative samples. Gayford's took place in a refuge. Marsden and Owen's ('Jekyll and Hyde Marriages', *New Society*, 1975) relied on a very small number of women who gave evidence as a result of an appeal for information. (Indeed, Marsden and Owen's account contrasted significantly with Gayford's.) Steinmetz and Strauss (*Violence in the Family*, 1974) interviewed couples who were seeking a divorce. The most useful research in this respect is that by Gelles, who investigated families who had sought help from the police and from social workers but used as a control group the nextdoor neighbours of those families. He found a good deal of evidence to suggest that, despite the stigma attached to admitting violence, an appreciable amount of it existed, not only in the 'problem families' but within the families of the control group as well.

When it comes to explanations about what causes domestic violence, there is a good deal of disagreement between the researchers and those organisations like the National Women's Aid Federation, which spend a lot of time with battered women. There exists a number of hypo-

theses, which are largely uncorroborated, and a variety of heated de-
nials. In brief, the contentions revolve around the following fairly
common but also fairly debatable ideas.

1. That battering is often the result of a 'marital tiff' which 'gets
out of hand'. The NWAF argue conversely that 'domestic violence
has existed throughout most societies long before it was defined as a
crime'. In Britain it has been 'kept quiet' by the reluctance of police and
welfare service officials to intervene.

2. That domestic violence only occurs in 'problem families' already
known to the social work agencies. The NWAF claim that 25 per cent
of reported violent crime is wife assault and that more and more
women who have had no previous contact with social services refer
themselves to Women's Aid refuges.

3. That violence, because it is concentrated in 'problem families', is
also largely a working-class phenomenon. This is one of the allegations
most hotly disputed by the NWAF who claim to have contact with
the partners of doctors, solicitors, teachers and businessmen, etc. It is
their experience that 'battering affects women of all ages, races, classes
and lifestyles'.

4. That domestic violence is associated with masochistic and sadistic
tendencies which means that women either 'enjoy' being physically
dominated or 'deserve all they get'. The claim that women in refuges
have high adrenalin levels indicating the excitement they derive from
violent relationships is, according to NWAF, a degrading and insensitive generalisation to make, given the numbers of women
involved.

5. That women must enjoy the violence in a bizarre kind of way,
otherwise they would leave. The NWAF claims that this kind of argument fails to appreciate the difficulties many women face, especially if
they have children and no job, in leaving the family home and its
economic security. The Federation points out that 'until refuges were
open, there was nowhere for women to go and few places where a
woman could get help' in a society in which 'women are expected to
be financially, legally and emotionally dependent on men'.

6. A common explanation for all kinds of personally experienced
social problems is that of inheritance. Domestic violence is no exception and is frequently explained as the consequence of people witness-
ing violence as children and growing up to accept it as part of life.
Male children, influenced by a violent home, it is said, grow up to
practise violence themselves. And female children, it is argued, are
likely to seek out relationships with violent men. The evidence on
which this explanation is based depends on extremely small samples—
too small to be significant—and yet the 'cycle of violence theory' is
widely regarded as a significant factor in domestic violence. The

NWAF argues that the blaming of domestic violence on the inherited pathology of individuals, like the 'cycle of deprivation theory' (see page 97) to which it is closely related, fails to take account of the social and economic forces which are 'at work on these individuals— low income, bad housing, unsatisfactory work conditions, and particularly the unequal roles men and women are expected to fulfil, publicly in the community, and privately in the family'.

So far, therefore, the arguments attempting to explain domestic violence are inconclusive but whilst the causes and the extent of domestic violence may be in dispute, there can be no doubt about the awfulness of its repercussions. As Jan Pahl comments in her study of a Canterbury refuge, 'Some women are appallingly injured; they suffer broken bones, knife wounds, and severe bruising; some are hit over the head with furniture; some are thrown downstairs; and one had a nail hammered into her foot. But some women suffer in other ways and may have no bruises to show for it. One of the women who has stayed longest at the refuge, putting up with what are clearly for her extremely difficult circumstances, has never said what it was that drove her from her home; all that she has said is that she has not been physically battered; but her need for refuge is clearly great.'

Changing Roles Within the Family

One of the most significant changes in family life since the Second World War is claimed to be the changing relationship between husbands and wives. The increasing emancipation of women from the home, greater economic independence, fewer children and the emergence in the late sixties of ideas concerned to promote greater equality between the sexes have all contributed to a relaxation of rigidly defined marital roles. Feminists would probably argue that the changes have not yet gone far enough. Those of a more conservative disposition may feel that 'women's liberation' has presented a serious threat to the stability of family life.

Sociological research into the changing roles of husbands and wives since the war has revealed a less substantial shift in attitudes and behaviour than might be expected, however. Three studies which illustrate the research which has been done are Klein's account of Nottinghamshire miners and their wives in the early fifties, Jan and Ray Pahl's study of managers and their wives in the sixties and Ann Oakley's study of forty London housewives at the beginning of the seventies.

In Ashton in Nottingham, Klein described how miners and their wives lived almost separate lives. 'If the woman's place is in the home, the man's place is definitely outside it. After work the men go home for a wash and a meal, and then go out again to meet their friends at the club, the pub, the corner, the sportsground.

'Except at the weekend, when the men's clubs and the Miners' Welfare Institute allow women in, the women keep together much as the men do. For women as for men, the enjoyment of the company of others is a major source of leisure-time satisfaction. At one or other house in the street, the women will be "callin", taking a cup of tea, with family, neighbours or both, and spending some time in the morning or the afternoon regularly in this way. At these women's gatherings there is endless gossip about the neighbours, about their own husbands and children, about the past. . . .

'The wife's role is defined in terms of her husband's convenience. He pays his wife an agreed weekly sum called "her wages". She may not know how much he earns or what proportion of his earnings is given to her. Indeed one woman, when asked whether her husband worked in town or nearer home, had to call a neighbour to ask if she knew. With her wage, the woman rules the household and makes all expenditure decisions, except for big items, such as a new cooker, for which her husband will pay out a further share from his wages. This practice is a great help to the wife, for ordinary hire purchase items are paid for out of her wages.

'Restricted to the home as they are, wives do not appear actively to resent it. When pressed they will acknowledge jealousy of their husband's freedom, but many of them say that they find satisfaction in the care of their children.

'The husband has fulfilled his obligations when he has paid over the wife's wage; it is part of the woman's side of the bargain that the home must be a comfortable place to come back to after work, with a meal prepared, a room tidy and warm, and a wife ready to wait upon him. There must be no cold meals, late meals, washing lying about or ironing to do while he is at home. The duties should be performed while he is at work; when he is at home, the wife should concentrate on his comfort. The wife agrees with these stipulations; both acknowledge that a miner's work is hard and that it is a "poor do" if the wife cannot fulfil her part of the contract so long as the husband fulfils his. In one instance a wife had gone to the pictures after asking her sister to prepare a meal and serve it when the husband came home. The husband so confronted, threw the dinner "to t'back of t'fire". It was his wife's duty to look after him. He would accept no substitute.'

This account of married life among husbands and wives in a traditional working-class area represents a particularly rigid division of labour in the home which other sociologists have argued has declined, especially among younger couples and middle-class couples. Ronald Fletcher (*The Family and Marriage*), Blood and Woolfe (*Husbands and Wives*) and Peter Willmott (*The Symmetrical Family*) all attach a good deal of importance to the legal emancipation of women and to the increase in the number of married women working outside the home. They also agree that husbands participate much more in housework and bringing up children than they used to.

Ray and Jan Pahl* looked at the behaviour of middle-class nuclear families and asked the wives of managers to rate their roles in relation to those of their husbands. 'The majority of the wives saw their role in relation to their husband's work as being essentially a supportive and domestic one and only a minority took a more positive part in his work life. The typical wife saw herself as someone who cares for the house and children while her husband is at work and who helps him to sort out his worries and relax when he comes home to the nest in the evening.'

The Pahls made a distinction between supportive wives, independent wives and domestic wives but for the majority of them marriage was the most important thing in their lives, providing them with emotional as well as financial security. 'The wife who falls into the *domestic* category comes typically', they suggest, 'from a working-class background or has had limited work experience; she does not expect or want a role outside the home and feels more at ease in her home environment. The wife who falls into the *supportive* category comes typically from a lower-middle-class home, or from a job as a secretary. She too does not want a role outside the home, at least while her children are young, but she is familiar enough with the office world to feel that she has a role to play in relation to her husband's work life. The wife who falls into the *independent* category may be forced there by her husband's desire to keep home and work separate; more typically her middle-class home background and her higher education have led her to want identities apart from her identity as a wife and mother.'

The Pahls completed their fieldwork before the Women's Liberation Movement had attracted much popular attention in Britain. They found little evidence among the women they interviewed of any dislike of the nuclear family, and resentment about the marriage tie or any very great frustration in their chief roles of wife, mother and housewife.

Hannah Gavron's study of 96 urban housewives in the early sixties and published in 1966 (*The Captive Wife*) revealed, on the other hand, that the feeling of being tied to the house and isolated from meaningful social contacts was common to both middle-class and working-class women. Her study also suggested that 21 per cent of the middle-class and 54 per cent of working-class couples interviewed 'simply shared the housework between them'. But according to Ann Oakley (*The Sociology of Housework*), Gavron arrived at this conclusion by failing

---

* Managers and their Wives, J. and R. Pahl.

to distinguish between what husbands *actually* do and what they *might be prepared* to do. Her own study of forty housewives, twenty working-class and twenty middle-class, revealed less encouraging evidence.

So far as household chores were concerned, she found that only a minority of husbands gave the kind of help which could be called 'shared' or 'equal'. She found that decision-making and leisure activities were more likely to be shared in middle-class than in working-class homes, but that shared leisure activities and decision-making did not necessarily mean husbands also played an equal part in housework and childcare. 'In fact, many marriages that appeared to be egalitarian concealed a good deal of traditional role playing by the husbands and wives.'

Oakley examined the extent to which women's attitudes were changing on whether or not husbands should be more 'domesticated' in the home. Most of the men she interviewed agreed with the wife who said 'I don't agree with men doing housework. I don't think it's a man's job. I certainly wouldn't like to see my husband cleaning a room up. I don't think it's mannish. . . . I like a man to be a man.'

When asked about women going out to work and men staying at home, the answers showed a firm belief that it is 'natural' for women and 'unnatural' for men to be domesticated: 30 out of 40 women rejected the idea of a reversed-roles marriage. None of the others really approved of the idea but said that it depended on the couple and their circumstances. Asked why men could not take over the housewives' role most replied that women were better at domestic chores than men and could not earn as much as men outside the home. No one suggested that men are bad at domestic chores because, unlike women, they never had to learn how to do them, or that women's equal pay and job opportunities can and are being won by legal and political changes.

Oakley concluded from her research that men's and women's roles in the family, their attitudes to marriage and their beliefs about equal opportunities are not changing as quickly as it is often suggested. None of the women she interviewed questioned the assumption that a woman's first and most important duty is to be a wife and mother.

It could be argued, as with the research into domestic violence, that the evidence presented in these studies is based on rather small samples which may well be untypical. But the findings do seem to confirm the arguments presented earlier about the popularity of marriage despite the increase in the divorce rate, and the efficiency with which the family system as a social institution complements the requirements of a capitalist economy by separating wage labour from domestic labour. Some of the implications of this for women as paid workers outside the home, and unpaid workers whose 'caring services' inside the home bolster the provisions of the welfare state in times of stringency, will be examined in subsequent chapters.

Revision

1. Refresh Your Memory

Make sure you know the meaning of the terms: anthropologist, maternal deprivation, division of labour, socialisation, economic system, subsistence economy, illegitimacy, stigma, multinational companies, sex roles, 'reserve army', service industry, inflation, meritocracy, cottage industry, 'baby farmers', 'war babies'.

2. Check Your Understanding

Be able to explain in your own words:

(*a*) The difference between monogamy and polygamy.

(*b*) The difference between socialist and capitalist economic systems.

(*c*) The difference between Confucius' 'three obediences' and 'four virtues'.

(*d*) The main changes which came about in family live in China after liberation.

(*e*) The difference between nuclear and extended families.

(*f*) The difference between wage labour and domestic labour.

(*g*) The difference between geographical mobility and social mobility.

(*h*) The legal distinction between divorce and separation.

(*i*) The difference between custody and maintenance.

(*j*) The difference between prenatal and perinatal mortality.

(*k*) The 'pros and cons' of the 'cycle of violence' theory used to explain domestic violence.

3. Essay Questions to Try

(*a*) What evidence is there to suggest that family organisation and behaviour is immensely flexible?

(*b*) Explain some of the ways in which family organisation in different societies reflects the needs of different economic systems.

(*c*) Outline some of the main differences between wage labour and domestic labour in a capitalist economic system.

(*d*) What pressures to conform are exerted upon those who live 'outside the nuclear family' in British society?

(*e*) 'The disturbing increase in divorce in recent years presents a serious challenge to the stability of family life.' Discuss.

(*f*) Examine some of the factors which have contributed to the labelling of illegitimacy as a social problem.

(*g*) Discuss the extent to which the research concerned to account for domestic violence is accurate and acceptable.

(*h*) To what extent have egalitarian matrimonial roles replaced segregated matrimonial roles in recent years in British family life?

Further Reading

A Refuge for Battered Women, Jan Pahl, DHSS, 1978.
Coming of Age in Samoa, Margaret Mead, Penguin, London, 1943.
Examining Sociology, Jane L. Thompson, Hutchinson, London, 1980.
Family and Kinship in East London, Michael Young and Peter Willmott, Penguin, London, 1969.

Finding a Voice, Amrit Wilson, Virago, London, 1978.
Growing Up in New Guinea, Margaret Mead, Penguin, London, 1942.
Managers and their Wives, R. and J. Pahl, Penguin, London, 1972.
Married Life in an African Tribe, Isaac Shapera, Pelican, London, 1971.
Samples from English Culture, J. Klein, Routledge & Kegan Paul, London, 1965.
Scream Quietly or the Neighbours Might Hear, Erin Pizzey, Penguin, London, 1974.
The Captive Wife, Hannah Gavron, Routledge & Kegan Paul, London, 1966.
The Sociology of Housework, Ann Oakley, Martin Robertson, Oxford, 1974.
The Sociology of the Family, Michael Anderson (ed.), Penguin, London, 1971.
Wedlocked Women, Lee Comer, Feminist Books, London, 1974.

4

EDUCATION

Informal and Formal Education

Most of the things which people learn, from the second they are born, throughout the many phases of their lives and in the varied and numerous situations in which they find themselves, happen 'outside' the formal education system, from people not usually regarded as teachers and through experiences not always defined as educational. From the very moment of birth, children begin to learn and develop the behaviour, values and attitudes which are considered to be acceptable in our society. The family is the first context in which learning occurs, and parents and other relatives act as the first 'teachers'. As the child grows older friends and neighbours become more influential, as do adult contacts and work mates in later life. All of these interpersonal relationships provide the opportunities for individuals to learn information, acquire knowledge and skills and modify or change their behaviour as a consequence.

But it is not just a matter of personal relationships. Teaching others and learning from them, in the many and varied encounters of everyday life, happens in a social context. Put simply, society has already decided a good deal of what it considers to be 'appropriate' behaviour, attitudes and values, and uses a variety of methods to ensure that these become accepted by and get transmitted to new recruits. Other agencies of 'informal education' besides the family and personal contacts in different groups and at work, are influences like the media, cultural traditions and customs, and the kind of moral guidelines, legal rules and social values enshrined in the ideology and practice of legal, religious, economic and social welfare systems in society. None of these is a natural or neutral operation, though. All of them are 'man-made' and reflect the accumulated attitudes and interests of those individuals and groups who, over a period of time, have been most closely responsible for formulating their philosophies, shaping their policies and directing and enacting their decisions. The individuals and groups in question have tended historically to be those whom I referred to in Chapter 2 as the ruling class. But more of this later. The point to note here is that however important or effective the influence of these 'informal' educational agencies might be—for good or ill—these are not usually the experiences which are seriously considered and recognised when 'education' is being defined or discussed.

For most people education is what happens in schools and colleges and all the other easily identifiable institutions which are part and parcel of the education system. So far as sociologists are concerned, most of their attention has been focused on schooling and related issues, as the only part of the education process which is both universal and compulsory. For this reason, most of what follows in this chapter will be concerned with the main aspects of the sociology of education as they relate to the organisation and experience of schooling.

The Historical Context

Strange as it may seem, despite appeals to 'tradition' the experience of education for most people in Britain is a fairly recent development. The first real intervention by the state in the business of providing universal, free and compulsory schooling only really began to take effect towards the end of the last century. The history of the last hundred years has been one of conflicting views about the merits of different ways of organising schools, one of struggle to expand educational provision and equalise educational opportunities and one of tension between the roles of education as an agency of social control and social change. Before considering some of these arguments in more detail, it is useful to list some of the main developments that have taken place in the organisation of schooling over the last hundred years or so and some of the views which have influenced them.

Beginnings

The legacy which nineteenth-century educational provisions gave to this century was the deliberate development of two separate educational systems: public and grammar schools on the one hand, providing training in leadership for the children of social and wealthy elites, and a variety of cheap, mass schools, providing training in basic literacy and appropriate values for the majority and future workers on the other.

In 1870 the Forster Education Act created locally elected school boards and encouraged them to build elementary schools. In 1880 elementary education was made compulsory for all children but parents had to pay between 2 and 8 old pennies a week in fees. In 1891 the Free Education Act allowed most children to receive a free elementary education and in 1899 the minimum school-leaving age was raised to 12. None of these developments particularly pleased the factory owners who had become used to employing children in the nineteenth century for half the wages paid to adults. Some poor parents also complained because they needed the wages their children earned, and in 1893 a 'half-time system' was introduced which meant that children of 10 or 11 could attend school on a half-time basis and spend the rest of the time in paid employment. Right from the beginning, then, the 'economic considerations' were often in competition with 'educational considerations' when the development of schooling was being considered.

Secondary Education for All

The Education Act of 1902 laid the foundations for a national system of secondary education in Britain by allowing local authorities to build secondary schools, but did not, as many people hoped, provide secondary education for all. Rather than offering an extension of elementary education, secondary schools clearly operated as a parallel but separate system.

Elementary schools kept the majority of children from five until they could officially leave, or until financial pressures at home and the 'half-time system' took them out of school. The all-age elementary schools were still governed by the elementary code, their buildings and facilities were inferior to those of secondary schools. Their teachers taught larger classes, were paid less and were less well qualified than their counterparts in the secondary system.

The old grammar schools consolidated by government aid and the new ones which were opened after 1902 were intended to continue the business of 'educating the minority'. They took as their model the objectives and traditions of the old endowed grammar schools and public schools. And entry to all of them, until at least the Second World War, was based on social and economic considerations, rather than intellectual ones, for these were fee-paying schools which admitted the children of the upper middle class, usually quite regardless of ability. After 1902 the local authority grammar schools were obliged to take a proportion of scholarship children but the number of scholarships remained relatively small and competition for places was fierce.

This differentiation of elementary and secondary schools had little to do with intelligence. It was based on the assumption that different classes of children needed different types of education to fit them for their future economic position in society.

During and after the First World War the demand for genuine secondary education for all increased. R. H. Tawney was a leading critic of the influence of industry on educational concerns, which he regarded as advocating division for economic ends. In an article in the *Daily News* in 1918 entitled 'Keep The Workers' Children in Their Place' he criticised the Federation of British Industries' opposition to the Fisher Education Act of that year which stopped the half-time system and raised the school-leaving age to 14. The Federation welcomed better secondary education 'for the more able children' but felt that for the working-class child in elementary school, school life should be 'directly vocational' and 'geared to the industry he will enter at fourteen'. 'Selecting children for higher education should not create, as was done in India, a large class of persons whose education is unsuitable for the employment which they eventually enter.'

The increasing demand for secondary education for all provided the brief for the Hadow Committee's report on the 'Education of the Adolescent', published in 1926. But any suggestion of altering the practice of having different schools for different classes was not the issue and education in secondary grammar schools was deliberately excluded from their terms of reference. Hadow's main recommendation was the break between primary and post-primary schooling should take place at 11 on the grounds that there is 'a tide which begins to rise in the veins of youth at the age of 11 or 12' by which time children have given 'some indication of difference in interests and abilities sufficient to make it possible and advisable to cater for them by means of schools of varying types'.

Psychological support for this essentially organisational convenience came from the work of people like Francis Galton, Charles Spearmen, Godfrey Thomson and Cyril Burt, who claimed to be able to 'identify and measure' the abilities in children which they had 'inherited in a fixed and unchanging amount at birth' and which were 'impervious to influence by subsequent education'. This ability could be measured with 'accuracy and ease' at 11 so that by 12 the 'children could be grouped, not merely in separate classes and standards, but in separate types of schools'.

The committee was completely convinced by the psychologists and was also keen to recommend streaming by ability within schools as a preparation for the division at 11 into separate schools. So the principle of differentiation, originally a social and economic device, was given scientific respectability and became the official justification for putting different children into different streams and different types of schools.

Views on Segregation

There were, however, plenty of 'non-official' groups ready to challenge this viewpoint and, as Rubenstein and Simon show in *The Evolution of the Comprehensive School*, the various teachers' unions were quite in advance of the politicians at this time in arguing for common schools which all children could attend.

At this stage the theories of the psychologists were not questioned but it was felt that 'multiple bias' or 'multilateral' schools would be a less divisive and more socially acceptable way of bringing all children together under the same roof. Their different abilities could still be catered for by separate courses within the school.

In 1938 the Spens Report was published. By now support for the single school had increased and if legislation was forthcoming the London County Council was all set to develop schools along multilateral lines. But Spens was not convinced. Despite the evidence of teachers' unions and the TUC the doctrine of the psychologists was still given precedence, perhaps because it said what the establishment in education wanted to hear. Intelligence was 'identifiable', 'measurable' and 'predictable' and could best be catered for in three different types of schools: grammar, technical and modern. The argument that such a division would 'institutionalise class barriers' and effectively prevent educational, social and economic parity was largely ignored by an official ideology which was based on a tradition of class divisions in educational provision and which could see no good reason to change.

Such an arrangement would also be administratively convenient. Grammar and technical schools had already been built and it was assumed that they would be too small for the purposes of multilateral schools. Perhaps this too was a rationalisation.

The rejection of multilateral schools was also based on a good deal of ideological prejudice about the value of grammar schools and the wish to preserve them for those who were either 'wealthy enough' or 'intelligent enough' to deserve them. In short, the multilateral idea was considered by Spens to be 'too subversive a change to be made in a long-established system'.

In 1943 the Norwood Report on Curriculum and Examinations in Secondary Schools also came out in support of 'separation'. It identified the existence in the child population of 'three broad types of mind' suitable for the three types of schools: 'the pupil who is interested in learning for its own sake, who can grasp an argument or follow a piece of reasoning . . . the pupil whose interests and aptitudes lie markedly in the field of applied science or applied art . . . the pupil who deals more easily with concrete things than ideas'. The quality of Norwood's reasoning aroused a good deal of anger at the time because it was based on such obvious oversimplifications and prejudice, but again it played an influential part in giving respectability to a decision which had already been taken to keep children separated in different kinds of schools.

Tripartite Schooling

The system of state schooling which evolved after the 1944 Education Act owed a great deal to the recommendations of Norwood and Spens. Secondary education was provided by three different types of schools: grammar, technical and secondary modern. Despite increased demands for 'equality of educational opportunity' and access to common schools, the Labour Government which was returned to power in 1945 with a majority of 200 seats over all other parties, saw the tripartite system firmly established.

Again administrative considerations played an important part. The economic situation after the war was difficult. Different types of schools already existed and it was no doubt easier to utilise them as they were than plan radical reorganisation.

The first pamphlet published by the new government's Ministry of Education, 'The Nation's Schools', in 1945, drew heavily on the assumptions of Norwood and actually underlined the fact that modern schools were intended for working class children 'whose future employment will not demand any measure of technical skill and knowledge'. The labour rank and file were critical of their government's policy but whilst 'The Nation's Schools' was withdrawn fairly rapidly, its successor 'The New Secondary Education' differed very little in its assumptions and ideology and was reprinted without alteration as late as 1958.

The pamphlet warned that 'the distinction between the three main types of secondary school is bound to appear much more definite and rigid on paper than it need be in practice . . . there is a need to avoid exaggerating and stereotyping the differences between types of education that have, and must always have, a great measure of common ground'. Be that as it may, the 'common ground' never developed into 'parity of esteem' and the history of these schools over the next decades was one of a continued separation which showed all the qualities of divisiveness predicted by opponents of the system at the outset.

Experience of the tripartite system in practice stimulated yet another phase in the debate about equal opportunity. Since grammar, technical and modern schools did not provoke equal esteem, it was increasingly thought unlikely that combining them under one roof, in a single but divided multilateral school, would either. The demand changed to one for comprehensive schools.

The main difference between the notions of multilateral and comprehensive schools was that in the former the distinction between grammar, technical and modern sections would be retained and children would be kept quite separate under the same roof whilst in the latter all children would be regarded as being part of the same school and be mixed up together for at least some of their activities.

But not everyone was in favour of introducing comprehensive schools. When the Conservative Government took over in 1951 the notion of separate types of schools for separate types of minds had been replaced by separate schools for separate abilities. The task of 'measuring that ability' by an examination and by sorting the pupils in each locality, into **precisely the numbers required to match the number of places available** in the schools, became known as the 'Eleven Plus'.

But the fifties and sixties became the years of research, reports and critical writing which gradually undermined the firm belief in three types of children and in 'fixed ability' which could be measured to provide an accurate guide for dividing pupils at 11.

Research and Party Politics

In 1966 Alfred Yates recorded a distinct change in the psychological view of intelligence. The importance of environmental influences were now stressed in the definition of intelligence as 'a fluid collection of skills whose development is demonstrably affected by early experience and subsequently by the quality and duration of formal education'. Pressure had undoubtedly been brought to bear on the psychologists by sociological research into the effects of the education system.

Influential research by Floud and Halsey in the mid-fifties indicated the social factors involved in making use of educational opportunity and the barriers facing working class children in the education system. In 1957 Vernon's research questioned the validity of selection based on intelligence testing and reinforced the argument made earlier by Brian Simon in *Intelligence Testing and the Comprehensive School*. The implications of this were obviously great and were well documented by many sociologists, among them J. W. B. Douglas and his colleagues in *The Home and the School* in 1964. They were able to show the close relationship between, for example, streaming and social class and how the children of professional and managerial parents were over-represented in the high streams, whilst those of manual and semi-skilled parents were predominant in the low streams.

When government reports like Crowther, Newsom and Robbins also revealed that selection for high-status schools, examination courses and higher education showed a marked imbalance in favour of middle-class children, the case against the tripartite system and the eleven plus hardened.

In 1952 the ban against secondary modern schools taking GCEs until 16 was lifted and the achievements of those schools in terms of good examination results was a further indication of the fallacy of selection at 11.

But those who wanted to defend selection were also vociferous. Against an increasing barrage of social-scientific evidence about the failings of selection, the cause of the grammar school was taken up with increased fervour by writers like Eric James, Harry Ree and G. H. Bantock in terms of 'education for leadership', a rigorous induction into 'hard learning and studious application' and the production of 'an elite' on whose shoulders rested the responsibility for the 'health and vitality' of society.

Perhaps it was inevitable that the issue should also become party-political. In 1955 comprehensive schools appeared in the Labour Party's manifesto for the first time. But so far as the Conservative Government was concerned, they were prepared to allow only 'limited experiments' in comprehensive reorganisation, especially in country areas or new towns, and where they presented no challenge to the 'well established traditions' of the grammar schools.

By 1965, however, comprehensive education was no longer a minority concern. A quarter of all local authorities had made changes in their selection procedures between 1960 and 1964, and by 1964 a total of 71 per cent of all authorities had or were intending to introduce some form of comprehensive schooling. Comprehensive schools, established as experiments some years earlier, were now bearing fruit and this, together with the persuasive arguments of educationalists opposed to 'early selection' and economists concerned about a better educated labour force, led in the early sixties to what Simon and Rubinstein call a 'grass roots movement to reorganise secondary education on comprehensive lines'.

In July 1965 the Labour Government issued its famous Circular 10/65 in which it 'requested' local authorities to submit plans within a year for the comprehensive reorganisation of their schools. No direct compulsion was implied by the circular but its successor a year later made money for school buildings available only for the purposes of comprehensive redevelopment. Encouraged by this initiative from the Ministry, sympathetic authorities got to work quickly. This was a period of rapid growth in the numbers of comprehensive schools established. From 262 in 1965 the number increased between four and five times to 1145 by 1970.

But the absence of obligation in Circular 10/65 permitted recalcitrant authorities to use delaying tactics of various kinds to avoid making any irrevocable commitment to comprehensive education. The introduction of a bill which attempted to give teeth to the Government's intentions was mismanaged in its committee stage and failed to see the light of day before the Government lost power in 1970.

An analysis of the 'gains' for the comprehensive system during these years shows they are not as impressive as they may at first appear, however. The typical arrangement of comprehensive schools in the sixties was as part of a mixed system. Although by 1970 it appeared that one third of the secondary school population was in comprehensive schools only a proportion of these were 'genuine' comprehensive schools—that is, those which took *all* the children from the area and which were not 'creamed' of their more able pupils by grammar or independent schools. Seen in this light, only 12 per cent of the school population attended fully comprehensive schools. The rest were in what were still really secondary modern schools, renamed as comprehensives. The grammar and independent schools still flourished and, according to Rubinstein and Simon, 'had not as yet experienced any radical change'.

Conservative Government

The election manifesto of the Conservative Party in 1970 proclaimed that a Conservative Government would 'maintain the existing right of local education authorities to decide what is best in their areas'. One of their first actions in taking office, therefore, was to withdraw Circular 10/65 and to replace it by Circular 10/70, which was supposed to let local education authorities 'be freer to determine the shape of secondary provision in their areas' judged in terms of educational criteria, 'local needs and wishes' and 'the wise use of resources'.

Research by the NFER, the NUT and the Campaign for Comprehensive Education has shown that in just over three years of Conservative rule, the overall effect of its policies was to slow down the changeover to comprehensive education. The main architect of Conservative policy during this period was Margaret Thatcher. By 1972 she had approved 2,000 comprehensives but she had also reprieved 92 grammar schools. She had increased government aid to direct grant schools at a time when cuts in expenditure were being made in the state system, and she had re-popularised the notion of 'parental choice' as a way of justifying the protection of grammar schools. The effect of her policies was wherever possible to preserve selection and to impede the development of genuine comprehensive education.

By August 1st, 1973, 310 schools out of 3420 applications had been rejected. In six months between February and July 1973 the rejection rate had risen to 29 per cent, i.e. one in four schools proposed by local education authorities. The effect of keeping even one school selective in a local authority's area implied the retention of selection for the whole area since it inevitably 'creamed' that area. On the basis of a survey carried out by the NUT and the Campaign for Comprehensive Education in 1973, Caroline Benn was able to highlight some of the implications of comprehensive and selective schools coexisting side by side. For example, of the coexisting comprehensive schools in the survey, 89 per cent said coexistence deprived their schools of 'high ability' pupils and increased the numbers of 'low ability' pupils; 80 per cent said they were deprived of a social mix—in practice middle-class pupils; 86 per cent said it lowered the level of esteem of the school in the community; and 86 per cent said it caused many parents to feel their children in the comprehensives had been given a second choice school.

The Current Situation

At the time of writing comprehensive schools are considered to be 'a fact of life' by most sides of the political spectrum; arguments about 'going comprehensive' or not are largely a thing of the past. Now the vast majority of secondary school children in the state system are in comprehensive schools of one kind or another. Public schools and independent schools still cater for the children of a significant minority of wealthy and upper-class parents, and competition for places in them seems to be increasing as middle-class people try to 'buy their children out' of the state system, in case comprehensive schools do not turn out to be as good as the old grammar schools were thought to be. Government support for private education fluctuates depending on which political party is in office. In 1979 the Conservative Government reaffirmed its intention of protecting and encouraging the private education sector.

So far as comprehensive schools go, attention has turned to internal issues. The great debating points in education these days are about 'standards' and 'discipline' in schools. In 1977–8 Shirley Williams, the Labour Minister of Education, initiated a series of national public debates in which the views of teachers, parents, industry and the trade unions were sought on the state of education quality and performance in the state system. Cuts in public spending on education, especially after the Conservative Government took office again in 1979, have increased concern about the kind of education which schools facing cuts and teacher redundancies can be expected to provide (see p. 243).

The other main issue seems to be the concern expressed by some industrialists that the schools are not providing the kind of workers they require. This argument, of course, has to be set against the alarming increase in the numbers of unemployed school leavers over the last few years and the whole issue of the relationship between the education system and the economic system. The discussion about the economic and other functions which the education system is said to serve for society is an important one and consequently something which we ought now to look at.

The Social Functions of Education

The development of the education system over the last hundred years or so has not only been about changes in the organisation of schooling. It has also been about exposing more and more youngsters for longer and longer to the experience of formal schooling. This development has been true of all industrialised societies for whom a highly organised education system is a necessity. The more complex the socio-economic arrangements of society become, the more stress is laid upon the supportive and reflective roles of the education system.

The laymen's view of schooling as 'a means of learning subjects like maths, geography, French, etc.' is only a part of the picture, and possibly not the most important part. Sociologists are more concerned with the functions which the education system serves for society as a whole, and to identify the contending interests which operate through the education system. Perhaps it is easiest to look at this process in terms of four distinct functions—though of course, each is clearly related to all of the others. The four are the economic, the social, the political and that concerned with social control.

Education and the Economic System

A major responsibility of education is to provide the necessary workers for the prevailing system of production and level of technology which society requires. In a superficial way this may mean teaching the kind of subjects in schools which pupils will need to know in their future jobs, such as typing or technical drawing. But if you think about it, the content of most subjects taught in schools is very unrelated to the world of work. The relationship between the school curriculum and the needs of industry is more subtle than this. Rather, the school system acts as a kind of 'sorting-out agency' or 'clearing house' for employment, largely through the workings of its examination system.

The old divisions into public, grammar, technical and secondary modern schools performed this function much more visibly, with each type of school preparing workers for a different level of future employment. And whilst public and independent schools continue their traditional function of schooling the future ruling groups in society, the state system has increasingly to confine its contribution within organisationally common schools. From a relatively early age in secondary schools, therefore, pupils are channelled into the streams, bands, options or curriculum groupings which will prepare them for, or preserve them from, the range of public examinations which help to grade them for future employers into prospective professional, skilled or unskilled workers. The attention given to counselling and careers guidance in schools is a further refinement of this process and another indication of the increasing emphasis given by the education system to occupational selection.

Education and the Social System

In Chapter 2 it was argued that all societies have ways of organising the distribution of the resources which they value by one form of social stratification or another, and that in Britain resources like wealth, property and specialist skills are distributed in differing amounts to members of different social classes.

One of the major differences between a class system and other forms of social stratification like slavery, feudalism or the caste system, is that individuals can influence their position by their own endeavours. In industrial societies like ours, which rely very much on the organisation and development of human resources for economic progress, there needs to be a certain amount of movement of individuals between different occupational and class categories. There also needs to be the kind of 'encouraging' social climate which suggests that 'getting on' and 'doing well' in terms of job, prospects and lifestyle, is perfectly possible for talented and hard-working individuals. Part of the responsibility for reinforcing social class divisions whilst at the same time providing qualified opportunities for some degree of social mobility lies with the education system. Let's take the latter first. Apart from 'marrying the boss's daughter' or 'winning the football pools', the main enabler of social mobility for most people is as a result of their educational attainment—the working-class child who gets good A level results, goes to university and qualifies as a teacher, doctor or solicitor, for example. Despite the fact that the majority of recruits into the top professions still come from middle-class and wealthy families, there is a place for a few able working-class youngsters who do well in the school system.

Most of the movement is between groups further down the social scale, however, between skilled manual and white-collar occupations and between upper working-class and lower middle-class social classifications. And the shift is more technical than real. A good deal of the apparent improvement is as much to do with changes in the occupational structure and the growth in the middle-class service occupations as any real development in educational attainment or redistribution of skill. As Madun Sarup argues in *Marxism in Education*, it is not so much a question of the 'embourgeoisement of the affluent worker' (see above, p. 36) as 'the proletarianisation of the white collar worker'. In tempering some of the popular euphoria stimulated by notions of social mobility, he suggests that the application of scientific management and technology to office work has in fact reduced what was once regarded as a middle-class occupation to the same low status granted to manual labour when it is characterised by dependency on machinery, routine and automation.

Thus despite the ideology of social mobility and the restriction of its benefits to an intellectually competent minority, the prevailing pattern seems to remain one of a class system highly resistant to change and an education system not seriously concerned to change things.

One of the major preoccupations of the sociology of education over the last twenty years or so has been to demonstrate the extent to which the prevailing education system both reflects and reinforces the class system. Not only does the private sector allow those already in superior social positions to ensure that, for the most part, their children remain in superior positions, but the state system perpetuates—through its methods of streaming, curriculum arrangements, examinations and social location in specific neighbourhoods—a way of continuing to educate the children of middle-class, working-class and ethnic minority groups more or less separately.

It was the evidence which supported these kinds of observations provided by J. W. B. Douglas in *The Home and the School*, for example, and Brian Jackson in *Streaming—the Education System in Miniature*, in the 1960s that did much to enhance the arguments for comprehensive reorganisation as a way of equalising the educational opportunities for working-class and other children. It was possible to demonstrate in the 1970s that the proportion of working-class youngsters going on to university had not changed in fifty years, that working-class children were much less likely than middle-class children to find themselves in grammar schools, top streams, examination classes or staying on at school past the officially allowed leaving age. Explanations for this phenomenon were sought in the characteristics of different children, their upbringing and environment, and in the selection procedures and underlying assumptions which were employed by teachers and schools. But whoever was to blame, or if indeed either of these explanations went to the root of the matter, the facts were inescapable, schools were seen to be reflecting and reinforcing the social class divisions of the wider society. Perhaps it is too early to consider whether the 'opportunity of equality' provided by comprehensive schooling has significantly altered things. Certainly Julienne Ford's* early examination of the practice of comprehensive schooling in relation to its ideology of equality, increased opportunities and diffusion of class differences was not very encouraging about the power of the education system alone to change society.

Education and the Political System

The ability or inability of education to change society brings us into the realm of politics. Politics, of course, is a very loaded word, and one which is usually approached with caution when people are talking about education in case it is associated with indoctrination. But in the sense that all government activity is political in its purposes, and concerned with formulating policies about the way society should be run, introducing legislation, and working through social institutions to implement it, the education system is just one of the many support systems which serve a political need.

The reorganisation of schooling along comprehensive lines, for example, was partly done for educational reasons, but it was also undoubtedly to do with a political attempt to bring about greater social equality. Another illustration of the education system being used by the state to realise political policies has been the selective provision of extra staffing and funding and the identification of Educational Priority Areas in an attempt to reduce social and economic deprivation. Many commentators believe that the raising of the school leaving

---

* Julienne Ford, *Social Class and the Comprehensive School*, Routledge & Kegan Paul, London, 1969.

age to 16 in 1972 was more a political attempt to delay the problem of youth unemployment by keeping youngsters in school for an extra year than the provision of extra education for its own sake.

Attempts to achieve political goals through the education system are by no means always successful. Some would argue that they are not intended to be, and are merely there to give the impression that 'something is being done'. In America schools were used to help bring about racial integration and thousands of millions of dollars were poured into pre-school and nursery education in the attempt to reduce the social, economic and cultural deprivation said to be exhibited by poor white and black Americans in urban ghettos like Harlem. But in many cases the forced integration of schools was accompanied by riots, murder and the policing of school campuses, and ten years after 'Headstart' and other projects designed to provide positive educational discrimination in areas like Harlem, researchers could find no visible signs of any change in the distribution of social advantage or opportunity.

But whether or not the attempts to achieve political ends through educational means are successful, the important point to note is that the attempt is made. Government policies, whatever they might be, implemented through the schools, illustrate the essentially political nature of education, and the important role of teachers as the people responsible for putting them into practice.

But teachers and schools are also responsible for encouraging and stimulating behaviour and representing views that are less obvious than those mentioned above, though they can be described as being equally political. Think of the way in which the education system continues the process begun in the family of socialising society's new recruits into the kind of values, attitudes and types of behaviour which society wants to encourage.

Education as an Agency of Social Control

If you look back to p. 42 you will see that some sociologists have identified education as one of the principal ideological institutions which support and service the prevailing economic systems in society. The essence of this view of the relationship between base and superstructure is that an economically powerful group uses its power to define the values, attitudes and beliefs of the various support systems in the superstructure, and these in turn operate to both reflect and reinforce the interests of the economically powerful, so that any real challenge to their authority is made both difficult and unlikely.

Non-Marxists are more reluctant to describe the relationship between economic power and prevailing values in quite these terms, since it seems to suggest the manipulation and control of the majority by the cleverness and power of the few in pursuit of selfish interests.

Those sociologists who take a more conservative view of social behaviour as it is produced by social systems (see p. 11), emphasise the organic nature of society, the search for integration and cohesion between subsystems, and the need to organise socialisation and control as a way of preserving society and ensuring its maximum efficiency. Those sociologists influenced by a social action approach (see p. 11) tend to concentrate on socialisation and the development of social meanings and behaviour in an interpersonal context. They are reluctant to acknowledge the influence of 'huge' and 'impersonal' forces like institutional ideologies on human behaviour, but do accept that individuals are very susceptible to being moulded and influenced by subconscious messages and symbols in the process of social interaction.

Whichever view different sociologists take and whatever motives and implications they attach to their views, the activity of the school system in the business of socialising children into the values and beliefs of mainstream society is generally accepted. In this sense the education system is regarded as one of the main ways in which society inculcates values and beliefs and enforces some degree of social control.

This is not to suggest that schools teach children moral values and attitudes in the kind of overt way in which they teach history or mathematics, for example, but that they recognise, stand for, and reinforce mainstream values through the kind of 'atmosphere', 'ethos', 'rewards', 'punishments' and 'attitudes' which underpin the relationships of schooling. Competition in sport and academic achievement, stimulated by cups, badges and house points, for example, and the sanctions imposed on those who 'dishonour the reputation of the school' are simple illustrations of the 'hidden curriculum' of schooling in operation. The separation of boys and girls for different activities and the varying behavioural expectations that are attached to each of them are both preparations for their future lives as adults in a society which defines sexual roles differently. The presentation of knowledge in subjects which are taught as if they are separate and distinct from each other, and often in a way which emphasises the passive accumulation of information by the pupils, rather than their active and critical involvement in the creation of knowledge for themselves, also makes distinctions in status between those who have been exposed to 'academic' subjects like languages and science, as against those who have experienced 'only' practical or vocational skills. In later life these distinctions will be reflected in their employment opportunities and occupational status.

All of these, and countless other examples, together make up the social and moral climate of schools, and have the effect of communicating to pupils which of them are regarded as 'successes' and 'failures' in society's terms, and what behaviour will be expected of them in the future. Those pupils who truant from school or get involved in the kind of disruptive behavioural activities which attract public concern and criticism may lead to the conclusion that schools are not always very successful in inculcating appropriate behaviour and values. Indeed, the visible failure of many schools to 'control their pupils' behaviour' has been used to refute the view that the education system is a crucial agency of ideological control, operating on behalf of vested economic interests. If this were true, the argument goes, disruption on the scale currently exhibited would prove untenable and the vested interests concerned would move in to do something about it. The recent political backlash against all forms of 'progressive education' and the fear of declining standards plus the exodus of large numbers of middle-class pupils into the private sector could indeed be said to be an indication that this is happening.

But of course control in the sense of allocating future workers to different levels of employment, with the opportunity to exercise different degrees of initiative and responsibility, does not require them all to be 'successful' in the school's terms. If they were they might expect better employment prospects than the system is prepared to provide. Even unemployment as socially unpopular as it appears to be acts as a 'useful regulator' of the labour market, enabling wages to be kept lower than might otherwise be the case, keeping a reserve pool of labour always on hand to service the ups and downs of the economy's needs for expansion. This kind of interpretation of the relationship between schooling and control does not explain 'disruptive behaviour' as a threat, or an indication of the school's 'failure' to exercise the degree of ideological control demanded of it by vested interests. Rather, disruption, like apathy, is seen as a manifestation of alienation. Both are preparations for the alienation which workers deprived of any control over their labour or their lifestyle experience in the work situation. According to this view, it is the price society seems prepared to pay as a means of preserving the prevailing economic system, based on the unequal distribution of wealth, power and social justice. The education system operates as a way of 'regulating' and 'controlling' that process on behalf of the economically powerful and at the expense of many of those who are kept powerless by its activities.

Social Factors Affecting Educational Failure

During the last twenty years or so, sociologists of education have been preoccupied with questions of achievement in the education system—especially explanations of 'failure' in schools. As you consider these arguments you should be able to recognise rather different approaches and assumptions being used—both in the definition of terms like 'failure', 'achievement', 'success', 'ability', etc., and in the social factors which are considered to be significant.

Of course, it is much too simple to reduce the different arguments

Table 2. Differing explanations of educational failure

Assumptions	Types of explanation	Location of 'the problem'	Key concept used	Remedy
1 'Children fail because they're inferior.'	*Pathological: Psychometric* Failure arising from low IQ—innate psychological and mental inadequacy, transmitted from one generation to the next and capable of being measured by IQ tests.	In the mental deficiency of the individual.	Low ability	Remedial education.
2 'Children fail because they're deprived.'	*Pathological: cultural deficit* Failure arising from the 'deficient' cultural experiences and social pathology of 'deviant' groups.	In the social deficiencies of individuals, families and 'deviant' groups.	Deprivation	Compensatory education and social work intervention.
3 'Children don't fail—bad schools fail them.'	*Technical/maldistribution* Failure arising from the malfunctioning of some schools and the unequal distribution of resources and opportunities.	In the relationship between institutional and administrative 'mistakes'.	Disadvantage	Institutional change and positive discrimination policies.
4 'Society uses the education system to "create" and perpetuate failure. So long as failure exists, education is succeeding!'	*Structural* Failure arising from the need to protect an economic system based on private profit.	In the relationship between the working class and the political, economic and social structure.	Exploitation	Redistribution of economic power and control in society.

and approaches to the kind of diagram shown in Table 2, but it may help you to begin to see the differences between them and the shifts from one 'type of explanation' to another. Although each 'type of explanation' tends to lead from, and to some extent replace, the 'type of explanation' which precedes it, it is still possible to find all of them 'alive and well' and in current use.

Pathological: Psychometric

This type of explanation of educational failure went more or less unchallenged for at least the first half of this century. It relies on the view that most, and some would say all, of a child's ability is based on genetic intelligence that is both innate and inherited. Modifications to the view over the years have conceded the influence of the young child's family environment, and recognised that social factors can stimulate or restrict the development of ability.

But notions of intelligence and ability are rarely defined in this type of explanation. They are often used interchangeably and it is assumed that everyone knows and agrees upon what they mean. If challenged, they would probably be defined as those qualities of 'mental dexterity', 'verbal fluency' and 'logic' which make the 'learning of knowledge' relatively easy. Cyril Burt, writing in 1933 explained, 'By intelligence, the psychologist understands *inborn, all-round intellectual ability*. It is inherited, or at least innate, not due to teaching or training; it is intellectual, not emotional or moral and remains uninfluenced by industry or zeal; it is general not specific, i.e. it is not limited to any particular kind of work, but enters into all we do or say or think. Of all our mental qualities it is the most far reaching; fortunately it can be measured with accuracy and ease.' So sure of their ground were early psychologists like Cyril Burt, that a battery of Intelligence Quotient (IQ) tests were devised and used to measure this intelligence. On the basis of the results, decisions were made about the type of school and level of stream which would be 'best suited' to the intelligence of the child being tested. Those children who performed badly in the tests and who failed were considered to be lacking in the 'mental dexterity', 'verbal fluency' and 'logic' necessary to learn very effectively. They were termed children of 'low ability', who in extreme cases would need specially planned remedial education to help them make the best of their mental handicaps.

There are many criticisms levelled against this type of explanation of educational failure which seems to concentrate almost exclusively on the personal mental deficiency of individuals.* One of the main criticisms is the unproblematical way in which concepts like 'ability',

---

* See, for example, B. Simon, *Intelligence, Psychology and Education*, 1971, and D. Ingleby, 'The Psychology of Child Psychology', in *Schooling and Capitalism: a sociological reader*, edited by Dale *et al.*, Routledge & Kegan Paul, London.

'intelligence' and 'failure' are used. It seems as though intelligence is something which can be measured only by IQ tests and that ability is somehow 'defined' as a result of an individual's response to such tests. But research has shown how biased and one-sided apparently neutral tests can be. It is argued that they favour the cultural experiences of white, Anglo-Saxon, middle-class children, and that consequently it is not surprising that black, West Indian, working-class children, for example, do not usually do very well in them. Similarly, research has shown that in completing IQ tests, 'practice makes perfect' and children are likely to do better in the tests if they have been given lots of experience of them beforehand. These types of criticisms are also made about the explanation of educational success and failure, that although it appears to rely on scientifically sound principles, it is considerably influenced by social and sometimes emotional factors which are not sufficiently taken into account.

You can follow up some of the arguments for and against testing for yourselves. The defensive position is still being put in the *Black Papers*, for example. But as an indication of the dangers of believing that IQ tests are 'culture free', try this question from an old 'eleven plus' scholarship paper for yourself:

Explain which of the following is the odd man out and why . . .
MEASLES, STEAMER, LEAVE, OMELETTE, COURAGE
(answer on page 109)

Pathological: Cultural Deficit

This type of explanation of educational failure lies rooted in the reports and sociological writings of the 1950s and 1960s, which emphasise the links between social class and educational achievement*. The outcome of all this research has been to stress the significance of the *home* in the educational process and to suggest that the home is, in fact, more important than the school in determining educational success and failure.

The argument goes something like this. There are several characteristics which together contribute to a 'good' home. They are such things as financial security, reasonable comfort, space and a pleasant physical environment. They include family stability and parents with a good understanding of the importance of educational play and language development. As the child starts school, a 'good' home continues to provide supportive educational experiences and a lot of encouragement and interest in what the child is doing at school. A 'bad' home,

---

* See, for example, the following reports: 'Early Leaving' (1954), Crowther (1959–60), Newsom (1963), Robbins (1963–4), Plowden (1967); and the following sociological texts: *Social Class and Educational Opportunity*, by J. E. Floud, A. H. Halsey and F. M. Martin (Heinemann, 1956), *The Home and the School* (McGibbon & Kee, 1964) and *All Our Future* (Peter Davies, 1968) by J. W. B. Douglas *et al.*, and *The National Child Development Studies* (1st Report 1966, 2nd Report 1972, National Children's Bureau).

on the other hand, is one in which there is no financial security, over-crowding and lack of space. There are often too many children, and sometimes a broken marriage to contend with. 'Bad' parents do not have 'the proper kind of attitudes' about education, or 'the right aspirations' for their children. Their language, and the language they teach their children, is 'restricted' in its vocabulary and sentence structure and provides a poor preparation for the child's subsequent learning experiences in school. Children from 'bad' homes have parents who show little interest in their schooling and they are usually very reluctant to visit teachers and to discuss their children's progress.

This is obviously an oversimplified version of the kind of characteristics which are used to depict 'good' and 'bad' homes, but the more you read the literature, the more you'll be able to identify these kind of judgements being made. In The National Child Development Study 'From Birth to Seven', for example, these comments are made:

'A great deal—if not the major part—of learning takes place outside the school and much of this is accomplished even before the child enters school. The vocabulary and concepts used by those around him are vital in providing a framework within which his own intellectual growth can take place. If this framework is bare or impoverished, his own development is likely to be slow, a rich framework of words and ideas will provide the food for more rapid growth. More advanced or abstract thought processes are usually clothed in a more elaborate and highly structured language (Bernstein, 1961). A home conducive to learning is one where there is a feeling for the spoken and written word as a tool for conveying precise meaning; and where children are stimulated to question the world around them and receive explanations appropriate to their age.

'There are two senses in which a child from such a home comes to school ready to learn. He is intellectually ready in that his language and concepts are already well structured, so that the school is building upon established foundations. But he is also psychologically ready to acquire new skills. For example, he has learned that reading provides pleasure and he wants to be a part of the literate community as soon as possible. His whole attitude to school is conditioned by his parents' high regard for education.

'*This kind of home is certainly not a monopoly of professional or other non-manual workers. However, it is more frequently found amongst occupational groups which possess a high level of education and skill.*' (author's emphasis)

Because of the association of 'good' and 'bad' homes with research that links educational achievement and social class, the two become collapsed into the association of 'good' homes with middle-class lifestyles and 'bad' homes with working-class lifestyles. In other words, it has become widely assumed that middle-class children do better in school than working-class children because they come from better homes and their parents make a better job of bringing them up.

This explanation of failure is firmly located in the social, cultural, linguistic and educational deficiencies which are said to be 'typical' of a good many working-class people. Children brought up in such circumstances are said to be 'seriously deprived' compared to their more fortunate 'brothers and sisters' from middle-class backgrounds. Terms like 'the culture of deprivation' are used to link the various characteristics of a way of life which seems to spell disaster. The sense of deprivation being passed on from one generation of 'feckless' and 'deprived' individuals to the next, is caught in the use of the term 'cycle of deprivation', in which it is thought to be almost inevitable that 'poverty and ignorance' will breed 'poverty and ignorance'. Indeed, the vocabulary of deprivation can reach almost epidemic proportions, as an American cartoon of the mid-1960s illustrates (Fig. 6).

From the point of view of 'remedy' this kind of pathological explanation of failure presents two alternatives. It is thought that in terms of heredity, parents' occupation and education, family size and the physical circumstances of the home, there is little that can be done, certainly not by education. But in terms of the 'culture environment' of the home, parents' attitudes, their knowledge of the education system, their use of language and the help they give their children with appropriate learning, some positive intervention can be made. It is this kind of belief that encourages social work initiatives, especially in pre-school activities in the home, and also the notions of 'compensatory education' for deprived children, to help repair the cultural 'damage' done by their upbringing.

The weakness of these explanations and remedies is, of course, the uncritical way in which the relationship between home, school and social class is treated, and the tendency to oversimplify, and indeed stigmatise, vast numbers of individuals, their families and their home circumstances because they do not conform to the prevailing norms defined and agreed upon by the researchers and report writers.

The other major weakness lies in the recommendations about 'social intervention' and 'compensatory education'. In a famous article by Basil Bernstein*, in which he tried to put right the way in which his earlier analysis of language had been used to reinforce notions of middle-class 'cultural superiority' and working-class 'cultural deficiency', he argued that education cannot be expected to 'compensate for society'. If the prevailing social structure is unequal in its distribu-

* Basil Bernstein, 'Education Cannot Compensate for Society', *New Society*, February 26th, 1970.

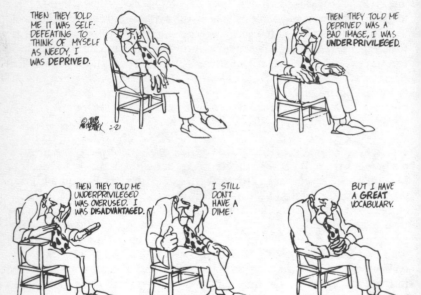

Fig. 6. The 'cycle of deprivation'.
(Reprinted by permission of Jules Feiffer)

tion of resources, and operates a class system which discriminates against working-class people, no amount of educational compensation can alter their experience of social and economic disadvantage. He also challenges the notion of 'cultural deprivation', arguing that, since everyone has a culture, no one can be said to be deprived of their culture. Nell Keddie develops his argument in her introduction to *Tinker Tailor—The Myth of Cultural Deprivation*. She argues that the cultural background of so-called 'deprived' groups reflects, in fact, *different* assumptions and practices about child-rearing, not *deficient* ones. She shows how in schools teachers define what is meant by ability, success, failure, achievement, etc., and organise their schools to reflect their definitions. They are the same definitions that serve the interests of socially powerful groups in society. If those are the yardsticks which are used to measure educational achievement and educational potential, then it is hardly surprising that the children of socially powerless groups fail to match up to the criteria that have been established.

With the added 'authority' of sociological research and government reports, cultural deficit explanations of educational failure become virtually institutionalised, in the sense that children become progressively disadvantaged educationally. Since they are thought to be 'deprived', little is expected of them from the day they enter school. The remedy is not 'compensatory education' and 'social intervention' to change children's cultural behaviour, but rather, the fundamental reform of the assumptions, practices and educational values which operate in schools. According to Keddie, it is in the organisation of schooling that the responsibility for failure lies, not in the deficiency of individual children and their upbringing.

Technical/Maldistribution

Both of the pathological versions of educational failure rely upon a micro analysis of social behaviour and assume that failure is somehow located in the individual. The technical/maldistribution model takes a slightly broader perspective.

One version of this kind of explanation echoes Nell Keddie's view that schools are 'middle-class institutions' which represent assumptions, values and behaviour that alienate working-class children, and which in a variety of obvious and less obvious ways systematically ensure that the majority of them fail. Sources of failure are looked for in the ways in which schools operate. It may be that their curriculum is badly organised or badly taught, their rules and regulations may be inappropriate, the 'hidden curriculum' of their teachers' attitudes may have the effect of denigrating the ability and potential of many of their children. An examination of specific schools, like Hightown Grammar* and Lumley†, have illustrated some of the ways in which the organisation and expectations of the schools help to administer success and failure to different pupils.

The implication of this kind of analysis is that if the values and practices which cause failure can be identified, they can be altered. This view relies a good deal on the assumption that failure has to do with

---

* *Hightown Grammar*, Colin Lacey, Manchester University Press, Manchester, 1970.
† *Social Relations in a Secondary School*, David Hargreaves, Routledge & Kegan Paul, London, 1967.

'technical' weaknesses in the system which can be remedied. Failure is in the failure of parts of the system to operate effectively or fairly, and once it is accepted that 'systems failure' creates, or at least contributes to, pupil failure, then institutional change should be able to improve matters.

This type of explanation and remedy seems more appealing to many liberal-minded people than the one which relies on 'blaming individuals' for their cultural deficiency. It seems less daunting to change the attitudes and practices of a few thousand teachers and schools than the cultural behaviour of several million children. But a lot of teachers and some sociologists would argue that institutions like schools are no more in a position to check the distribution of failure in society than those who experience it: teachers and schools are merely pawns in an altogether more complicated game.

Another version of this explanation looks at the distribution of educational and other resources in society. The argument presented by Byrne, Williamson and Fletcher, for example, in *The Poverty of Education* shows how different social classes, located in different areas of the city and in different parts of the country, receive different resources.

In practice this means things like the age and quality of the schools, the amount of money spent on equipment and materials, the size of the staff-pupil ratio, the provision of pre-school nursery classes, educational grants to help needy families, good sixth-form facilities, etc. In *The Poverty of Education* the writers show how uneven is the distribution of these resources between schools and between local education authorities. Like the more general resources of housing, transport, employment and environmental planning, middle-class areas and more prosperous regions tend to be much better served than working-class neighbourhoods and poorer and more remote parts of the country.

Many of the decisions about the allocation of resources are dependent on local and national government policies, and in times of economic crisis the tendency is to save in areas in which there will be the least organised and least effective opposition to expenditure cuts. In practice this hits working-class communities particularly hard.

The effect of unequal resource distribution according to Byrne, Williamson and Fletcher is to exacerbate the social and educational differences between children from different social environments, since the performance of the neighbourhood schools in which they find themselves is thought to be directly related to the provision of resources they receive. Fig. 7 shows how. . . .

In this argument, educational success and failure are directly related to local authority spending, which is in turn affected by local and national government decisions. The assumption is that different decisions and more spending could reduce the amount of educational fail-

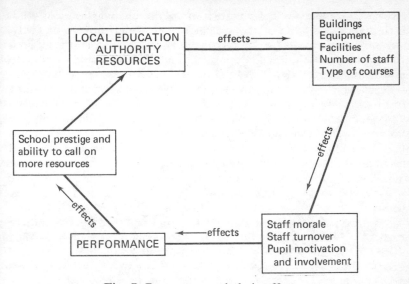

Fig. 7. Resources and their effects.

ure recorded in poor areas and badly resourced schools. The remedy is seen to be in terms of 'positive discrimination', so that schools in disadvantaged areas, in which pupils and their families experience the cumulative effects of receiving fewer of society's resources than in the more advantaged middle-class areas, should receive proportionately more educational funding, better facilities and more favourable staffing ratios to restore the balance between them. In other words, a significant reallocation should occur—not just in education, but in other social and environmental provision too—to counteract the prevailing inequalities which keep some communities in a state of serious disadvantage.

Structural

All of the explanations so far assume that educational failure is either a personal or a technical problem which can be remedied, compensated for, altered by institutional change, or modified by positive discrimination. In all of these circumstances failure is regarded as 'regrettable' and reforms are advocated to ameliorate its effects.

Those sociologists who advance a 'structural explanation' of educational failure, however, take a more pessimistic view of the source and persistence of failure in our society. Key contributors to this kind of explanation in recent years have been the American historian Clarence Karier and the political economists Bowles and Gintis. All of them emphasise the central importance of the economic system in society. Karier, for example, argues that through the tool of education,

American schools have been used principally to teach the attitudes and skills necessary to adjust pupils to the changing needs of the economic system, and to reinforce the values of a 'business ethic' in American society.

Bowles and Gintis develop this view in their book *Schooling in Capitalist America*, which though argued in terms of American society, is considered highly relevant to the operation of all advanced industrial nations. According to Bowles and Gintis, the education system in society exists to produce the labour force for capitalism, both in terms of the qualities and skills needed and also the attitudes and values likely to endorse capitalist practices. The function of education, they argue, is to anticipate and reproduce the conditions and relationships which exist between employers and workers in the relationships of production (see pages 8–9).

They recognise that capitalism has considerably advanced since Marx first identified its main characteristics in the nineteenth century. Then, a view of education 'to gentle the masses' on behalf of the ruling class seemed a simple correlation between education and society. Today, the relationship is much more complex, as the massive expansion of capitalist influence and state intervention in people's lives has become commonplace. Man's experience of work has been transformed over the last hundred years and today the majority of productive workers are the employees of vast multinational concerns, with factories and investments in various countries, operating outside the control of individual governments. Their 'local managers' have in turn become very small cogs in incredibly big wheels. Automation and technology have developed to such an extent that machines and computers have gained precedence over workers in the work process and altered and eradicated the jobs they once did (see Chapter 7).

In these circumstances, in which economic growth and social change are both extensive and rapid, education, according to Bowles and Gintis, is used to maintain order and control. Far from being 'egalitarian' and 'reformist', as so many educators suggest, schools are about 'inequality' and 'repression'. Capitalism does not require everyone to fulfil their educational potential or become highly qualified and intellectually critical. In fact, any of these indicators of educational 'success' would on a large scale seriously challenge the distribution of employment, profit and power in a capitalist society. People have to be educated 'just enough' to become dutiful workers, citizens and consumers, but 'not enough' to understand, or seriously challenge, the prevailing economic and social system.

The key term is 'behaviour modification'—the skills and attitudes which schools reward are docility, passivity and obedience. And there is a 'correspondence' between the social relations of production and the social relations of education so that children in school begin to

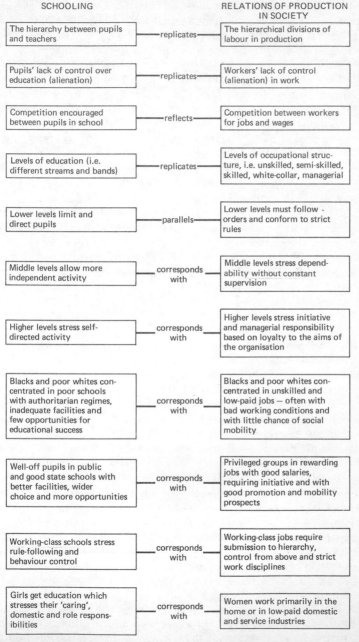

Fig. 8. Bowles' and Gintis' Correspondence Theory.
(Copyright Open University Press; E202, Unit 32)

learn the values and functions they will later repeat as workers. This is achieved, according to Bowles and Gintis, by schools modelling themselves on the economic divisions of society so that the relations of schooling 'replicate' the relations of production (for example, see Fig. 8).

Bowles and Gintis do not attribute the responsibility for creating an unequal society to the education system, however. The root cause of inequality is firmly attributed to the structural divisions of a capitalist society which needs to maintain its working-class labour force. But just as capitalist society exploits the labour power of the workers, and controls so much of their social and cultural lives, so too does schooling 'exploit' the child-workers and ensure their alienation from real learning. In different schools and in different streams, the future managers and shop-floor workers are rehearsing their future roles as organisers and organised. And all the while, a façade of equal opportunity and meritocracy exists to confirm that educational success is alive and well, and to explain failure in terms of poor motivation and personal deficiency.

Of course all of this is strong stuff and there are many sociologists who feel that Bowles and Gintis overstate their case! But certainly the limited achievements of recent educational reforms like positive discrimination policies in Educational Priority Areas, the raising of the school-leaving age to 16, and changes and innovations in the curriculum seem to have done little to alter radically the sense of failure which many children experience daily in our schools.

Given this kind of analysis, Bowles and Gintis are very pessimistic about remedies couched in terms of remedial education, compensatory education or even 'positive discrimination' when in practice the sums of money involved are minute compared to the size of the problem needing to be tackled. Since most educational problems are not caused by the school system but by the workings of the capitalist economy, reforming institutions in a piecemeal kind of way, without changing the wider economic and political structures of society, is, in their view, doomed to fail. They argue that liberal reformers in all walks of life, not just education, have failed to understand this. They act as though social problems can be ameliorated by the sympathetic intervention of the state. They try to reform individuals and institutions by social-welfare and legal initiatives, but without questioning the basic structure of property and power in economic life, which are the root causes of these problems. None of these reforms, according to Bowles and Gintis, places social problems in their real social and economic context of a knowledge that capitalism depends on institutionalising inequality, poverty and educational failure as a means of surviving and flourishing. Schools and the education system are so important to capitalism in this process that they are unlikely to change in any radical way unless there is the most massive political onslaught on the economic and political base of capitalist society. Failure will never be eradicated from the school system so long as capitalism requires schools to reproduce the majority of its labour force with limited horizons and limited achievements. The most that schools can attempt to do, if they actually want to challenge the function they have been given by society, is to alter their relationships, so that instead of re-plicating 'the social relations of production' and helping to perpetuate the capitalist system, they dedicate themselves root and branch to promoting the personal development of all their pupils and social equality between them.

In Conclusion

This chapter has attempted to explain in some detail the organisational changes which have taken place in schools over the last hundred years or so, some of the main functions which the education system is thought to serve in society, and the ways in which different sociologists explain educational success and failure. The sociology of education has a vast and growing literature and a variety of other concerns which have not been touched upon here. You may be interested, for example, to follow up some small-scale studies of individual schools, or examine the literature which analyses different teaching methods. Studies of the curriculum in schools are also prolific and have been given a recent 'kick in the pants' by the 'sociology of knowledge' which questions how subject knowledge comes to be selected and how it gets transmitted in the educational process.

By taking a slightly more 'macro' view of the relationship between schooling, education and society, however, you will have the 'back-cloth' and wider context in which you can locate any of these, or other, educational concerns, should you want to pursue them.

Revision

1. Refresh Your Memory

Make sure you know the meaning of the terms; eleven plus, IQ test, social mobility, Educational Priority Area, social pathology, psychometrics, cultural deficit, cultural deprivation, remedial education, compensatory education, positive discrimination, the cycle of deprivation, multinational industry.

2. Check Your Understanding

Be able to explain in your own words:

(*a*) The difference between informal and formal education.

(*b*) The difference between elementary and secondary education before the 1944 Education Act.

(*c*) The difference between multilateral and comprehensive schools.

(*d*) The difference between grammar, technical and secondary modern schools after 1944.

(*e*) The main provisions of the Forster Education Act of 1870, the Balfour Education Act of 1902 and the 1944 Education Act.

(*f*) The main recommendations of the Hadow Report, the Spens Report and the Norwood Report.

(*g*) The difference between Cyril Burt's and Alfred Yates' definition of intelligence.

(*h*) The difference between notions of 'cultural deficit' and 'cultural difference'.

(*i*) The main difference between 'pathological' and 'structural' explanations of educational failure.

3. Essay Questions to Try

(*a*) Explain why intelligence is not the only factor which determines a pupil's progress at school.

(*b*) Explain how the development of neighbourhood schools might provide further educational advantages for the middle-class child.

(*c*) Examine the links between education and social mobility in our society.

(*d*) Explain the growth of comprehensive education in post-war England and Wales.

(*e*) Discuss the view that the main function of educational institutions is to transmit the values of society between generations.

(*f*) Evaluate the explanations advanced by sociologists to account for the relative failure of working-class children in the school system.

(*g*) How far is it accurate to view Britain as a meritocracy?

(*h*) Attempt sociological explanations of two of the following:

  (i) The raising of the school-leaving age.
  (ii) Educational priority areas.
 (iii) Comprehensive reorganisation.
 (iv) Criticisms of streaming.
  (v) Parents on the governing bodies of schools.

(*i*) 'The lower-working-class child is doomed to failure before he or she enters school. The next eleven years merely confirm earlier irredeemable processes.' Discuss.

(*j*) Examine the relationship between education and social stratification.

(*k*) Is the progress of pupils in schools better explained by what happens to them in school or out of it?

(*l*) Discuss the view that the education system changes primarily in response to 'economic needs'.

(*m*) 'I do not understand how we can talk about offering compensatory education to children who in the first place have not, as yet, been offered an adequate educational environment' (Bernstein, *Education Cannot Compensate for Society*). Explain and discuss.

(*n*) What can sociologists contribute to an understanding of programmes of compensatory education?

(*o*) Girls, blacks and the lower class are less successful in the education system than boys, whites and the non-lower-working-class children. Select one of these pairs (e.g. girls/boys, blacks/whites, working class/non-working class) and explain their relative 'success' or 'failure'.

(*p*) '... consequently attempts to eliminate inequality of educational opportunity by removing the child from the influence of the family are on the face of it likely to be more successful than changes in the structure of secondary education. It is equally clear, however, that such changes are unlikely to be implemented or even seriously considered, in most industrial societies where they would offend other, deeply held, values.' (Hurd, *Human Societies*) Discuss.

Further Reading

Education and Poverty, Philip Robinson, Methuen, London, 1976.

Equal Opportunities in Education, Harold Silver, Methuen, London, 1973.

From Birth to Seven. A Report of the National Child Development Study, R. Davie, N. Butler and H. Goldstein, Longman, London, 1972.

Priority Education, Eric Midwinter, Penguin, London, 1972.

Social Relations in a Secondary School, David Hargreaves, Routledge & Kegan Paul, London, 1967.

The Evolution of the Comprehensive School 1926–72, Brian Simon and David Rubinstein, Routledge & Kegan Paul, London, 1973.

The Home and the School, J. W. B. Douglas, McGibbon & Kee, London, 1964.

The Sociology of Educational Ideas, Julia Evetts, Routledge & Kegan Paul, London, 1973.

Women and Schooling, Rosemary Deem, Routledge & Kegan Paul, London, 1978.

(The answer to the 'eleven plus question' on p. 97 is *steamer* because all the others have 'national' connotations, i.e. German measles, French leave, Spanish omelette and Dutch courage.)

5

STUDIES IN YOUTH CULTURE

Defining Culture

Culture is a term used frequently by sociologists—but in various ways. In 1952 Kroeber, Alfred and Kluckhohn identified 164 different definitions of culture, not counting the various statements they found about culture, which ran into thousands. No doubt in the intervening years since their review was carried out, and given the increasing interest in different kinds of cultural behaviour during this period, countless other definitions can be added to the list.

In general terms, notions of culture tend to reflect two main tendencies:

Culture as Art

One tendency reflects a conservative view of culture which considers 'high art', classical music, great literature—in short 'the best which has ever been thought, said, written or produced'—as the epitome of excellence, against which everything else is measured. Those who share this rarefied and elitist view of 'high culture' consider it to be superior to mass culture or popular culture, which they consider less civilised, less intrinsically worthwhile, and ultimately threatening in its superficiality to the quality of human existence.

A more liberal view of 'culture as art' still holds 'high art' as the yardstick against which other cultural forms must be measured but takes a more romantic and sentimental view of some popular culture. The claim is made that 'it isn't *all* bad'— or, alternatively, that most of the mass culture *is* bad, especially if it is crude or commercialised, but there *are* some illustrations of 'good' and 'authentic' popular culture. To some extent this represents a pluralist view of society which concedes that other cultural traditions deserve due recognition, though not necessarily due respect.

Since comparison between different cultural standards is the major characteristic of this use of the term culture, it relies on implicit assumptions about 'good' and 'bad', and upon value-judgements about what is best, most civilising, most enduring, most significant. It operates, on the whole, with little if any reference to social context, to history, politics or economics.

110

Culture as Life

A second tendency is to define culture not merely as art or the production of artefacts but as 'a whole way of life'—something which includes language, beliefs, attitudes and values as well as the more visible characteristics of social behaviour, dress and appearance and general lifestyle. This use of the term culture has enabled sociologists and anthropologists to identify the general social characteristics of national cultures which those born and brought up in different societies have in common. Using this definition, it is possible to describe social differences between industrial and pre-industrial societies, for example, between rich and poor countries and between the Eastern bloc and the West. Culture as 'a total way of life', incorporating different social, political, economic and moral characteristics, passed on from one generation to the next by socialisation, enables sociologists to describe how Eskimos, for example, are different from Red Indians, who in turn are very different from Bushmen or Aborigines.

Subculture and Culture

Some sociologists, notably A. K. Cohen,* make extensive use of the term subculture. For Cohen, subcultures are 'cultures which exist *within* cultures' and have three major characteristics:

1. The group identified as a subculture shares a distinctive way of life and possesses knowledge, beliefs, values, codes, tastes and prejudices of its own.
2. These are learned from others in the group who already exhibit these characteristics.
3. Their way of life has a historical dimension and has 'somehow become traditional' among those who inherit and share the social conditions to which the subcultural characteristics are a response.

Cohen of course is referring almost exclusively to teenage gangs but the use of the term subculture has also been applied to a whole variety of other groups, including social class, neighbourhood, political and racial groups.

Culture and Economics

Marxists tend to explain the cultural characteristics of different societies and groups within societies as a reflection of the economic division of labour in different societies, so that in analysing cultural characteristics, precedence is given to the nature of the economic relations, to the characteristics and relationships of production, and to the process

---

* *Delinquent Boys: The Culture of the Gang*, Albert Cohen, Free Press, 1955.

by which powerful groups try to maintain their power and less power-ful groups are driven to oppose them.

This economic and social analysis of the origins of culture has led some sociologists to differentiate between dominant or mainstream culture, which reflects the behavioural patterns, values, beliefs and vested interests of those holding economic, social and political power in society, and subcultures of various kinds which derive their social characteristics from, and in response to, the subordinate relationship of their members to more powerful groups in society.

The Creation of Culture

For the purposes of this chapter it is important to be clear what de-finition of culture is being used. Culture is not simply art, or objects, or behaviour or even 'a whole way of life' if this is regarded as something which is predetermined, and which does not change.

It is important to remember that people do not merely *receive* their culture from others, they also make it and remake it continually in a process of interaction with others in a variety of social relationships and social settings. When talking about the lifestyle and behaviour of different groups, as an indication of their culture, it is important to remember that these all have historic and present dimensions as well as future possibilities. It would be too simple to argue that the way people behave is entirely the result of their socialisation by families, workmates and friends, education and the mass media on behalf of economic interests. Clearly social, economic and political forces of various kinds have a tremendous power to influence and mould indi-vidual behaviour and to structure the situations in which people learn the kind of cultural responses which are characteristic of the different groups they belong to in society—but it is a two-way process of nego-tiation. The institutions which attempt to influence and control people are themselves influenced and controlled by people. They *are*, in effect, 'people in action' and not impersonal forces or inanimate objects. Their philosophies and decisions and actions and behaviour are given character and meaning by different people. Frequently they are given *different* meanings. Just as they influence, so too can they be influ-enced. Society is far from being a 'consensus system' in which different subgroups share without question the same values, attitudes and be-haviour patterns. It is a hierarchical system, though, as we have seen, and one in which some are able to exercise control over the behaviour of others and to define the boundaries of 'acceptable behaviour' much more influentially than others. But just as surely, there are other groups whose social and economic interests lie in resistance to these attempts at control. It is the interplay between the two, worked out in cultural as well as economic terms, which highlight the conflicts and contradictions inherent in a stratified society.

The interesting area of investigation so far as sociologists are concerned is to examine the relationship between these contradictory and competing cultures, to question from where they originate, how they respond to and reflect social and economic relationships in society and how they are continually in a state of being and becoming. Bryn Jones in *The Politics of Popular Culture* puts it like this:

'Culture is an instrument of social control. The capacity of a dominant group to reproduce its dominance over time depends on its ability to control the means by which the world is made sense of, i.e. culture and ideology. But culture is also the site of struggle and conflict, of negotiation which constantly re-defines (and usually reproduces in a new form) the existing relationships of domination and subordination in a society. The power to create and manipulate culture as a means of controlling others is well entrenched in the social, economic and political institutions of a society but it is also continually resisted by opposing cultural forms.'

The classic example of an 'oppositional culture', so far as Jones and other sociologists engaged in cultural studies are concerned, is that of the industrial working class who have struggled over time and in different historical circumstances to make their existence bearable and better—not only in their relationships at work with their employers but in the struggle for control over their own non-work time. Some of their institutional responses have been trade unionism, professional football, working men's clubs, the music hall, etc. For many working-class youngsters their opposition has been in the non-formal, but none the less coherent, resistance of counter-school culture, teenage gangs and ritualised youth culture.

Adolescence and Culture

It has been in the period since the Second World War that teenagers have become of major interest to social scientists—largely as a consequence of their increasing affluence and independence and as a result of the preoccupation in society generally with those forms of youthful behaviour associated with trouble—drugs, sex and violence.

Early studies of teenage behaviour were very influenced by psychological and behaviourist considerations in which 'the problems of adolescence' were explained in relation to the physical changes taking place in growing bodies and the discontinuities between physical and social maturity. This extract from 'Who is the Adolescent?'* is typical of many such accounts:

'The common psychological features of early adolescence include a sensitiveness about appearance, anxiety, a striving for approval and a

---

* From The Marshall Cavendish Learning System: *Man and Medicine*.

lack of confidence. There is also an awakening interest in sex, a general restlessness, boredom and disinclination to work. Some degree of awkwardness and clumsiness is common in teenage boys and girls. Mannerisms are common and lead to some embarrassment. For example, blushing with very little provocation is a common feature of this age period. Boys and girls of this age also have emotional ups and downs with rapid changes from laughter to tears; giggling is frequent. Adolescents are particularly sensitive to comments from parents and others and are easily offended, taking everything said as implying criticism. They are particularly likely to be infuriated by parental criticism of their clothes, appearance, hairstyle, or still more, of their friends. Failure of the parents to recognise the sensitiveness of the adolescent is one of the major causes of friction at home.

'One obvious reason for friction is the transition from dependence to independence, and the more the parents try to keep control—the more they underestimate the maturity of the teenager—the more rebellious he becomes. Not unnaturally, parents find it difficult to relax discipline, to balance overprotection with unjustifiable carelessness. If they go too far one way, the adolescent rebels; if they go too far the other way, he may get into trouble.

'Another source of friction is the difficult behaviour of adolescents. Moody, sulky, quarrelsome and obstinate behaviour are common features and lead to friction with their parents who cannot understand why they should act so. They are apt to be rude, to snarl and snap. They look for faults in their parents, they quarrel with their brothers and sisters. They become furious when teased in the gentlest of ways. Adolescents want to think for themselves. Previously all decisions were made for them by their parents and now they rebel against this. They rebel against the ways and the thoughts of the older generation and hence adopt fantastic hairstyles and unconventional clothes as a token of rebellion against their elders. This rebellion against tradition may have more serious consequences—sexual licence, illegitimate pregnancy or venereal disease.

'Adolescents are now no longer willing to accept all that their parents say as absolute truth. They want to know the reasons for everything. When they were younger they were forced to do as they were told. Now that they are becoming independent they want to think for themselves and they are no longer willing to accept the "because I say so" approach.'

Accounts like this which seem to treat anxiety and gaucherie as the 'normal traits' of adolescence are balanced by those who see teenagers as the enlightened and crusading champions of social progress, ever ready to join campaigns and fling themselves with enthusiasm into idealistic causes.

In equally romantic vein, Theodore Roszak* and Jeff Nuttall† explain the use of drugs, sex and underground politics as a replacement of cultural values which are corrupt, lifeless and boring by alternative standards, libertarian values and fresh affiliations.

But in most of the literature, and the reports of psychologists, criminologists, journalists and social workers, young people are invariably portrayed as troublesome and as 'a problem group' in society. Many of the commentators seem to forget their own youth and exaggerate the significance and the extent of what young people are said to habitually be engaged in—drug-taking, football hooliganism, mugging, punk, sexual orgies, glue-sniffing, vandalism, crime, etc. The sociologist Stanley Cohen calls all of these 'moral panics' and shows how they are used to stereotype the bad and the dramatic behaviour of young people out of all proportion to their actual significance.

The Social Class Factors

What is missing from these different analyses, of course, is any serious attention to social class as a significant variable in the behaviour of teenagers. The tendency has been to explain teenage rebellion in terms of 'psychological turmoil' or a 'generation gap' or as the commercially-induced allegiance to pop music and fashionable fads. The assumption seems to be 'that when you've seen one teenager, you've seen them all'. But what is frequently overlooked is the similarity as distinct from the difference in attitudes, values and expectations of most youngsters and their parents, and the very real difference which characterises the behaviour of different groups of young people.

The tendency to lump together all young people as part of the same generation and to assume that they are all the same as each other because they listen to the same music or have similar leisure interests ignores the extent to which social class influences what people learn, for example, who their friends are, how they view the world and what opportunities are available to them. Social class divides and creates differences among youngsters just as significantly as it does among adults.

Similarly, although teenagers may feel closer to their friends than their parents and actively resist the authority of their parents during adolescence, the majority of young people, when they leave school, go on to college or get a job, decide to marry and make plans for their future, tend to do all of these within the same general social and economic context as that which has given character to their parents' lifestyle. This is not to say that society is not changing and has not changed considerably since the war. Clearly there is visible and

---

* *Making of a Counter Culture*, Theodore Roszak, Faber & Faber, London, 1969.
† *Bomb Culture*, Jeff Nuttall, Paladin, London, 1970.

material evidence of changing lifestyles over the years. But whilst increasing affluence, for example, and greater geographic mobility, smaller families and the increasing tendency of women to work outside the home, may all have created changes *within* social classes, the disparities *between* different classes still continue. Nor has the tendency of middle-class and working-class youngsters to remain more or less within the same social class categories as the ones they were born into changed significantly. It is the differences which distinguish one social class from another rather than those which differentiate a younger generation from their parents that are still the single most important factor in any analysis of social change.

Youth Culture

How best then to study the behaviour of teenagers in relation to youth culture? John Clarke and Tony Jefferson of the Centre for Contemporary Cultural Studies at Birmingham University, writing in 1973, describe the creation of youth culture as the attempt 'to exert some control over one's life situation'. What characterises youth culture, according to them, is the search for excitement, autonomy and identity—the freedom to create 'cultural meanings' rather than simply accept what is presented by those representatives of officialdom and authority.

Youth can best be seen as the time in which young people, in different ways, depending on their social class background, attempt to negotiate with their elders and within the context of a society in which dominant and mainstream culture is the arbiter, their own definitions, and to give meaning to the world they find themselves in. In the process of negotiation and in the attempt to define for themselves what is important, different youth cultures can exploit two principal opportunities that are extended to young people in our society: the opportunity to 'have a fling' before taking up the adult responsibilities of 'earning a living' and 'settling down', and the opportunity to join in activities encouraged by commercialised leisure pursuits. Both opportunities have their limitations, however, in the sense that 'doing your own thing' is usually tempered by the demand for a proper respect for adult rules and regulations, and the organisation of leisure activities is considerably influenced by commercial interests concerned with making money rather than encouraging teenagers to make their own choice and define their own tastes without external interference.

The fact that the distinctive and visible signs of youth culture are most noticeable in leisure-related activities and 'non-work' time demonstrates the extent to which school and work provides the most obvious restrictions on individual and self-determined action, though non-conformity to the mainstream culture of the school and the workplace is also evident, as we shall see presently.

Why Study the Workers?

One of the interesting characteristics of recent studies of youth culture, now that social class has been recognised as being an important variable, is that they are almost exclusively studies of working-class boys. There has been little written about working-class girls (see below) and virtually nothing about middle-class adolescents.

It is interesting to speculate why middle-class adolescents have attracted so little attention. Perhaps it is because the majority of them have presented no particular problem to society. Preoccupied with schooling and post-school education, they have appeared conformist and quiescent, and their non-conformity, compared to the behaviour of delinquent gangs, soccer hooligans, teds, skinheads and bootboys, seems to offer little threat to property and public order. In consequence, the emergence of student unrest at the universities and the hippy movement of the middle and late sixties took sociologists almost unawares—especially in Britain. With rare exceptions, postwar studies of youth cultures have concentrated almost exclusively on the behaviour of working-class groups. The extent to which sociologists have tended to focus on the behaviour of 'subject populations', especially if they are defined as 'social problems' as distinct from the behaviour of ruling groups, is an interesting characteristic of sociological enquiry which merits more attention!

Ruling by Consent

In their study *Working Class Youth Cultures*, John Clarke and Tony Jefferson begin by reminding us of the tendency of the dominant class in a society like ours to rule by consent rather than coercion. You will remember from Chapter 4 the arguments of Bowles and Gintis which link the education system to the economic system and the recognition that a vital function of schooling is to prepare young people for the labour market—not simply in terms of skills, but also in terms of attitudes and expectations. This is just one way in which dominant groups in society, having won control of the education system, use it in their attempt to influence the behaviour of others.

Economic and social dominance also depends upon ensuring that as many people as possible learn to see and to accept the way society is organised in the same way as the ruling class and to believe that these patterns are not only natural but inevitable. In achieving the consent of subordinate classes the ruling class is seeking to minimise the effects of conflict and organised opposition to its interests and to discredit any alternative pattern of life which might threaten its position (see Chapter 10).

The Swinging Sixties?

Rule by consent was bolstered in the fifties and sixties by the expansion of affluence. Increased production and higher wages made new patterns of consumption a reality for many working people. Conservative politicians proclaimed the end of inequality with slogans like 'You've never had it so good' and 'We're all middle class now'. Sociologists talked in terms of the embourgeoisement of the working class (see p. 36) and so far as anyone could tell the problem of capitalism had been solved.

The advertising industry helped to shift the focus of attention from the workplace onto consumption in the home, at leisure and in the family, and the government reinforced rising expectations about prosperity with promises of an increasingly 'open society' which would operate as a 'property-owning democracy'.

For the majority of working people increasing affluence was a matter of degree rather than significant change, however. They were generally better off than their parents had been. But in comparison to other social groups, the gross inequalities of everyday life continued. For them, this was the period not of private ownership of property but of redevelopment. Families were moved out of traditional working-class areas onto new estates and into new towns. Or their neighbourhoods were cleared and replaced by high-density, low-cost housing—mostly flats and tower blocks. In either case the effects on the local community and its cultural base established over generations were enormous.

In the creation of new estates and the redevelopment of old areas, planners based their decisions on assumptions about the nuclear family as distinct from those who had always been used to living in close social contact with relatives and neighbours in extended family arrangements (see p. 58). Families and neighbours were separated and split up, and important local meeting places like the street, the pub and the corner shop ceased to exist.

The significance of 'working-class community' as one of the cornerstones of working class culture is well documented by sociologists. The destruction of social communities by redevelopment in the fifties and sixties is seen by Frank Parkin,* among others, as a major attack on the independence and identity of working-class people.

At the same time as local meeting places were being pulled down, the general aura of increasing affluence helped to encourage the development and expansion of an organised and highly sophisticated leisure industry. People at leisure became 'consumers' of leisure activities, in much the same way as they were encouraged to consume

---

* *Class, Inequality and the Political Order*, Frank Parkin, Paladin, London, 1972.

manufactured goods and foodstuffs, and in everything from pub interiors to the organisation of professional football increasing attention was given to ways of packaging entertainment in a commercially profitable way (see Chapter 6).

But although the politicians and the representatives of commercial enterprise did their best to portray the late fifties and the 'swinging sixties' as an era of increasing classlessness and affluence, cracks were appearing in the façade.

The Re-emergence of Class

The first soundings of alarm came from a number of commissions of enquiry set up by the government to consider London's housing (Milner-Holland), children and young people (Ingleby), primary education (Plowden), the personal social services (Seebohm), and people and planning (Skeffington). One after the other the reports told the same sad story of bad housing, urban decay, educational disaster areas, unacceptable levels of poverty—in a phrase, urban deprivation.

Local councils found themselves increasingly criticised for their housing policies and dissastisfaction among those consigned to badly planned estates and tower blocks multiplied—as did vandalism and delinquency.

The discovery of 'the problem of urban deprivation' led in rapid succession to a vocabulary of complementary diseases: 'areas of special need', 'pockets of deprivation', 'twilight zones', 'priority areas', etc. Their inhabitants were variously referred to as 'the disadvantaged', 'the underprivileged', the 'culturally', 'environmentally', 'linguistically', and 'educationally deprived', 'the needy', 'the maladjusted' and 'the handicapped'. In fact, they were all members of the working class.

Once class was 'rediscovered' in the sixties and the complacency of prevailing assumptions about affluence were challenged, the government had to be seen to intervene. Comprehensive reorganisation, Urban Aid, Educational Priority Area and Community Development Projects were just some of their responses to circumstances in which class and racial inequalities might provoke threats to the social order (see Chapter 9).

The Response to Social Changes in the Fifties and Sixties

The social changes of the fifties and sixties caught the majority of the working class between two contradictory ideologies: the new ideology of conspicuous consumption and the traditional ideology of work and production. Whilst affluence was largely a myth, so far as the majority of working-class people were concerned, the enticements to indulge in consumerism and materialism were well orchestrated by the advertising and credit industries.

At the same time, changes in technology and the replacement of traditional work skills by automated production undermined the pride which many had previously taken in their jobs.

For those who were experiencing the effects of rehousing on new estates or redevelopment, another prop—the extended family—was progressively removed. According to Clarke and Jefferson, 'the focus of all the anxieties engendered by these changes, and which resulted in both an increase in early marriage and the emergence of specific youth cultures in opposition to parent culture . . . was worked out in terms of generational conflict'.

Of course the anxieties and contradictions experienced by working-class parents were also shared by their children, in that their common membership of the same oppressed class served to promote common problems. But differences in age presented an added dimension to what seem to be the same problems. Changes in the structure of employment, for example, and the prospect of redundancy, affect you differently if you have been in regular employment for most of your life compared to the effects on an unemployed teenager. Similarly, the solutions you might seek to counter frustration or alienation may well be different depending on your age group.

Youth Cultural Response: Mods and Skinheads

Two of the youth cultures which emerged at the time, and which represent the struggle of the groups involved to exert some control over their own life situations in the face of social changes apparently outside their control, were the mods and the skinheads. Both of them can be seen as the attempt to retrieve some of the socially cohesive elements of community which were being destroyed in the parent culture.

The mods came first and reflected the aspirations and style of the socially-mobile, white-collar workers, with fashion and music that measured up to their hedonistic search for affluence and glamour. The skinheads, on the other hand, adopted reggae, the protest music of the West Indian poor, and a form of dress that caricatured the appearance of manual workers. According to Clarke and Jefferson they were a 'reaction against contamination of the parent culture by middle-class values' and served to reassert the most reactionary traits of traditional working-class culture—puritanism and chauvinism. The puritanism crystallised in opposition to the hedonistic greasers and hippies and the chauvinism in 'queer bashing'.

In analysing the cultural characteristics of the mods and the skinheads Clarke and Jefferson make excellent use of the notion of 'style' which they use to mean the appropriation of apparently neutral objects and symbols from a 'normal' context which are then reinvested with different meanings and significance. The creation of style by different youth cultures involves the identification of objects like clothes, types of music, hairstyles and so on, which are relevant to the central concerns of the group in question, but which are then given new meaning and significance as the symbols of group identity.

The mods, although they aspired 'to better things', were mainly unskilled and semi-skilled workers or in routine white-collar jobs. The reality of their boring work compared to the affluent aspirations of the swinging sixties was one of the main contradictions which encouraged their search for action. 'If the daytime world was controlled by a succession of "grey adults", then the leisure time of nights and weekends offered the possibility of autonomy and excitement.' In the social context of aspiring working-class culture this was translated into a style which took on characteristics likely to disarm adult criticism, notably smartness and neatness, but which rapidly developed into a form which seemed to subvert adult values and which appeared to be both normal and incomprehensible at the same time. They seemed smart and respectable and yet they did things adults would not like. In creating their own style they gave new meaning to what were formerly harmless and neutral objects as Dick Hebdige illustrates in his article, 'The Meaning of Mods':

'The scooter, a formerly ultra-respectable means of transport was appropriated and converted into a weapon and a symbol of solidarity. Pills, medically diagnosed for the treatment of neuroses, were appropriated and used as an end in themselves. And the negative evaluations of their capabilities imposed by school and work were substituted by a positive assessment of their personal credentials in the world of play, i.e. the same qualities which were assessed negatively by daytime controllers, e.g. laziness, arrogance, vanity, etc., were positively defined by themselves and their peers in their leisure time.'

But despite their innovation and style and their originality the mods could not hold out against commercialisation for long. Just as the distinctive and authentic styles of dress and behaviour developed by the hippies were rapidly commercialised for economic gain, so too did the mods find their innovations being taken over by private enterprise. In the process, the potential of their opposition and resistance to mainstream cultural values was diffused and new converts to their cause were increasingly 'manufactured' rather than self-determining.

So far as the skinheads were concerned, the traditional working-class allegiances to football and the pub and the celebration of masculinity provided the inspiration for their creation of style. Whereas the mods had frequented discos and clubs, for the skinheads the pub was the place to meet up and spend time. The support of a favourite local team provided them with a focus for their loyalties and a way of expressing their solidarity. But football matches were as much about

getting drunk and fighting with opposing gangs as any simple enthusiasm for the game. The significance given to different ends of the
ground was more than custom, it represented territorial rights—'our
territory'—and common ownership. It was important to be able to
'count on your mates' and to demonstrate your toughness in the thick
of a fight.

A much publicised characteristic of skinhead chauvinism was 'Paki-
bashing' and 'queer bashing'. Pakistanis provided the scapegoat for
the aggression and frustration of skinhead kids in down-town areas,
out of work, in rough schools or dead-end jobs and in competition
with each other for scarce resources. West Indians were respected by
the skinheads because of their toughness and their masculinity and
their shared disrespect for the forces of law and order, but the Pakistanis, apart from racial dislike, demonstrated the kind of quietly
aspiring, 'respectable', family-orientated values associated with
middle-class culture. 'Queers' were also despised. Their definition of
'queer' included all those males who looked odd in a way which was
unmasculine. Homosexuals were obvious targets but so too were
hippies and students if they had long hair and wore uni-sex clothes.

Clarke and Jefferson explain the violence of skinhead culture as an
expression of toughness and a characteristically working-class self-
concept of masculinity. Their concentration on 'hard masculinity' was
also symbolised in their appearance—cropped shaved heads, heavy
denim jeans, braces and boots.

As Clarke* concludes, working-class youth cultures like the skinheads need to provide both a strong feeling of control and a strong
sense of identity to their members, as both of these things are denied
them in their subordinate class position. Two comments from skinheads illustrate his point:

'You got a terrific feeling of power, when a group of 200 of you
were running down the street, nobody would dare touch you, even the
police kept out of the way.'

'Well, it got you a lot of attention didn't it—the press and things,
everybody knew who the skinheads were . . . if we hadn't done those
things nobody would have noticed us.'

Youth Cultures in Context

Working-class youth cultures, like those of the mods and skinheads,
have to be seen, therefore, within the wider historical, social and
economic contexts in which they exist. They are partly a creation of
those contexts and partly a creative response to them. In the 'process

---

* 'The Skinheads and the Magical Recovery of Community', in *Resistance Through Rivals*, S. Hall and T. Jefferson
(eds.), Hutchinson, London, 1976.

of becoming and being' a distinctive subculture, a struggle for control is taking place. The ruling class, in the guise of the state, and represented in cultural terms by the ubiquity of mainstream culture, is attempting to impress its definitions of normality and values upon others, as a way of influencing and controlling their behaviour. The aim is to create a political and social consensus so that rule by consent can be strengthened.

Subordinate groups on the other hand, of which working-class youth cultures are just one example, continually resist the definitions and impositions of the state and the interests it represents. They struggle to give their own definitions and meanings to their life situations and the world they find themselves in. This in turn gives rise to values, beliefs and behaviour patterns that are frequently in opposition to those required by dominant groups in their concern to achieve consensus.

Sometimes their 'sense of difference' from other social groups and the norms of mainstream culture they reject is selfconscious and though unpoliticised is clearly 'oppositional' to the interests of mainstream culture (see below the discussion of Paul Willis' book *Learning to Labour*). Often their behaviour is incorporated and 'made safe' by a commercialised version of the real thing. Commercially promoted pop culture—clothes, music and leisure activities—can serve to distract youngsters away from a potentially more threatening and authentic oppositional culture and along avenues which make the consumption of mass produced pop culture 'seem like' the challenge they want to make to mainstream culture. The fact that ultimately the commercial interests and mass-produced pop culture emanate from the same economic concerns as those which seek to preserve a hierarchical society in which profit can flourish, illustrates the pervasiveness, variety and effectiveness with which ruling groups exercise their control and reinforce their power.

Clarke and Jefferson find it difficult to identify any youth cultures which are 'truly oppositional' in the sense of having a political dimension. Those members of the adult working class, for example, who do not accept the legitimacy of their subordination to other groups, and who are 'in opposition' to the structures which reproduce that inequality, have traditionally practised their opposition through organised political action and a strong sense of trade union militancy. The opposition of their children is confined to only one area of life—the leisure area. They are not geared up to the total transformation of their social conditions as politicised adults would be. Paul Willis reveals how working-class kids can be mightily resistant to the dominant culture of schooling, however, suggesting that oppositional consciousness is more developed and more all-embracing than Clarke and Jefferson seem to be conceding, but like them, he has to conclude that the counter-culture of schooling has yet to be transformed into any kind of generalised political resistance to the organisation and practices of an unequal society.

Counter-School Culture

In his book *Learning to Labour*, Paul Willis begins by standing a fairly common observation 'on its head'. It is not difficult to understand why middle-class kids get middle-class jobs. What is more perplexing is why others let them. Similarly, 'the difficult thing to explain about working-class kids getting working-class jobs is why they let themselves'.

The usual approach of sociological studies which set out to examine why working-class youngsters fail in the school system, although they may involve different perspectives and come to rather different conclusions, all tend to examine the performance and behaviour of youngsters from an objective rather than a subjective perspective. Some researchers make use of questionnaires, structured and unstructured interviews and the extended observation of classroom behaviour to corroborate their observations. Willis' study is different in that he attempts to build up a picture of 'the lads'' counter-school culture in the words and images and responses of 'the lads' themselves, rather than take as given the interpretations made by teachers.

The cultural responses which he describes, and which 'the lads' actively reproduce and recreate in their day-to-day relationships with each other and in collective opposition to the dominant culture of the school, are those which are described conventionally—and especially in the media—in terms of violence and indiscipline in the classroom. They are the kind of responses which are commonly attributed to 'trouble makers' and which in their extreme forms have encouraged a number of schools to establish special classes, withdrawal units and even quite separate 'sanctuaries' for those whose behaviour has become 'uncontrollable' in the conventional classroom.

In practice this means that 'the lads' do not regard school as a place in which education, learning and deference for teachers and their knowledge has much meaning. School is a necessary evil which has to be 'endured' and 'got through' as pleasurably as possible. And 'the pleasure principle' usually revolves round the creation of opportunities to 'have a laff'. It would be wrong to see school as a place of torture, however, or as an institution which inflicts symbolic and often actual violence upon its victims. At least not in 'the lads'' eyes. They expect nothing ennobling from school or from teachers. Their rules and rationalisations, their moral imperatives and rituals are to be resisted. They have no significance and rarely penetrate the cultural experience and subjective realities of 'the lads'. The best thing about school is the opportunity to rehearse with other working-class youngsters the loyalties and possibilities for defiance and resistance which they will later sustain as wage labourers on the shop floor. From the neighbourhoods they live in, the company they keep, the experiences of their fathers before them and the historic conditions of working-class labour 'the lads' have learned from generations of workers to expect nothing from work except wages. Wage labour, like school labour, is for them essentially meaningless. Exhortations to 'industry' and 'commitment to the company', to 'productivity and loyalty', to 'hard work and self-sacrifice'—indeed to the whole 'work ethic' which is continually and variously expounded by those who stand to profit from its acceptance—is largely meaningless to 'the lads'.

According to Willis, 'When "the lads" arrive on the shop floor, they need no telling (from those already there) to "take it easy", "take no notice" or that "they" (the management) always want more; you've had it if you let them get their way.' Their experience of schooling has attuned them to the relationships of work. No wage they could earn would be a fair wage for what they do. What is common to all wage labour work is more important than what divides it. 'The common denominator of all such work is that ... it yields to capital more in production than it costs to buy. Capitalism is organised for profit rather than use. ... It does not matter what product is made, since it is money which is really being made. The labourer will be switched with alacrity from the production of one commodity to another no matter what his skills or current activity when "market conditions" change.'

Given this view of work, experienced daily as a shared reality on the shop floor, no amount of official exhortations from either employers or teachers about 'the intrinsic satisfactions of a job well done' will cut much ice with 'the lads'. They know that the difference between 'doing enough to get by', 'having a laff', 'skyving', 'wasting time' and 'making the best of all possible worlds' is more to their advantage, and immeasurably preferable, to believing that harder work and more loyalty will improve their chances of success or amount to any significant redistribution of the wealth, power and authority which derives from their labour. In fact, their real power lies in failing to acknowledge and refusing to accommodate the values on which the ultimate security of capitalism depends.

Of course many working-class kids and their parents are seduced by the values of middle-class culture and its illusions of social mobility and educational success. Other sociologists have referred to 'false consciousness', 'embourgeoisement', 'incorporation' and 'conformity' to explain this condition. 'The lads' are more explicit. In Willis' study these are the 'ear 'oles'. And their 'betrayal' to both the counter-school culture and the shop-floor culture is despised by 'the lads' and their dads.

Hammertown Boys

The evidence on which Willis' study is based is a study of a group of 12 non-academic working-class lads from a working-class council estate in a working-class Midlands town which he calls Hammertown. They attended an all-boys school and were selected on the basis of their friendship with each other and their behaviour, which displayed visible opposition to the mainstream culture of the school. Willis was in close regular contact with 'the lads' for their last two years at school and for their first six months at work.

Hammertown Boys', the school they attended, served an exclusively working-class area, had a reasonably good reputation locally, and the educational provisions and physical resources which it enjoyed were as good as, and in some ways better than similar schools in other parts of Britain. In order to compare the responses of 'the lads' in his main study, Willis also made five comparative studies of predominantly working-class youngsters from the same town: a group of 'conformist' working-class boys in the same year at Hammertown Boys; a group of 'conformist' working-class boys from a mixed secondary modern nearby; a group of 'non-conformist' working-class boys from a single-sex grammar school; a similar group from a comprehensive school; and the last a mixed social class group of 'non-conformist' boys from a high-status grammar school in the suburbs. In addition to 'the lads', Willis also held detailed discussions and interviews with their parents and teachers.

The Teachers' View

The teachers' views of 'the lads' will be familiar to those who have ever heard teachers discussing 'troublesome pupils', of those who attempt to explain their behaviour from a position which is not a part of 'the lads'' culture. According to the teachers 'the lads'' attachment to a counter-school culture becomes blatant as they begin 'lording it about' and developing 'wrong attitudes' because they have become exposed to 'bad influences'. The problems are generally explained in terms of various character deficiencies which encourage the majority of 'misguided' and 'impressionable kids' to be 'led astray' by a small but disruptive 'minority of troublemakers'.

In the face of such difficulties, teachers frequently resort to belittling and sarcastic encounters, which exacerbate the distance between them and 'the lads'. Willis refers to the manifestations of this as the 'class insult'—which occurs 'in class' but for which the reference point is 'social class'. In the conventional teaching exchange an important dimension is the respect of one side for the other. In terms of the counter-school culture 'the lads' stop being polite to staff and the staff lose respect for pupils. So far as 'the lads' are concerned the recourse by teachers to either authoritarianism, sarcasm or progressivism are all different versions of an attempt to control and contain their resistance.

These 'institutional dynamics' are interpreted by 'the lads' as 'class dynamics'. They are strategies which are frequently demeaning, insulting and invariably resented and are experienced as cultural attacks upon their class identities. The intransigence of 'the lads' and their recourse to behavioural resistance is provoked by their impotence in the face of eloquent and sarcastic teachers. Teachers provoked into exasperated and ridiculous outbursts like 'Shut your mouth when you're talking to me' are fleeting triumphs won by 'the lads' in an arena in which teachers still have 'the mastery of formal words and expression'.

'The Lads'' Response

In an increasingly vicious circle 'the lads' hit back against attacks on their culture in any way they can. This might mean disruptive and deliberately provocative behaviour designed to wreck lessons, irritate teachers and amuse each other. It might mean registering, with careful precision, the amount of writing, reading and school work *not* undertaken. It might mean vandalising property and doing everything they can to 'go against' those who rapidly come to represent the enemy.

Class Conflict in the Classroom

Clearly the antagonisms are worked out in class terms and the reaction of one side to the other has a good deal to do with different cultural definitions and allegiances. To judge the one *in terms* of the other is always to find the other wanting. It is just that in education— as in class society generally—the cultural yardstick is usually 'the affronted sensibilities' of middle-class culture, when faced with forms of resistance which it cannot understand.

Willis comments: 'It is of the utmost importance to appreciate that the exchange relationship in the educational paradigm is not primarily in terms of its own logic a relationship between social classes, or in any sense at all, a self-conscious attempt on the part of teachers to dominate or suppress either working-class individuals or working-class culture as such. The teachers, particularly the senior teachers at the Hammertown school, are dedicated, honest and forthright—and by their own lights doing an exacting job with patience and humanity. Certainly it would be quite wrong to attribute to them any kind of sinister motive such as miseducating or oppressing working-class kids.' It is simply that their behaviour takes the form of class control and is interpreted—if not articulated—by 'the lads' as a class relationship based on notions of 'them' and 'us'.

So far as 'the lads' are concerned the progressive teachers, concerned with 'relevance', 'individual learning', 'self-discovery', etc., are merely variations on a common theme. They provide opportunities for 'the lads' to celebrate their own values and independence and to perfect their resistance to study and the official school culture in a way which is largely unmoved by the relative 'kindness' of 'progressive' teachers compared to their more traditional colleagues. They may provoke confrontation less frequently but 'for all their much lauded differences, in the real situation, both traditional and modern techniques are bas-ically about winning a form of consent from students within as tightly controlled an axis as possible. . . . Progressivism as it is practised can be seen as a continuation of traditionalism, in the sense that it attempts to preserve a version of the consent (of the governed) which has always been at the heart of the older method'. Willis dismisses progressive strategies as merely another way of attempting to exert control rather than being a renunciation of notions of control. One of its effects has been partially to legitimise counter-school culture 'and therefore also the processes which it sponsors'. The tactical withdrawal from con-frontation actually ensures 'a much more massive and less illicit presence for the articulation and sustenance of counter-school culture'.

If Willis' analysis is correct, it points to a significant difference be-tween the school and the shop floor and a much more indulgent en-vironment within education than the de-schoolers and anti-schoolers would have us believe. The indulgence or impotence of the education system to control the counter-school culture suggests the possibility that schools not only reproduce success, power, influence and favour, but also that they reproduce resistance—a resistance which might contribute to strengthening the already 'inherited' characteristics of an oppositional class culture.

'The lads' in Willis' study, for example, display and have developed 'to a fine degree in their school counter-culture, specific working-class themes: resistance, subversion of authority, informal penetration of the weaknesses and fallibilities of the formal; and an independent abi-lity to create diversion and enjoyment'. This, if it is true, leads to an important observation and, of course, to a single and critical ques-tion.

The 'Strengths' of Counter-School Culture

The observation is that although commonplace, explanations con-cerning 'educational failure' which rely on individual deviance or per-sonality defects of various kinds as causal factors, do not provide adequate social explanations of the factors leading to the adoption and development of an anti-school culture—a culture which may have regional and generational variations but which has remarkable consis-tency and similarity when viewed in social class terms. Notions of individual failure are closely allied to notions of individual success.

But whilst schools promote strategies which assume that the attitudes and abilities needed for individual success are necessary 'in general', the contradiction is rarely admitted that in a class society not all can succeed, and that there is consequently no point for the unsuccessful in following prescriptions for success based on hard work, diligence and conformism. 'The lads' know this. Some can 'make it' and conformity for them might have its attractions—but for the working class as a whole, conformity holds no rewards. For the majority of working-class men and women the ideals of equality and opportunity are illusory.

The counter-school culture, in its display of disdain for the cultural and moral values of the school, is an illustration—as are other working-class cultural forms—of an important and profound critique of middle-class notions of individualism, meritocracy and equality in our society.

If, as Willis argues, the counter-school culture acts as a rehearsal for shop-floor culture and contains within it the important elements of an oppositional class culture, it presents the potential for, not merely a partial and cultural challenge, 'but for a total transformation' of capitalism. The important question, therefore, is what prevents this transformation happening?

The 'Weaknesses' of Counter-School Culture

The main reason, according to Willis, is that although counter-school culture, like the shop-floor culture for which it is a preparation, is full of 'political significance' it is in practice essentially unpolitical. No organised political activity, be it the trade union movement or the Labour Party, actually attempts to interpret and mobilise cultural opposition.

Equally important are the internal divisions within the culture which prevent it from making connections between common interests and which in consequence prevent it from achieving its full potential as a coherent political challenge to the status quo. The most significant of these divisions are those between mental and manual labour and those of race and gender.

The rejection of school by 'the lads' can be seen as a rejection of 'individualism' but it is also a rejection of mental activity in general. Since an important cornerstone of the power of ruling groups in our society is based on the distinction between 'those who are good with their hands' and 'those who are good with their heads', the failure to challenge the authenticity on which these categories are based helps to perpetuate them. 'The lads' consciously disassociate themselves with mental labour both in school and as a future job. For them it is 'cissie' and 'effeminate'. The manual labour which they respect is associated with masculinity and strength.

This links to another divisive element in the culture of 'the lads' which weakens their potential to transform their world in political terms. It is highly sexist. So long as wives, girlfriends and mothers are regarded as restricted and inferior and incapable of certain important masculine strengths and perceptions, then what they provide, and what they do, is undervalued. The suggestion that they could do anything else is rarely conceded. If women were revalued within the culture by 'the lads', and by the women themselves, not only would the sexual oppression and subordination of women in the culture be removed, but the denigratory associations of feminine characteristics with mental labour would also be in question.

Racism provides a third divisive force in the cohesion of working-class culture in general and 'the lads'' culture in particular. Racial divisions provide a group which Willis refers to as an 'underclass, which is more heavily exploited than the whole working class, and is indirectly and partially exploited by the working class itself'. It provides another example (like women) of an 'inferior group' against which the 'superior self' can be measured. Despite the fact that the subordinate economic condition of the majority of black Britons closely resembles the economic conditions of working-class whites—a feature which becomes even more pronounced as second-generation blacks grow up, get educated and seek work alongside white working-class kids—a strong sense of difference and antagonism persists between them.

Others have simplified the complexity of inter-racial hostility as the tendency of exploited groups to seek other groups which they can in turn disdain. And clearly, so long as they are prevented from recognising their common conditions of exploitation, and are kept in competition with each other for scarce economic resources and cultural respect, then the challenge to the dominance of ruling economic groups and to the ubiquity of mainstream culture will be diffused.

'Voluntary Control'

Thus despite the fact that many of the values of mainstream culture are 'minced up, inverted or simply defeated' by the counter-school culture of 'the lads', when they leave school 'the factories are filled on Monday morning, and on every Monday morning, with workers displaying the necessary apparent gradations between mental and manual capacities and corresponding attributes necessary to maintain, within broad limits, the present structure of class and production'. 'The lads' do not ultimately use their 'oppositional potential' as a political challenge to transform the prevailing distribution of power in society because of limitations like sexism, racism and the strong celebration of masculinity which leads to 'the willing acceptance' of manual labour as a legitimate work role. 'In contradictory and unintended ways the counter-school culture actually achieves for education one of its main though misrecognised objectives—the direction of a proportion of working-class kids "voluntarily" to skilled, semi-skilled and unskilled manual work.'

The irony is—as with the girls described by McRobbie (see below)—the culture of the kids seems in the end to provide the most effective social control of all. Whilst the unruliness of 'the lads'' counter-school culture may in one way be defined as part of 'the crisis' in education which represents them as unteachable and unbearable, it could equally be argued that the process it sponsors has actually helped to prevent a real crisis, the challenge to capitalism, from taking place.

Girls and Youth Culture

One of the most striking characteristics of the literature about youth cultures is the absence of interest in girls. Although there has been a variety of studies since the war dealing with schooling, race and delinquency as well as youth culture, the appearance of girls has been largely confined to their role as 'girlfriends' or 'birds' and has been interpreted principally through the words of the boys the studies are really concerned with. When girls are considered, it is usually in relation to 'the lads'' view of them as domestic comforters or sexual partners. 'The lads' in Paul Willis' book *Learning to Labour* differentiate between 'birds' and 'scrubbers', who are sex objects for their use—an 'easy lay'—and 'the missus' who is *their* girl, sexually attractive but not sexually experienced. The familiar old double standard becomes restated in contemporary cultural terms. 'The missus' is regarded quite differently from the 'easy lay'. She is the loyal domestic, 'the belonging', who though respected is none the less 'property'. Any suggestion by others that she is promiscuous presents a first-rate challenge to the masculinity and pride of the lad she belongs to. The model for 'the missus' is, of course, mother. 'Good as gold' she is, but like mother, inferior, 'a bit thick—she never knows what I'm about'. Like dad, waited on in *his* home by mum, in the relationship between the lad and his missus, he is boss.

But what of the girls—how do they interpret their relationships and how do they feel about their lives? In Willis' book we see them through the eyes of 'the lads'. We do not hear from them in their own right.

Does the fact that the majority of post-war studies of youth culture ignores girls completely, or refers to them only fleetingly in passing, mean that girls have *really* not been involved in those cultures? Or have they been present but invisible—not seen as worthy of special attention by either the cultures or those who have researched them? Or have they been involved in *different* subcultural responses?

The main reason why it is difficult to answer these questions, and to discover whether or not girls have been significantly involved in the youth cultures which have been most widely studied, is that sociological investigation in general has been less than interested in women. Most academic sociologists are men and are themselves the products of a society in which academic study is largely controlled by men. It is a society which has also consistently relegated women to marginal and subordinate positions. As writers like Sheila Rowbotham and Ann Oakley have pointed out, women have been both 'hidden from history' and 'invisible in sociology'. In sociology their appearance is largely confined to studies which reinforce their stereotype roles as mothers, wives and in relation to family life. With the exceptions of promiscuity and prostitution, they have been largely ignored in studies of deviance, criminology and law. And as workers, the main focus of interest has been the conflict with domestic responsibilties which their work roles might produce.

So far as youth cultures are concerned, female invisibility tends to be something of a self-fulfilling prophecy, in that the popular press and the media have always concentrated on the most sensational aspects of youthful behaviour—vandalism, soccer hooliganism, gang fights and clashes with the police. Usually it has been the aggressive and violent aspects of youth culture which have hit the headlines and these are precisely the kind of cultural activities from which women have tended to be excluded. Since these are the forms of behaviour that are principally identified with youth cultures it is often assumed that they constitute the *only* behaviour—a behaviour in which girls do not take part.

Another factor, of course, is the socialisation and conditioning that girls receive in our society. Working-class girls in the fifties and sixties, for example, were obviously subjected to the same general social and economic conditions as their brothers, but their responses were worked out in different settings.

Whilst the male culture emphasised the work place, the pub, and the football ground, the girls' attention was more focused on the home, on mum and on marriage. Girls certainly did 'dress up' and go out and have boyfriends, but they would be less likely to hang about street corners. Boys were allowed more licence and were expected to do less in the home. Those who gained their sexual experience early were tolerated 'so long as they brought no trouble home'. Working-class girls who 'got themselves into trouble' in the fifties and sixties suffered a good deal of censure from parents and neighbours alike.

For boys the cultural spaces which had meaning were the streets and alleyways, pubs and football stands. For girls their cultural space was more likely to be in the home or at a friend's house. Angela McRobbie and Jenny Garber* suggest that a good deal of girls' culture happened within 'the culture of the bedroom—experiments with make-up, listening to records, reading and magazines, sizing up boy friends, chatting, jiving: it depended on some access by girls to room and space within (rather than outside) the home—even if the room was uneasily shared with an elder sister'.

But of course some girls did see themselves as 'teddy girls', as mods and hippies and have identified with the cultures of these different groups in very real ways. In most respects the identification seems to have been in a supportive role, however. Whereas the boys' reaction to the rise of rock and roll, for example, was often to become an amateur performer, girl participants would more likely become fans or groupies, record collectors or magazine readers. If greasers chose to ride motor bikes and mods to ride scooters, their girls sat on the back, they did not take charge of the machines in their own right. The classic 'motor bike girl' of the sixties' and seventies' ads—'leather-clad, a sort of subcultural pin-up, with pan stick lips, blackened eyes, numb expressionless look and the slightly unzipped leather jacket'—promised a new and threatening sexuality but was only a hair's breadth away from the classic fetishism of old-style pornography.

Thus the role of girls in subcultures, as in society generally, has tended to reflect their subordinate relationship to boys or their abuse as sex objects.

Of course the re-emergence of the women's movement in the late sixties and the increasing attention given to women's liberation in the seventies has made many more aspects of women's lives visible and more public than in the fifties. The media during this period have been fond of attributing increasing aggressiveness and crime among girls to the influence of women's liberation. Perhaps this is an altogether different argument, but if the self-fulfilling prophecy idea is accurate, it could help to explain the apparently greater involvement of girls in subcultural activities in recent years. Also the commercialisation of mod and hippy styles in the late sixties and early seventies helped produce a uni-sex and even transsexual dimension to popular culture. But whilst men were increasingly allowed to be 'more feminine' in their appearance and dress, it is doubtful whether girls were allowed complementary liberation from the dominant constraints of the female image. It has taken the 'gay women's' culture of the middle and later seventies to really challenge the conventional images of women—but for the majority of working-class girls, changes in clothes style have not been significantly matched by changes in their stereotyped relationships to boys. Certainly so far as the punks are concerned there is an egalitarianism in the dress and social behaviour which would not have been so evident in the fifties but a strong element of male chauvinism still persists.

---

* 'Girls and Subculture', A. McRobbie and J. Garber, in *Resistance Through Rivals*, S. Hall and T. Jefferson (eds.), Hutchinson, London, 1976.

Girls' Alternative Subcultures

McRobbie and Garber conclude that where girls take part in male-dominated and male-orientated youth cultures they do so generally in a subordinate role—as appendages to 'the lads' they are with. The chauvinism of the subculture reflects the chauvinism of the wider culture of which it is a fragment.

A further important area of investigation so far as they are concerned is the alternative cultures which girls are involved in and in which they interact not with lads but among themselves. One such culture is that of the teeny boppers. Unlike the other subcultures we considered earlier, there is little sense in which teeny bopper culture can be regarded as an oppositional response by a subordinate group to the dominance of mainstream culture. It has, in fact, been one of the most highly manufactured forms of available youth culture. It represents the commercialised pop industry at its most persuasive and effective and is packaged, filtered and controlled through the promotion of films, television, advertising, records, magazines and chain store fashions. What was significant about the teeny bopper syndrome of the seventies was the allegiance it won from an even younger market of kids than those traditionally involved in youth cultures. And what was perceptive about its promotion and packaging, so far as commercial interests were concerned, was its direction at the home and bedroom and boyfriend world of little girls as prospective 'consumers of femininity' and as future wives. As McRobbie and Garber point out, the teeny bopper culture needed only a bedroom to invite friends to, and a record player, to be accommodated. It was flexible enough to attract the limitless spending of the affluent, but competitive enough not to restrict entry to those with less money. At home 'with the girls' and 'in communication' *through* the printed page and *via* the record player with romance and glamour it was essentially safe and provided no risk of being 'stood up' or 'put down'. The identification with pop heroes provided alternative role models and sources of obsession to the authoritarian adults who controlled the girls' lives at school and in the family. Being a fan, especially if the enthusiasm was shared with others, gave solidarity and a defensive position from which to manage the 'meaninglessness of school'—especially for those conscious of themselves as academic failures.

There is a contradiction here, however. Teeny bopper culture *did* enable girls to create a cultural space of their own separate from boys' youth cultures and it *did* provide a form of resistance to parent and school culture, but its existence was cleverly manufactured and manipulated by the media and dependent for its very existence on the early and continuing conditioning of girls into submissive roles. Teeny bopper culture reflected mainstream culture in that it endorsed submissiveness in girls and dominance in boys. It also served to anticipate and prepare girls for future 'real' relationships in which magazine versions of romance and an idealised view of marriage are key influences in the conditioning of girls for the ready acceptance of motherhood and domesticity.

The Mill Lane Girls

In 1975 Angela McRobbie carried out a survey among 56 teenage girls who attended the same youth club, went to the same school and lived on the same council estate. As other researchers have done with boys, she attempted to identify the main ways in which they experienced and made sense of the world they lived in, and to consider in some detail their relationships with each other.

She began with the assumption that whatever she discovered it would be in part caused by, and certainly linked to, the social class position of the girls, their future role in production, their present and future domestic roles and their economic dependence on their parents. She also recognised that whatever form and style the girls' culture adopted, it would be within an already established context of socially defined femininity. Needless to say, what she found was 'an ultimate if not wholesale endorsement of the traditional female role of femininity simply because to the girls this seemed to be perfectly natural'.

Since childbirth was considered to be inevitable by most of the girls, housework and childcare also seemed to be unavoidable. These were the unalterable 'facts of life' which, although not always very exciting in prospect, were accepted so long as there would be friends to see them through and so long as the 'ideology of romance' helped to compensate for reality.

The girls' leisure outlets were constrained by their parents' earning capacity to a large extent, so that for the majority of them the more expensive world of organised leisure 'up town' had to wait until they left school and were earning money of their own.

The girls were very conscious of their age and what was possible at different ages. This measuring of possibilities in terms of ages and phases is of course reinforced by teenage magazines which pretend that 'life goes in phases' rather than 'differences exist between classes'. (The fact that the majority of popular teenage magazines are implicitly directed at working-class girls is never explicitly stated in those magazines.) Girls are led to expect to do different things at different ages and each progressive phase is one step further along the inevitable female trail through dating, courtship, 'going steady' and getting wed—'a linear career culminating in marriage'.

Age consciousness does not preclude a sense of separation from others who are different, however. The girls studied by McRobbie were working-class and she noted the extent to which common ex-

pectations and common experiences of being working-class and female
bound them together. Most of the girls spent between 12 and 14 hours
a week in some form of domestic labour which helped their mothers,
relatives or neighbours in return for pocket money. These were sex-
specific chores which were not shared by their brothers. They rarely
left the estate on which they lived, they bought their clothes from the
estate shopping centre or mail-order catalogues, and apart from occasional visits to relatives, their cultural space was confined to the home,
the school and the youth club.

Not only were the girls' experiences limited in this way, but any
other women they might meet, apart from friends and female relatives,
were figures of social control—teachers, social workers, youth leaders,
careers advisers and so on. Possibilities of alternative lifestyles seemed,
and were, remote.

School as an experience for working-class girls provides a number
of contradictions. The extent to which the school continues the process
of socialisation begun in the family and dedicated to the preparation
of girls for careers in domestic labour is well documented. We know
from Sue Sharpe* and many others that this process is encouraged,
both in the official and the 'hidden curriculum' of schooling. For girls
who consider themselves to be academic failures, the culture of the
school can be an alienating experience. Like 'the lads' in Willis' account of Hammertown Boys', the girls in McRobbie's study had
evolved strategies which enabled them to denigrate as 'snobs' and
'swots' those who were more successful than them in the school's
terms. Like 'the lads' of Hammertown, many had been able to transform the school into an arena in which they could, on their own
terms, develop their social life, fancy boys, learn the latest dance, have
a smoke together in the lavatories and 'play up' the teachers.

The main way chosen by the girls to oppose the mainstream culture
of the school was to assert their femaleness, 'to introduce into the
classroom their sexuality and their maturity in such a way as to force
teachers to take notice'. The rejection of authoritarian sexism in
schools (neatness, diligence, femininity and passivity, for example) was
achieved by the girls by adopting an even more sexist stance of sexuality.

'Marriage, family life, fashion and beauty all contribute massively
to the girls' anti-school culture and in doing so nicely illustrate the
contradictions inherent in so-called "oppositional" activities. Are the
girls in the end not simply doing exactly what is required of them?
And if this is the case, is it not *their own culture* which is itself the
most effective agent of social control for girls pushing them in exactly
the direction that capitalism and the whole range of institutions which
support it wish them to go?'

---

* *Just Like a Girl: How Girls Learn to be Women*, Sue Sharpe, Penguin, London, 1976.

To expect working-class girls, conditioned by their class position and pressured into gender roles appropriate to their future lives as working-class housewives, to offer resistance to forces in society which have oppressed women, and working-class women in particular, for centuries is perhaps unrealistic. It is not difficult to see how the process happens but why they continually allow it to happen, even appear to choose it, is a more complex question. Most of them realise that for them marriage is an economic necessity and delusions about romance help them for a while to avoid facing up to the fact that the realities of marriage and childbearing are not always quite as the magazines suggest. But whilst middle-class girls may enjoy 'the elbow room' of a few years spent at college or university, where thoughts of marriage can be at least temporarily suspended and where experiences of sexual and other relationships can be enjoyed in relative freedom for a while, 'there is not much place for a single working-class woman in society. This is not simply a question of economics—though it will mean a life lived on the low wages of women in working-class jobs . . . but being forced to live as a marginal person in working-class society'.* Working-class girls, therefore, are doubly bound both by the material restrictions of their class position, and also by the sexual oppression of women in general.

In Conclusion

All of the illustrations discussed in this chapter are of distinctive youth cultures which have emerged in Britain since the war. Each of the groups, in different ways, is characterised by a lifestyle with its own values, attitudes and behaviour patterns which are to some extent a reflection of, but in many respects a form of resistance against, those of mainstream culture. Whatever their origins, in social class subordination, in the manipulation of popular culture by the consumer society, in reaction to the social, educational and economic changes affecting the life experiences of young people—they are characterised by a considerable amount of public anxiety. 'Increasing permissiveness', 'increasing violence' and 'increasing disrespect' for adult values are the moral panics which the adult world has consistently used to label youth cultures as 'meaning trouble'. But of course the picture of young people 'out of control' has to be tempered by a recognition of the passivity of teeny bopper culture, for example, and the massive conformity which most youngsters display as they go to school, go to work and take part in routine family activities with considerable predictability.

The conflict becomes heightened in direct relation to the savagery

---

* 'Youth in Pursuit of Itself', in *Working-Class Youth Culture*, G. Mungham and G. Pearson (eds.), Routledge & Kegan Paul, London, 1976.

of the social circumstances in which youth cultures confront dominant culture. Where young people are permanently unemployed, looked down upon by more affluent social groups, confined to bad housing, poor schools, run-down neighbourhoods and frequently in conflict with the various state agencies of control, then youth cultures take on different significance. The struggle for material resources is also the struggle for cultural meaning: the attempt to find excitement, autonomy and identity. In this context youth cultures cannot be separated from the wider discussion of inequality and conflict in society generally.

Revision

1. Refresh Your Memory

Make sure you know the meaning of the terms: popular culture, socialisation, subculture, youth culture, consensus system, pluralist view of society, 'moral panics', embourgeoisement, conspicuous consumption, scapegoat, meritocracy, sexism, racism, oppositional culture.

2. Check Your Understanding

Be able to explain in your own words the difference between:

(*a*) 'Culture as art' and 'culture as life'.
(*b*) 'Mainstream culture' and 'subculture'.
(*c*) Rule by consent and rule by coercion.
(*d*) Economic dominance and cultural dominance.
(*e*) Puritanism and chauvinism in traditional working-class culture.
(*f*) 'The lads' and 'the ear 'oles' of Hammertown.
(*g*) Mental labour and manual labour.

3. Essay Questions to Try

(*a*) What do you understand by the term culture? In what sense can culture be described as 'a negotiation between conditioning and creation?'

(*b*) 'Culture is an instrument of social control. The capacity of a dominant group to reproduce its dominance over time depends on its ability to control the means by which the world is made sense of, i.e. culture and ideology. But culture is also the site of struggle and conflict, of negotiation which constantly re-defines (and usually reproduces in a new form) the existing relationships of domination and subordination in society. The power to create and manipulate culture as a means of controlling others is well entrenched in the social, economic and political institutions of a society but it is also continually resisted by opposing cultural forms.' (Bryn Jones, *The Politics of Popular Culture*.) Discuss.

(*c*) Describe some of the main ways in which psychological and sociological discussions of adolescence differ.

(*d*) Why is an understanding of social class relationships in society an important factor in the study of youth culture?

(*e*) 'One of the interesting characteristics of recent studies of youth culture is that they are almost exclusively concerned with working-class boys. There has been little written about working-class girls and virtually nothing about middle-class adolescents.' Suggest reasons why this concentration on working-class boys in youth cultural studies has come about.

(*f*) Compare and contrast the cultures of the mods and the skinheads in relation to the social changes of the late fifties and sixties.

(*g*) To what extent can any of the post-war youth cultures you have studied be said to provide 'true opposition' to the dominance of mainstream culture?

(*h*) To what extent are the counter-school cultures of working-class kids a rehearsal for their future adult roles?

(*i*) Analyse the significance of the role of girls in any of the subcultures you have studied.

(*j*) To what extent can the lives of teenage girls be said to be 'a linear career culminating in marriage'?

Further Reading

Learning to Labour: How Working-Class Kids Get Working-Class Jobs, Paul Willis, Saxon House, Farnborough, 1979.

The Meaning of Mod, Dick Hebdige, and *Girls and Subcultures*, Jenny Garber and Angela McRobbie, in *Resistance Through Rituals*, Stuart Hall and T. Jefferson (eds.), Hutchinson, London, 1976.

Working-Class Girls and the Culture of Femininity, Angela McRobbie, in *Women Take Issue*, Hutchinson, London, 1978.

Working-Class Youth Cultures, J. Clarke and T. Jefferson, in *Working-Class Youth Culture*, G. Mungham and G. Pearson (eds.), Routledge & Kegan Paul, London, 1976.

6

THE MASS MEDIA

Perhaps the simplest definition of the mass media is 'those forms of communication which are directed towards mass audiences of people'. The main media of communication will be familiar to you: television, radio, advertising, newspapers, film and recordings. Their significance in a society like ours is obviously very important. Denis McQuail in his book *Towards a Sociology of Mass Communications* identifies some of their main characteristics:

1. Mass communications usually require complex organisations for them to be able to operate properly. The production of a newspaper or a television service involves the need for huge capital resources and calls for the employment of highly skilled personnel. Everything has to be well organised, with a clear structure of authority and responsibility. Mass communications organisations, therefore, are very different from informal, face-to-face communications.

2. The mass media are directed towards large audiences. This results from the application of technology geared to mass production and widespread dissemination. The exact size of audience or readership group receiving mass communications cannot be specified, but it is large in comparison with audiences for other means of communication (e.g. a lecture or a theatre play), and large in relation to the number of communicators.

3. Mass communications are public—the content and distribution is open to all. But there is seldom the opportunity for complete open access because of the constraints imposed deliberately or arising from the social structure.

4. The audience for mass communications is heterogeneous in composition. It is made up of people living under widely different conditions, under widely varying cultures, coming from different sections of society, engaging in different occupations and hence, having different interests, standards of life, degrees of prestige, power and influence.

5. The mass media can establish simultaneity of contact with large numbers of people, at a distance from the source, and widely separated from each other. Radio and television achieve this result more completely than the print media, since the latter are likely to be read at different times and to be used more selectively. Two features of this

immediacy of contact are important. The first is the speed, distance and immediacy of impact that is possible. The second is that it tends to produce uniformity in the selection and interpretation of messages.

6. In mass communications the relationship between the communicator and the audience is impersonal in that an anonymous audience is being addressed by people known only in their public role as communicators. Mass media are organised to allow communication flow in only one direction on the whole, and despite attempts to get to know about the audience by audience research, correspondence and the evidence of sales and box office returns, little is really known at the moment about an audience's response to the communications it receives.

7. The audience for mass communication is a phenomenon unique to modern society. It is made up of individuals who are focussing on a common programme, film, report or recording; taking part in an identical form of behaviour and likely to be directed towards similar responses. Yet the individuals involved are unknown to each other, have only a limited amount, if any, interaction, and they are in no way organised as a group or an association. The composition of the audience is continually shifting, it has no leadership or feelings of identity.

Certainly with the introduction of sophisticated media, designed to communicate information and messages to a large number of separate individuals simultaneously, an important change takes place in the relationship between those who are communicating. Mass communication no longer represents a face-to-face exchange of information. Mass media imply the production of information, news, ideas and entertainment by a source such as the BBC, a publishing house or a record company, and then directed towards a mass audience. The source gathers the information, decides what will be passed on and how it will be passed on, and the audience, with few exceptions, does little more than receive what is sent. In other words, those who are in control of the various mass media initiate and process the communication of messages to a large and essential passive audience.

Clearly this situation is one which intrigues sociologists. They are interested to know what effects, if any, the various media have on people generally and whether or not they reflect the social, economic or political interests of certain groups at the expense of others in society.

One-Way Communication

The view that the mass media only provide for one-way communication, to an audience which has little influence or control over what they receive, is obviously a controversial one. It implies that the relatively few people who control the media and who work as journalists, film-makers, record producers and advertisers, have enormous power to decide what the majority of us will read, look at and listen to.

Clearly an audience has the right not to watch television or to choose one newspaper in preference to another. Television viewers, radio listeners and newspaper readers can write letters of complaint or seek advice and can express their own points of view in radio phone-ins or television interviews. But these are nearly all ways of reacting to programmes or articles which have already been produced and decided upon. Comments from the audience usually come as the postscript to a presentation by the media, rather than at the time when decisions are being made about what to include, what to leave out and what approach to take.

Of course it would be well-nigh impossible to involve all of the audience all of the time in discussions about the best method of communication. And many of those responsible for the media claim that in their programmes and newspaper presentations they are 'giving the public what they want'. But exact information about 'what the public wants' is hard to come by and most radio and television companies have really very little detailed information about what people think about their programmes. Frequently their definition of 'what the public want' is based on motives more closely linked to making money than to satisfying the varied interests and needs of individuals.

The charge sometimes made that the mass media actually prevent communication by only providing a one-way flow of information is often held to be a technical inevitability. But in their study of *The Sociology of Mass Communications*, McQuail and Enzensberger point out that 'every transistor radio is, by nature of its construction, at the same time a potential transmitter!' In other words, there is no electronic difficulty in making receivers like radios and television sets into instruments which could also be used to transmit messages back to the sources of information. However, the mass communications business, as we all know, has not developed like that. It has always been assumed that, with a few exceptions, mass communications will be largely a one-way process. In practice, those who own, control and work in the media decide what is news, who has something to say that is worth listening to, and how information, ideas, values and entertainment shall be presented.

A number of sociologists have speculated upon the reason for this kind of development. It could be interpreted merely as a consequence of the division of labour in a complex society, in which not everyone can be equally involved in what is essentially a specialised and professional job. Or it could be seen as a way of ensuring that a very powerful source of influence is kept within the control of a few people, who can use it to inform and entertain others in ways which best serve their own interests.

The Media Business

The charge is often made that the media represent the interests of 'big business'. The interests of 'big business' are probably best served when people spend a lot of money on their products, learn to accept their station in life without complaining about injustice or inequality, and believe what others tell them when it comes to formulating opinions about different social, political and cultural issues. In terms of the advertising industry this is not a difficult claim to substantiate but what about the other most important forms of mass communication?

In its evidence to the Royal Commission on the Press, the TUC pointed out that eight men control 90 per cent of Britain's newspapers (see p. 151). In 1972 the five leading commercial television companies—London Weekend, ATV, Granada, Thames and Yorkshire Television—served 73 per cent of all homes in Britain. The top five paperback publishers—Pearson–Longman, Granada Publishing, Collins, Thomson and Pan—controlled 86 per cent of the home market. EMI, Decca, Pickwick International, K-Tel and Ronco controlled 69 per cent of the market in mid-price LP record sales. Eighty per cent of the box-office takings at British cinemas went to seven companies: EMI, MGM, Fox–Rank, Columbia, Warner, Granada and Laurie Marsh. In all of these instances the main aim of the companies involved is to make financial profits and keep the customers spending.

It is not just that most of the market for a particular form of media is controlled by a handful of companies; most of the big companies have financial interests in a number of different media. EMI, for example, owns the country's biggest record company, second biggest cinema chain, a good deal of Thames Television, numerous leisure centres and has significant interests in the production of industrial and consumer electrical equipment; Rank owns the largest cinema chain in Britain; Butlins, countless hotels and bingo halls, radio, television and hi-fi manufacturing companies and a large part of Southern Television. It would not be unusual in fact for you to switch on the television, go to the cinema, turn on the radio, put on a record, or join in a game of bingo, and in every case be receiving information and entertainment from the same source.

Independent Television and Radio

Independent television and radio consists of 15 different television companies and a growing number of local radio stations. They must all apply for contracts to produce programmes from the Independent Broadcasting Authority (IBA). The IBA was established by an Act of Parliament in 1954 and members of its board of governors are appointed by the government. The IBA grants contracts and transmission facilities to the various independent commercial companies who pay back part of their profits to the IBA in rent. The IBA has the right to ensure that companies provide television and radio which is 'informative', 'educational' and 'entertaining', to keep an eye on advertising standards and to make sure that there is a proper balance in what is presented. So long as the various companies abide by their contracts with the IBA and do not get into financial difficulties, they have a good deal of independence, especially if they make a lot of money and can demonstrate that a lot of people turn in to their programmes.

The main source of revenue for independent television and radio depends on advertising. Advertisers have no direct control over programmes, but just as they are prepared to pay more money to newspapers with large circulations, so too do they pay more money for advertising slots in popular programmes at peak viewing and peak listening times. This inevitably encourages the companies to concentrate on popular and entertaining programmes which are likely to have a mass appeal rather than serious or innovative programmes which only attract a minority audience. In order to fulfil their contracts with the IBA, however, all the independent companies, even local radio stations, have to provide informative and minority interest programmes. Some companies take this responsibility very seriously and produce excellent documentary, serious drama and news programmes; others prefer to do the 'public service broadcasting' late at night or early on Sunday mornings when few people are tuned in. And despite the claims of many local radio stations to be 'serving their local community', most discussion and 'serious' programmes are reserved for the evenings when listening figures are about a fifth of those earlier in the day.

The government has given the go-ahead to a second ITV channel to begin broadcasting in 1982. Like ITV1 it will depend on advertising revenue for its source of income but the government has made it clear that ITV2 must be more educational, more experimental, less dominated by the 'big five' independent companies, and it must not place making money from advertising at the top of its list of priorities!

The BBC

The BBC was established in 1923 by royal charter as an independent, non-profit-making public company and like the IBA has a board of twelve governors appointed by the Home Secretary. The first Director General of the BBC was Lord Reith, who established early on an educational and moral role for broadcasting. He believed that broadcasting should not pander to 'low public taste' but should seek to educate, improve and elevate the tastes of those listening. He considered the development of broadcasting to be a 'mighty instrument to instruct and fashion public opinion, to banish ignorance and misery, to contribute richly and in many ways to the sum total of human well being'.

Those who worked with him and succeeded him were very influenced by this kind of paternalistic and moral attitude to their work. Stories of radio news readers dressed in evening suits, the insistence on high standards of spoken English and the censorship of any kind of slang or vulgarity make quaint reading in today's more permissive atmosphere. But before the BBC had to compete for audiences with independent television and radio it could afford to be disdainful of popular, commercial and trendy presentations. Today there is much less to choose between independent television and radio and the BBC than there once was. The BBC has received a good deal of criticism for reducing its serious and educational programmes in favour of light entertainment and more trivial presentations. But its lack of dependence on advertising revenue and the use of BBC2 as an outlet for programmes of a more educational and experimental nature, mean that, at its best, the BBC plays a responsible and pioneering role in producing good television which does not necessarily attract a large audience.

Unlike independent television and radio, the BBC depends directly on the state for money. Some finance comes from government grants and some from the sale of licences. Clearly this dependency limits the independence of the BBC. The Home Secretary is legally allowed to prevent the BBC broadcasting anything which he considers to be detrimental to the government or to the interests of the country. More often cautious directors cut out the programmes which they fear might annoy the government.

The independent companies are also vulnerable if they annoy governments too much. The IBA, as a government-appointed body, can refuse to renew a company's licence to broadcast, and the amount of tax the company has to pay on advertising revenue could be increased to the point at which profits were considerably reduced.

Broadcasting and the State

In Britain broadcasting institutions have an apparently unlimited amount of independence from the state and the government but in practice broadcasting has been open to government manipulation from the beginning. So far as the BBC and the IBA are concerned their ultimate right to broadcast derives from the state and in the last instance it is to the state that they are responsible. The BBC was established in 1923 and was subsequently joined by commercial television in 1954 and commercial radio in 1972. Each time the law was made clear: ministers could tell the BBC and IBA to broadcast or to withhold whatever the government wanted. The government may have seldom exercised this power—but the power to do so remains.

Stuart Hall* argues that in general broadcasting institutions operate within the dominant ideological and cultural perspectives of the state. They serve to corroborate prevailing opinion and values rather than to challenge them.

Areas of Concern

In times of public discontent the controversies surrounding the media's relationship to the state become more visible and more critical. Hall identifies the features which he considers to be the main areas of concern in this respect:

1. The fact that all mass communication systems—whether state controlled, semi-state controlled or commercially controlled—are part of huge monopolies.

2. The fact that broadcasting institutions in terms of size, complexity and recruiting policies are highly bureaucratic. They are inaccessible to the general public and the logic by which they function is only partly visible in their programmes and day-to-day operations.

3. The fact that broadcasting provides essentially one-way communication in which small professional elites speak to widely dispersed and heterogeneous audiences. The opportunity for audiences to complain or to respond is usually ineffective and is carried out 'on the broadcasters' terms'.

4. The anxiety surrounding the media's capacity to influence opinion, to form attitudes and to depoliticise essentially political issues.

5. The increasing concern of those with influence—politicians, government, experts and institutional spokespeople—to monopolise the media for their own purposes. It could be argued that some individuals and groups have always had greater access than others to the media—but this process has become increasingly sophisticated as the potential influence of the media has expanded.

6. The fear that the media help to undermine social and moral order. The critics of the media produce conflicting evidence in this respect: those who believe that popular broadcasting serves to erode public authority and decency on the one hand, and those who accuse the programme producers of clinging to useless and reactionary cultural traditions on the other.

7. The extent to which media have the power to define issues of national significance on which opinion is divided—for example, the position of blacks in a white society or the proper role of the army in Northern Ireland.

---

* *External Influences on Broadcasting*, Stuart Hall.

8. The extent to which the media favour power groups and establishment spokespeople in commentary on issues as against less powerful and less organised groups (e.g. ethnic minorities). In circumstances in which powerless groups are being discussed Hall suggests that they tend to have 'their problem defined for them' by other 'experts' or commentators.

9. When such groups become politically organised and articulate in defence of their own interests (e.g. black power groups, claimants unions or Gay Liberation) the ideological conflicts and tussles within the media become most public.

10. The media's role in providing the 'fitful images and stereotypes' on which we rely to make sense of complex and unknown cultures, especially non-western cultures (see p. 165).

According to Hall, questions raised by factors like these have to be taken into account in any discussion about the role of the media because they all add dimensions and shades of significance which cannot be explained in simple terms. Society is not a simple consensus system in which values and interests are shared, but it is usually only in periods of social discontent that intrinsic conflicts and contradictions become very apparent. 'Emergent forces whittle away the framework of consensual institutions, the values and beliefs which sustain the social order and challenge, the take-for-granted "rules" which neutralise social conflict and make the political-moral order legitimate.' As in other institutions, conflicts and contradictions become most visible in circumstances in which their taken-for-granted operations are challenged. In this respect broadcasting is no different from other social institutions currently facing critical examination.

The Effects of Broadcasting

In a complex and rapidly changing society like ours the passing on of information, values, attitudes and opinions by word of mouth, in the family or even via education is only part of the process of socialisation. In a society in which over 93 per cent of homes have a television set and almost everyone had a radio, the media of radio and especially television are by far the most effective ways of getting a variety of messages to thousands of people in the intimacy of their own homes.

James Halloran, a sociologist who has done perhaps more research than anyone else in Britain on the impact of television, suggests that television is more likely to be influential when it is dealing with subjects or situations which are often either very new to people or about which they have very little direct experience. People tend to believe what they see more than what they read, and compared to newspapers, for example, most people believe television to be more reliable and less biased in its presentation of information. Halloran suggests that this encourages many people to use television as their main source of evidence and as the basis of an increasing number of their opinions and attitudes. Certainly the state recognises the influence of television in formulating opinion and the government, for example, is one of the largest buyers of advertising time. But if Halloran is right then there is also the danger that television could help to misinform people as well as to inform them. If, for example, black Britons are featured only in programmes about the 'problems' of a multi-racial society, or used in so-called 'comedy' shows in a way which confirms prejudice and stereotypes about black people, then television could be seen as encouraging and perpetuating biased and ill-informed attitudes among many of its viewers.

If Halloran is right and television is most influential in those areas in which people have little other evidence or experience to balance the opinions they glean from television, then young viewers are likely to be even more impressionable than adults. The fact that young people between 5 and 14 seem to watch more television each week than almost any other group, as the figures in Table 3 show, has led sociologists and others to speculate about the effects of television and sex and violence upon young viewers. The same kind of question is also asked about pop music, in which an increasingly younger audience is possibly learning more in terms of attitudes and values than a superficial interest in pop stars and the pop charts might suggest.

Table 3. Television: Average Number of Hours Viewed Each Week

Age group	1975	1976	1977
5–14	24.0	22.0	22.0
15–19	19.3	18.4	17.6
20–29	18.2	19.1	18.2
30–40	18.4	19.0	17.9
50+	19.6	20.4	20.0

Although there has been a good deal of research into the effects of the various media on people's reactions to sex, violence, consumerism and politics, the results are varied and as yet inconclusive.

Some people point out that there is more real violence shown in news programmes than in television fiction; others claim that for many people television merely provides 'company' and a background noise which they really do not watch closely enough to be influenced one way or the other. The Chief Constable of North Wales, Philip Myers, speaking at a conference in 1978, linked the increase in violent crime to films and television programmes. He told the joint conference of police chiefs and local authority representatives, 'The violence portrayed today is alleged to be part of real life and likely to be copied.' He compared the crime and entertainment patterns of 1967 and 1977. 'In 1967 there were clear lines of what could or could not be shown on the cinema screen. Violence in the westerns of the day was removed from reality.' But he said, 'Nowadays violence is such an integral part of adventure programmes that heroes have to continually display their physical superiority and sexual prowess. I don't think it's any accident that crimes of violence are on the increase.' When he was a child he said neither he nor other children hit people with bricks. He wondered if this was because he was not fed on violence from a television set in the living room so often that violence became normal to a six-year-old.

So far as sociological research shows, the effects of films and television on crime and violence are inconclusive. Here is what sociologist Denis McQuail has to say:

'Mass communications research is probably most closely linked in its public reputation, with concern over the possible harmful effects of the media. The most persistent concerns have been with the danger to children, who cannot easily be protected from exposure to adult content in the cinema or on radio and television. The rapidly and seemingly uncontrolled growth in human activity has changed as a result of new developments in mass communications. It seems hardly in doubt that some significant social changes must accompany the revolution in communications and that these changes would be outside the control of those who try to preserve public order and morality. However, such research as we have had in these questions has proved to be generally disappointing to those who welcome firmer policies of social control.

'The expectations that crime and violence will be increased derives from the well documented fact that the mass media tend to over represent the portrayal of acts of crime and violence. This has led to the speculation that mass media fans might come to accept crime and violence as "normal", they might learn the techniques of crime, they might imitate what they see or read about, they might have deeply hidden emotions "triggered off" or they might come to regard violence as a perfectly acceptable way of getting what they want.

'Research carried out in Britain by Himmelweit and others after the introduction of commercial television was inconclusive about the effects on children on TV violence, however. It was concluded that "television is unlikely to cause aggressive behaviour, although it could precipitate it in those few children who are emotionally disturbed". A more recent American study by Schramm largely confirmed the

British findings. Whether or not children learn violence from television depends largely on what the child brings to television. Halloran does not altogether agree. He argues that portrayals of aggression are more likely to encourage rather than to release aggressive behaviour.'*

*Another widespread concern about the mass media and television is that some generally undesirable tendencies will be encouraged, includ-*ing 'passivity', 'escapism', 'unsocialibility' and loss of 'personal creativity'. Others believe that the present generation is better educated and informed than any other generation has been because of the educational benefits of television. McQuail has this to say:

'Again there are well documented observations to support the view that the mass media are time consuming and their content is directed towards fantasy more often than reality. The question is whether an over-concentration on fantasy may reduce the individual's capacity to handle reality and whether by getting "drawn into" the fantasy world of the media people lose their initiative and withdraw from personal action and social intercourse.

'Again studies on children have been the most common. And again the findings have been inconclusive. Himmelweit found that television had neither encouraged passivity nor stimulated interest. Schramm found that it depended to a great extent on the personality characteristics of the child-viewer.

'Belxon found a slight reduction in "initiative" and "interests" among "new" adult viewers. His research into the effects of television on family life and sociability in Britain, despite the thoroughness of the research, found that whatever effects had occurred they were either slight, variable or both!'

One thing is certain though: businessmen, advertisers and politicians would not spend so much time and energy keeping control of television if they did not think it was a very influential method of communication.

The Press

The fact that the entire British press is owned by a small group of individuals who are not democratically elected or accountable in any significant way to millions of people who buy and read their newspapers raises two important questions about the power of the press in Britain. Do they merely provide an information and communications service based on principles of free speech and objective reporting which adds to the store of general public knowledge and helps

---

* *Towards a Sociology of Mass Communications*, Denis McQuail, Collier Macmillan, West Drayton, 1969.

to create a better informed public opinion? Or does the concentration of the sources of information and communication in so few hands provide the potential for enormous control of the many by the few?

Geoffrey Sheridan and Carl Gardner* take the view that the concentration of newspaper power in the hands of those who could be described as part of the ruling class 'has led to a systematic misinterpretation in the reporting of the lives and activities of the large majority of the population, including several significant oppressed minorities'. The suggestion that that any form of communication can ever be neutral or objective is of course difficult to substantiate. All expressions of opinion, selections of relevant information, ideas and interpretations of facts derive from a social context and serve to satisfy particular social ends. So far as the press is concerned, it is important to be clear what these ends are. The interests of the owners and the controllers must surely be high on any such list of priorities.

In its evidence to the Royal Commission on the Press, the TUC commented: 'The fact that eight men control 90 per cent of Britain's papers means that the concept of freedom of expression or independence of editorial is somewhat Orwellian.' In fact, although there are a few family firms which still own provincial papers, the days of individual proprietors like Lord Northcliffe and Lord Beaverbrook are over. With the exception of the *Guardian* and the *Daily Telegraph* all national newspapers are owned by UK conglomerates or foreign-based multinational companies. The actual distribution of power which the TUC was referring to is that six companies publish 80 per cent of all daily and Sunday newspapers in Britain. The companies concerned are Reed International, News International, Trafalgar House (formerly Beaverbrook), Associated Newspapers. The Thomson Organisation and Pearson Longman.

News International owns the *News of the World* and the *Sun* as well as a chain of evening and weekly newspapers (Berrows) in Worcestershire and Hertfordshire. The company is presided over by Rupert Murdoch and is also the largest shareholder in London Weekend Television. In 1981 Rupert Murdoch also bought *The Times*, the *Sunday Times* and *The Times* supplements from the Thomson Organisation.

The Thomson Organisation owns a chain of important regional newspapers including those produced in Aberdeen, Belfast, Blackburn, Burnley, Cardiff, Edinburgh, Hemel Hempstead, Newcastle and Reading. When Roy Thomson died in 1977 full control of the com-

---

* *Media, Politics and Culture*, Geoffrey Sheridan and Carl Gardner, Macmillan, London, 1979.

pany switched to Canada. The company also has substantial interests in oil and the travel business.

Reed International is the biggest UK based multinational with newspaper interests. One of its subsidiaries—the Mirror Group—owns the *Daily Mirror*, the *Sunday Mirror*, the *Sunday People* and the *Scottish Daily Record* and *Sunday Mail*. The company also owns a chain of provincial papers in Devon. The International Publishing Corporation (IPC), which publishes over 200 magazines, comics and trade journals including *Woman, Woman's Own, Woman's Realm* and the *New Musical Express*, is also owned by Reed International.

Pearson-Longman owns the *Financial Times* and the *Economist*. Its subsidiary Westminster Press has the largest single share of provincial morning, evening and weekly papers. It also has publishing interests in Longmans and Penguin Books. The Hon. Michael Hare is the Chairman of Pearson–Longman and in 1977 the company donated £10,000 to Conservative Party funds, £1,500 to British United Industrialists and £1,000 to Aims of Industry.

Associated Newspapers owns the *Daily Mail*. The company is presided over by Lord Rothermere who lives in the South of France. The group's provincial newspapers include those published in Cheltenham, Derby, Exeter, Gloucester, Grimsby, Hull, Leicester, Plymouth, Swansea, Stoke and Torquay. The company also has interests in restaurants, oil and transport. In 1977 it made £12,000,000 profits.

Trafalgar House took over the *Daily Express*, the *Sunday Express* and the London *Evening Standard* in 1977 and launched the *Daily Star* in 1978. The company also owns the Cunard shipping line and hotels like the Ritz. In 1977 the company had a turnover of £587 million and contributed £20,000 to Conservative Party funds.

Six of the 'so-called' Independent television stations are owned substantially by one or other of these newspaper giants. News International is the largest shareholder in London Weekend Television, Associated Newspapers owns 37.5 per cent of Southern Television and the Thomson Organisation had, until 1973, a 25 per cent share in Scottish Television. Similarly, News International, Trafalgar House, Associated Newspapers, Thomson and Reed all own substantial shares in local radio.

Given this kind of evidence, Sheridan and Gardner* conclude:

'This strong proprietorial monopoly, interwoven with both subtle

---

* *The Politics of the Media*, G. Sheridan and C. Gardner, in *Media, Politics and Culture*, Macmillan, London, 1979.

and crude financial pressure on the part of advertisers, rather emphatically undermines the whole pretence of "Press freedom". What "press freedom" means to a Thomson or a Murdoch is the freedom to appoint the person of his choice, to decide autocratically what shall and shall not reach the eyes of millions of readers. In turn his (and it is invariably *his*) subordinates understand the general limits within which to report, and trim their copy accordingly. Much of this is unspoken—many journalists share their editors' social and political assumptions. But in any case there is not a lot of "freedom" involved in such a process. En route the paper is expected to make money, generally by satisfying the capitalist advertiser.

'At present both goals are in principle satisfied at a national level by a conservative editorial policy: seven of the nine major Fleet Street dailies more or less support the Conservative Party; one, the *Daily Mirror*, supports Labour; and one, the *Guardian*, is never quite sure. Not a lot of 'freedom" there either, at least in terms of political expression. The political spectrum represented—from centre Labour to right wing Tory—is probably the narrowest of *any* national press in Western Europe.

'The argument that the British Press—because it remains exclusively in private hands and because private ownership is a cornerstone of Conservative political philosophy—guarantees that newspapers, those who own them and those who work for them will be predominantly Conservative in sympathy, seems well supported in the literature. This has not prevented some newspapers—the *Observer* in the 1979 elections, for example—coming out in support of Labour, however. But there are forms of Conservatism other than advocating a Conservative vote at general elections. In issues which are less explicitly political— coverage given to religion, social ideas, sport, the arts and fashion, for example—it may well be that newspapers are more likely "to uphold the ordering of society much as they find it . . . if a suitable calculus could be arrived at, it could probably be used to show journalists tend in general to assume that the way society is at present organised is the right way—that it may need improvement, but not overthrow".'

Circulation Figures

Roughly 15,000,000 copies of the nine national daily papers are sold every day and it is estimated that about three people read every copy sold. The circulation figures of the eight Fleet Street dailies in the first half of 1978, before the *Daily Star* was launched in November of that year, are shown in Table 4.

Table 4.   Circulation of British National Dailies (1978)

Sun	3,930,554
Daily Mirror	3,778,038
Daily Express	2,400,907
Daily Mail	1,932,808
Daily Telegraph	1,344,968
The Times	293,989
Guardian	273,201
Financial Times	180,793

The fact that some papers sell many more copies than others does not necessarily mean that these are the most influential newspapers. Something which has also to be taken into account is who reads which papers. A rather satirical analysis of the main readership characteristics of well-known dailies was given by Cyril Plant, the President of the TUC, in 1976:

'*The Times* is read by the people who run the country.

The *Daily Mirror* is read by people who think they run the country.

The *Guardian* is read by people who think they ought to run the country.

The *Morning Star* is read by people who think that the country ought to be run by another country.

The *Daily Mail* is read by the wives of the people who run the country.

The *Financial Times* is read by the people who own the country.

The *Daily Express* is read by people who think the country ought to be run as it used to be run.

The *Daily Telegraph* is read by people who still think it is.

—and then of course there are the readers of the *Sun*—they don't care who runs the country so long as she has big tits!'

Those concerned with market research, advertising and the communications media generally have a slightly more specific way of identifying their consumers and assessing their purchasing power. A grading system based originally on the Registrar General's five-point scale gives six categories of consumers:

A—senior administrative and managers
B—middle managers, professional people
C1—senior clerical, supervisory staff
C2—skilled craftsworkers
D—semi and unskilled workers
E—casual labourers

Table 5.   National Newspaper Readership Profile (1978)

		A	B	C1	C2	D	E
Percentage of population over age 15		*3*	*13*	*22*	*32*	*21*	*9*
	Readership			Percentages			
Sun	12,267,000	1	5	17	41	29	7
Daily Mirror	11,841,000	1	6	17	39	29	7
Daily Express	6,735,000	3	15	29	30	18	7
Daily Mail	5,465,000	4	16	31	28	15	6
Daily Telegraph	3,171,000	13	37	30	13	6	2
The Times	925,000	18	34	28	12	6	2
Guardian	861,000	9	41	30	14	6	1
Financial Times	707,000	16	36	33	9	5	1

The readership groups in 1978 for different newspapers is shown in Table 5. It is clear from these figures that the people with the most authority, influence and power in Britain are more likely to read *The Times*, the *Telegraph* and the *Financial Times*, and together with the *Guardian* these papers certainly provide a good deal more in-depth reporting of political, social and economic issues than is considered necessary to include in the popular dailies intended for a mass audience. The same distinction between a mass readership and an influential readership also occurs in the main Sunday papers (Table 6).

Table 6.   Sunday Newspaper Readership Profile (1978)

		A	B	C1	C2	D	E
Percentage of population over age 15		*3*	*13*	*22*	*32*	*21*	*9*
	Readership			Percentages			
News of the World	13,297,000	1	5	16	40	39	9
Sunday Mirror	12,149,000	1	7	20	40	26	6
Sunday People	11,304,000	1	7	19	39	27	8
Sunday Express	8,582,000	5	21	32	24	12	5
Sunday Times	3,777,000	13	33	31	15	7	2
Sunday Telegraph	2,500,000	11	31	32	16	7	2
Observer	2,282,000	9	32	31	17	8	3

The time may have gone when, as happened to the *Pall Mall Gazette*, a London evening paper in 1893 was sold to a Conservative politician, W. W. Astor, and changed from a Liberal to a

Conservative paper overnight whilst the Editor was on holiday. But the allegiance of national newspapers to political parties is still fairly common (Table 7).

Table 7. Partisanship of the British Press (National Dailies)

Partisan Conservative	Moderate Independent		Partisan Labour	Partisan Communist
	Right	Left		
Daily Telegraph	The Times	Guardian	Daily Mirror	Morning Star
Daily Mail	Sun			
Daily Express				
Financial Times				
Star				

In terms of those who have power and control in society, therefore, it is interesting to speculate about the political and social influence papers with a conservative bias like the *Express*, the *Daily Star* and the *Daily Mail* have on their essentially working-class readers.

The Growth and Development of the British Press

One of the main differences between the press in Britain and in other similarly capitalist countries is that our press is much more centralised and more tightly controlled by a relatively small number of owners. Allegations about the opportunity given to the few wealthy capitalists who own the press to indoctrinate the rest of the population with their views and in ways which best serve their own interests are frequently made. But this notion needs a little more careful analysis because if the aims of the press under capitalism are simply to indoctrinate then why are the characteristics of ownership and competition between papers in Britain different from other capitalist countries? And why do some newspapers like the *Daily Mirror*, for example, seem to align themselves with working-class readers in ways which are also politically partisan?

To answer these questions it is necessary to look back at the circumstances in which the press developed in this country and how the press responded to these circumstances. The Industrial Revolution took place earlier in Britain than elsewhere. Capitalism was developing at the same time as the railways were making Britain into a much more accessible country and at the same time as the press itself was developing. The railway network enabled the national press to compete with the provincial and local press in a way which was never possible in the United States and which was never attempted in France and Germany.

A second important historical factor is that the British press was created in the eighteenth century by the bourgeoisie. But they had a struggle that went on for at least a generation with the old ruling class to become established, to win the right to report on parliamentary debates and to establish freedom and commercial independence. The battle against state interference and state control, and the right to establish an independent press with freedom of speech, lasted for at least a hundred years. It was not until 1855 that stamp duty was finally removed—although by that time the bourgeoisie were much more powerful as a class than they had been in the eighteenth century. (The stamp was a special postage rate imposed on all newspapers by the government—whether they were sent by post or not. Its effect had been to restrict the development of provincial papers and papers which working-class people could afford.)

At the same time as the national press was developing, local papers serving much smaller communities did exist, however, and at the beginning of the nineteenth century an independent radical press emerged concerned mainly with political campaigns for the vote and with issues relating to economic, educational and political conditions. The radical press—like *The Political Register*, *The Black Dwarf*, *The Poor Man's Guardian*, *The Pioneer*, etc.—were all quite independent from commercial control, though not from state repression, and provided one of the first forms of accessible, independent, popular reporting for working people.

The Sunday papers, which predated daily papers as a national institution by several years, were also fairly independent in their early days and were intended for a popular audience. Their contents reflected the popular culture of the growing urban centres. They included reports of crime and scandal which, considering that we are talking about the 1820s, make an interesting comparison with popular Sunday newspapers today—but also radical politics. They certainly could count on a wide popular readership and were often shared around and read aloud to others in the local pubs and political meeting places. Historians often make the mistake of assuming that because of illiteracy, newspapers made no real impact on the masses until the end of the nineteenth century, when the Forster Education Act of 1870 had had time to increase literacy and the Northcliffe revolution in the production of daily papers took place. In fact, this view is quite mistaken. Obviously there was a good deal of illiteracy, among the poor especially, but at any time in the nineteenth century there were more than enough people who could read for themselves and read to each other to make both the radical press and Sunday newspapers quite popular institutions.

So far as the radical press was concerned it was not all plain sailing, however. Since most of the papers were attached to specific campaigns like the Chartist Movement, for example, they were attacked and re-pressed by the state in the same way as the movements which they represented. But in the end it was not political repression alone which precipitated their decline. They soon found themselves in competition with the commercial press and finance obviously became a problem. Between about the 1820s and the 1860s the cultural and political inter-ests of the urban population, including radical politics, were pro-gressively incorporated into the content of the Sunday papers, leaving the radical press in a fairly isolated position, attacked by the govern-ment on the one hand and unable to compete with commercial news-papers on the other.

By the end of the century the destruction of the radical press was complete as commercially-owned and commercially-run evening papers and daily papers became more common.

Centralised Control

Another feature of the development of the press during this time was the shift away from independence towards more centralised ownership and control. Papers which had been independent until the 1880s—probably belonging to one family or one printing house—were gathered over the next twenty years or so into monopoly holdings by the corporate press houses we have today. The ownership of several papers by one owner or one firm was strengthened by parallel de-velopments in the concentration of advertising money. Most of the advertising that went on in the nineteenth century was in the form of not very lucrative classified advertisements and papers had to be sold at cost price. Northcliffe's revolution was to introduce display adver-tising and to use advertising revenue based on the promise of wide circulation to a mass audience to subsidise the costs of production. On this basis he could sell papers well below cost to more people and provide in the process a most effective form of commercial advertising. This economic principle has guided the British press ever since.

Although the subsidy of advertising ensures that the cost of news-papers can be kept fairly low so far as readers are concerned, the principle has obvious weaknesses so far as the guarantee of a varied and relatively independent press is concerned. Today the effect is quite simply that papers which cannot guarantee a mass circulation to at-tract advertising revenue cannot survive. This constraint obviously affects both the quality and the content of the newspapers. Advertisers also have a vested interest in sustaining the philosophies and practices of capitalism if they are to receive lucrative profits from the sale of their goods. With owners and advertisers in political unison it is per-haps not surprising that of the nine daily newspapers available nationally, the slightly left-of-centre *Guardian* is politically the most left wing of British newspapers. Although this may not be surprising it is very unusual and is not true of other comparable capitalist countries. The *Morning Star*, which is owned and produced by the Communist Party of Great Britain, has a very small national circulation in comparison to the other national dailies and has to rely on revenue not from advertising but from donations, sales and fund-raising campaigns.

Those papers which have closed in recent years have closed not because they lacked interested readers but because they could not attract sufficient advertising revenue or compete with the big newspaper monopolies. The *News Chronicle*, the *Daily Herald* and the old radical Sunday paper the *Reynolds News* all had large circulations of between one and two million when they closed—circulations much larger than newspapers in similar countries. Raymond Williams in *Media, Politics and Culture* argues that the viability of newspapers in Britain is directly related to the availability of advertising money. He concludes that papers like the *News Chronicle* and the *Daily Herald* died because they had large numbers of elderly and, 'in advertising agents' terms', D and E readers—in other words, semi-skilled, unskilled and casual workers. For advertisers these were not the people likely to spend vast amounts of money and consequently the papers were considered hardly to be worth advertising in.

The concentration of advertising therefore helps to strengthen the process of press centralisation and control in the hands of a few individuals or a few companies.

Indoctrination or Incorporation?

The other concern, apart from the implications of centralisation and the influence of advertising, is of course indoctrination. The allegation that newspapers indoctrinate people into certain beliefs and act to sustain the class and political interests of ruling groups in society is frequently made. The process by which this occurs is of course much more complex than this simple charge suggests. After all, people do have a choice, however limited, between different newspapers. And they have the freedom to reject what they read—or indeed to read nothing at all.

Raymond Williams again says, 'at a certain level, if you look at the economic interests and political affiliations of the people who own the press, it is not surprising that the press puts the kind of political and social line it does'—by which he means the selection of news and the interpretation of events which sustain conservative, capitalist and commercial interests. But the influence of the press also operates in a more subtle and in the end a more pervasive way. Williams cites the *Daily Mirror* as an example:

'take the phenomenon of the *Daily Mirror*, which began as a simple picture paper, in a fairly typical ideology of the early twentieth century, for women. Women would not want to read about politics—in any case they did not have the vote—but they would like to look at pictures, they would like to read some gossip, they would like the events of the day treated in a lively way. ... Now take the transformation of the *Mirror* which occurred in the 1940s. ... The *Daily Mirror* campaigned in a radical way, as it said, on behalf of the men in the army. It campaigned at a certain level against the old ruling class. The adjective "old" is a very important one, because it is still a way of identifying radicalism—you campaign against the "old" ruling class and not the current one. But in any event it showed a distinct political shift which at a certain level did not correspond directly to the political affiliations or the economic interests of the owners.'

Roger Protz* describes a meeting between Cecil King, head of IPC for many years, and Guy Bartholomew, who helped to transform the *Daily Mirror* in the late thirties and early forties with the wartime cabinet. 'They debated whether a situation could arise similar to 1918–19, when an explosion of militant strikes throughout the country put British capitalism under challenge by the working class movement. ... After much soul-searching and head-scratching they were cheered to hear the opinion of one cabinet member who suddenly piped up: "There is a crucial difference between 1918 and 1945—today we have the *Daily Mirror*." It would be absurd to suggest that the relative stability of post-war Britain rested solely on the *Daily Mirror* but the cabinet minister had in one pithy sentence summed up the power of the press to head off the tide of discontent that millions of working-class people feel under capitalism and to direct that discontent into the safe harbour of reformism.'

The *Mirror* today—a subsidiary of Reed International, the biggest UK-based multinational with newspaper interests, which also owns IPC (see p. 151)—is still considered to be a paper for the working class. It knows it is talking to an audience with entrenched anti-Tory views and slants its propaganda accordingly. But its declared radicalism is superficial and clearly there are many ways of perpetuating conservatism besides advocating a Conservative vote at general elections.

In 1978 a new newspaper, the *Daily Star*, was launched in Manchester and began printing in Fleet Street in 1979. By June 1979 it had established impressive circulation figures of 1,011,116 among predominantly working-class readers. Although owned by the extremely conservative chairman of Express Newspapers, Victor Matthews, and very blatantly sensational and sexist in its coverage of news and events, many of its editorials are sympathetic to the interests and concerns of low-paid workers.

---

* Roger Protz in *Media, Politics and Culture*, G. Sheridan and C. Gardner (eds.), Macmillan, London, 1979.

What is happening in both these examples is not indoctrination; neither is it evidence of newspaper editors courageously supporting political opinions contrary to the interests of their owners. The process at work is the attempt to incorporate working-class readers—to appear to give them what they want and to appeal to their interests and concerns but subtly to shape, fashion and influence these interests and concerns in a way which actually depoliticises them. Williams points out that if this is done in too crude a way it will fail: it needs to appear to be harmless, entertaining, all good fun, and it typically requires people from outside the ruling class to do it. 'The whole language of the *Mirror* through that evolution from the 1940s to the 1950s was a very skilful miming—it is a miming—of colloquial English, to reassure people that these are not to be the all-too-familiar voices of the established culture but these are people like yourself. . . . It established the sales, and these were skills which were highly rewarded. Let us not underestimate them: they took a long time to work out—at a certain level you had to persuade people that you were speaking *for* them and in their way against the identifiable old culture which was not theirs, although obviously as an institution and on every decisive level of political stance and economic affiliation, the very organisation doing it was part of the class which it was presumably rejecting.'

The process is in many ways similar to what happened to the popular press in the nineteenth century—it was essential to its success to be concerned with the real interests of the people and to write in a style and in a way with which they could identify. The twentieth century has extended this incorporation of working-class culture and interests even further than merely learning the language in which to express the attention given to day-to-day politics, organised sport, fashion, scandal and crime: for example, it has also learned a 'language for its handling of news which at a very deep level involves the process of the self-identification of the reader with much of what is *apparently* being spoken . . . *apparently* from their position and *apparently* with their kind of lifestyle and interests in mind'.

This deliberate and conscious attempt to mime working-class feelings and concerns is not merely the newsmen's reflection of an authentic and coherent culture, however. For the majority of working-class people newspaper and television representations of their lifestyle, their social conditions and political interests are very different from what they would hear if they talked to those whose experience and class position is much closer to their own and who have become politically committed.

The *Sun* is a good but sad example of this process at work. When the *Sun* first appeared in 1964 it was as an attempt to take over from the old *Daily Herald*. It did not do very well and by the spring of 1969 had lost over £12,000,000. Its owners, Reed International, decided to close the paper but then decided to sell it 'at a knock-down price' to Rupert Murdoch of News International, who also owned the *News of the World*. Between 1964 and 1969 the *Sun* had continued in the *Herald* tradition of trying to provide a paper for working people which treated political and social issues seriously. Murdoch gave up this attempt and went for people's baser instincts. Sales soared. By May 1978 selling just under 4 million copies, the *Sun* was reckoned to have overtaken the *Daily Mirror* in popular appeal and in 1974 had encouraged a Tory vote at the general election.

The media at their most effective, so far as the interests of capital are concerned, serve to distract the attention of working-class readers from both an understanding of and a reaction to the economic disadvantages of their class conditions in ways which would encourage them to become politically rebellious. And the obvious popularity of the popular press measured in terms of patronage and circulation over the years is some indication of their success in this respect.

Lord Beaverbrook, who died in 1964, owner of the *Daily Express* and the *Sunday Express*, played an important part in politics for most of this century. He never made any secret of the reasons why he owned newspapers: it was minds not money he was after. He was a self-confessed Conservative and a major aim of his newspapers was to transmit his Conservative views to his readers. For similar reasons Roy Thomson was quite happy to run *The Times* at a loss for many years. In some respects, therefore, so far as newspaper tycoons are concerned, economic profit is not their sole motivation. Enzensberger * explains it like this:

'The products of the mind industry can no longer be understood in terms of a sellers' and buyers' market, or in terms of production costs: they are, as it were, priceless ... To concentrate on their commercialisation is to miss the point and overlook the specific service which the mind industries perform for modern societies. ... The mind industry's main business and concern is not to sell its product: it is to "sell" the existing order, to perpetuate the prevailing pattern of man's domination by man, no matter who runs the society, and by what means. ... An entire industry is engaged in ... eliminating possible futures and reinforcing the present pattern of domination.'

Enzensberger was referring specifically to radio and television in this analysis but his interpretation can equally well be applied to the British press. To explain the motivations of media proprietors as being simply to amass more and more personal wealth is to understand only part of their concern for power and influence.

---

* *Industrialisation of the Mind*, Enzensberger, Pluto, London, 1976.

John Whale* takes a rather different view of all this. Whilst agreeing that the British press is predominantly conservative, he also maintains that readers have significant influence in determining the form that newspapers take. His conclusion is that the press is predominantly conservative in tone because its readers are. 'If any substantial number of people seriously wanted the structure of society rebuilt from the bottom, the *Morning Star* would sell more copies than it does. The reason why national newspapers fall tidily into two bundles—popular and posh, with the popular ones all physically smaller than the posh but selling five times as many copies—is that British life remains similarly and obstinately divided.' Whatever shifts have come about in the economic differences between different classes, nothing has happened, according to Whale, to narrow the cultural gap. Different 'styles' are called for but in their different ways both middle-class and working-class culture reflect essentially conservative responses.

What is News?

Another aspect of television, radio and newspapers that interests sociologists is the way in which 'news' is selected. Each day there are an enormous number of things that happen in every part of the country and all over the world. Who decides which of these many events are newsworthy? And are the same news items considered to be equally relevant to all viewers, listeners and readers?

Harold Evans, editor of the *Sunday Times*, said in 1963: 'News is people. It is people talking and people doing. Committees and cabinets and courts are people; so are fires, accidents and planning decisions. They are only news because they involve and affect people.' Much earlier Lord Northcliffe, one of the original 'press barons', had made his position clear: 'News is what somebody somewhere wants to suppress; all the rest is advertising.' So far as the majority of journalists are concerned, for events to be 'newsworthy' they have to contain one or more of the following ingredients: conflict, hardship and danger to the community, unusualness (oddity, novelty), scandal or individualism.

The way in which journalists 'treat the news' is controversial in itself. Events like elections, protests, accidents, strikes, etc., do actually *happen*—but news is *made*. That which appears on your television screen or in the press is a manufactured product, and there is a whole chain of production to be gone through in its manufacture before the reader or viewer becomes aware of it through the media. At any point in this chain or production, the raw material—i.e. the actual event— can be substantially defined, reinterpreted and altered as it passes from one journalist to another. Let us take newspapers as an example. Reporters at the scene of the event produce copy which is their inter-

---

* *The Politics of the Media*, John Whale, Fontana, London, 1980.

pretation of what has happened. This gets passed on to subeditors who rewrite the copy, shorten it, give it a new emphasis—and all this without their having been to the scene of the event or having talked to any of the main participants. In a busy paper theirs will be the version which usually gets printed. If it is particularly controversial or especially newsworthy it may also get examined and altered by their section editor. In any event, it has passed out of the control of the participants who were involved in the event and the journalist who first reported it. The same process occurs in television except that it is film rather than 'copy' which is edited.

Before independent television was established, BBC news broadcasts were very staid affairs. News bulletins used a still photograph of Big Ben and this, until 1954, was their only illustration. It was not until December 1956 that the notorious Fourteen-Day Rule was abolished. This regulation was used to prevent the media from broadcasting discussion about any issue which was due to be debated in Parliament in the two weeks leading up to the parliamentary debate.

But news broadcasting took on a different character with the introduction of commercial television. John Whale describes how Independent Television News 'made a cult of comparative irreverence from the first. Whether the matter in hand was popular music or the balance of trade, the interviewer was the respondent's cheerful adversary, putting the questions which would rise in the mind of the sceptical outsider. That had not been the BBC's way. Its practice had been much more to choose what should be held up for respect, and hold it up; and the works and words of governments had fallen for the most part into that category. Now it was obliged to adapt itself to the new patterns of wide and yet quizzical coverage.'

For many years broadcasting the spoken word was simply a matter of reading the written word aloud. When politicians broadcast they had a script and it was only in the fifties and sixties that there was a steady movement away from the scripted to the unrehearsed interview. Again the more investigative and less reverent style of ITV had a lot to do with this. So long as they relied on advertising revenue, even news bulletins had to set out not to be boring because advertising slots had to be sold in and around these programmes just like all the others.

In deciding 'what is news' then, the selection and style of presentation is made by those who work in the media and is based partly upon their decision about what is newsworthy and important and partly on the opinions they have about their audience.

Because mass communications are designed to reach a maximum number of people rather than separate individuals in isolation, one noticeable tendency of the media is to stereotype their audiences—to think of them as large groups of people who are all more or less the same. This can lead, for example, to 'women's pages' in the press, which treat women as though they are all the same and as if all they are interested in is fashion, cooking, gossip, slimming and romance. It also means that television programmes and newspapers frequently oversimplify what they have to say—especially for working-class audiences—on the assumption that they are less well educated and less intelligent than middle-class audiences.

Bias and stereotyping can happen in other ways too. There is the tendency to go for stories that are 'sensational' and, as the Glasgow Media Study Group showed in their report *Bad News*, there has been in recent years a clear anti-union bias in news reporting and a concentration on the damaging effects of strikes, quite out of all proportion to the number of strikes that actually take place. While it is the case that more working days are lost each year because of industrial accidents and as a result of industrial injuries than by strikes, the study group could find little evidence in the press of this information being made available.

Murdock and Golding, writing in 1973, made quite a detailed study of broadcasting. They found a noticeable tendency in the media to appeal to ideas of patriotism, the 'national interest' and 'togetherness', as a way of stressing conformity and isolating outsiders and those who do not conform. They also noted how British concerns, British exploits and British achievements are considered to be more newsworthy and important than events which happen in other countries.

Two other sociologists Galting and Ruge, in a special analysis of foreign news showed how:

1. Coverage of events in other countries stressed fighting, natural disasters and accidents rather than everyday events.

2. When countries are not considered to be very important (e.g. Third World Countries) only their very important citizens were considered newsworthy.

3. When ordinary people in these countries were portrayed it was usually only in circumstances of famine, war or political unrest.

The effects of this kind of concentration, according to Galting and Ruge, is to emphasise 'bad news' and to present stereotype images of countries in which only the leaders are considered to be important and everyone else is either stupid or starving.

It Can't Be All Bad!

You may be feeling by now that all those involved in the media are fairly unscrupulous people who, in giving the rest of us a 'good time', are really concerned to take advantage of us. Clearly the links with private profit and the potential power to exercise influence and control means that media organisations have to be scrutinised carefully.

But there is another point of view which has to be put. No one can deny that in providing leisure activities, entertainment and pleasure for large numbers of people, the mass communications business does perform a valuable service in society. The important thing to remember, though, is that those who provide the services have a variety of motives for what they do, and enabling people to enjoy themselves is not always their first consideration.

So far as radio and television go, clearly no one should underestimate the important contributions they have made to popular education and to making people more aware of what is going on around them. Despite all the reservations outlined above, television particularly has helped bring drama, music, light entertainment, sport, knowledge and ideas to the attention of many more people than ever before. And despite the undue influence of advertising and government financing, there is enough evidence to suggest that conscientious journalism designed to expose corruption in high places and to give publicity to the plight of those who are often powerless to speak for themselves is also part of the contribution that the mass media can make to a complex society like ours.

Revision

1. Refresh Your Memory

Make sure you know the meaning of the terms: mass media, heterogeneous audience, monopoly, socialisation, political partisanship, incorporation, indoctrination.

2. Check Your Understanding

Be able to explain in your own words the difference between:

(*a*) Mass communication and face-to-face communication.

(*b*) The IBA and the BBC.

(*c*) 'Circulation' and 'readership' figures in relation to newspaper consumption.

(*d*) National and provincial newspapers.

(*e*) The 'popular' and the 'quality' press.

(*f*) Conservative with a big 'C' and conservative with a small 'c'.

(*g*) The 'radical' and the 'commercial' press in the nineteenth century.

3. Essay Questions to Try

(*a*) What are some of the main characteristics of mass communications systems in a modern society? What implications do these characteristics have for the transmission of information and entertainment?

(*b*) To what extent do you agree that audiences of the mass media are essentially passive and consequently susceptible to control?

(*c*) Discuss some of the main ways in which the mass media are linked to the interests of 'big business'.

(*d*) To what extent are television and radio independent of the state?

(*e*) Suggest reasons why research into 'the effects of television' on its audience is inconclusive.

(*f*) 'The concentration of newspaper power in the hands of those who could be described as part of the ruling class has led to a systematic misinterpretation in the reporting of the lives and activities of the large majority of the population, including several significant oppressed minorities.' Discuss.

(*g*) 'So far as the mass media are concerned there are forms of conservatism other than openly advocating a Conservative vote at a General Election.' How far do you agree with the view that the British press and broadcasting media are conservative with both a big 'C' and a small 'c'?

(*h*) What social and economic factors have influenced the growth, development and contemporary characteristics of the British press?

(*i*) Is there any truth in the suggestion that 'the news doesn't just happen—it is made'?

(*j*) According to television research each girl and boy spends on average more than two hours per day watching television. This is equivalent to one third of the time which 5–16 years olds spend in school. We assume that school has some effect on the lives of its pupils, but what do sociologists know about the effects of television on the lives of children and young people?

Further Reading

Media, Politics and Culture, Carl Gardner (ed.), Macmillan, London, 1979.

Towards a Sociology of Mass Communications, Denis McQuail, Collier-Macmillan, West Drayton, 1969.

The Politics of the Media (Second Edition), John Whale, Fontana, London, 1980.

7

INDUSTRY AND INDUSTRIAL CHANGE

The effects of economic forces on people's lives are both fundamental and complex. At the most elementary level, the opportunity to work and the nature of the work which people are engaged in has tremendous ramifications in terms of their spending power, their economic security, their degree of choice and their control over what they do with their lives.

Since the Second World War the ideal of 'full employment', or the right of everyone to paid employment, was seen as an important cornerstone of government policy. In the early sixties a national unemployment figure of around 400,000 seemed small enough to be contained. Twenty years later in 1981 unemployment had risen to almost 3 million, and the conviction that long-term, structural unemployment of between 2 and 5 million would become a normal condition of the 1990s was being anticipated with both anxiety and resignation.

In these circumstances the obvious question for sociologists to ask is 'what will the effects be on people's lives?'. More important, perhaps, is the question 'why has this happened?'.

In the early sixties the standard of living in Britain was one of the highest in Europe. In 1981 it was one of the lowest. Britain has always existed and depended upon its capacity to earn profit from its activities as a trading nation. But in 1979, for example, exports grew only one tenth as fast as imports. Take domestic appliances as an example: 45 per cent of washing machines, 99 per cent of dishwashers, 69 per cent of fridges and 56 per cent of electric mixers were imported from abroad; 56 per cent of new cars came from manufacturers outside Britain and every foreign car imported into Britain meant less work for British workers—not only car workers, but all those others involved in producing British steel, tyres, plugs, lights, carburettors, batteries, radiators and all the other components that go to make up a completed car.

At the beginning of the last century Britain made all the weaving machines for the world market. Today she makes virtually none. Whilst British manufacturers stuck doggedly to making old shuttle looms, foreign rivals pioneered high-speed shuttleless equipment. As a result, when British textile-weaving firms now re-equip their factories, they buy Swiss, German and French machines. In almost every case they are replacing looms made by well-known British firms which once led the world.

But it is not just the weaving looms. Britain no longer makes typewriters, sewing machines, motor-cycles or even cars on a large scale. The experience of a Croydon company of typewriter manufacturers called Oliver provides a good illustration of attitudes which have bedevilled this and other manufacturing industries in Britain. Between 1914 and 1918 they made typewriters 'for the troops', and they went on using the same basic design until the thirties, when Swedish and German ideas helped to modernise the models they produced. But in 1939 the British Army wanted the 'same models which had seen them through the First World War' and Oliver's returned to their old designs.

After the war, few people in the British typewriter industry observed what was happening abroad, or noted the spread of 'electrification'. By 1958 a third of the US production was electric typewriters. In Britain it was 6 per cent.

Imperial, Britain's most famous name in typewriter manufacture produced a fair proportion of its models for the civil service, 40 per cent of which was shipped abroad. Protected by government orders, the company made little effort to change its ways. Imperial did not introduce mass production techniques until the sixties and by the late seventies the consequences had become clear. In America and Germany, imports of typewriters accounted for 25 per cent of home sales. In Britain the percentage was 75 per cent. Today British Imperial no longer make typewriters.

The easy explanation, and the one favoured by the popular press, has been to attribute this decline as a trading nation to either laziness among the workers who go on strike too often, or to inefficient management. But the reasons go much deeper than this. The Birmingham Community Development Project, tracing the developments which have put many Saltley workers 'on the scrapheap', suggest that the explanation must be sought in the outdated organisation and equipment of British industry which they maintain is 'firmly stuck in the past'. Add to this the investment decisions of major employers which have resulted in large-scale redundancies, increasing competition from other industrial nations, the invention of new technologies, escalating oil prices and the expansion and development of international capitalism, and you will begin to see how the origins of our industrial malaise are many-faceted and why the costs of industrial change are likely to be unevenly distributed.

The Industrialisation of Britain

Britain was the first industrial nation and British capitalism was the first to develop. A number of conditions contributed to its early growth and development.

Abroad, Britain had built up a considerable empire by the middle of the nineteenth century which provided both cheap raw materials and a range of markets in which to sell manufactured goods. At home the 'enclosure' of agricultural land had made many land-holding peasants homeless and they became the first labourers attracted to the new industries and the towns which sprang up around them.

In the first half of the nineteenth century most manufacturing was still organised on a small scale in workshops, making full use of hand craft and individual skill. But as railways and shipbuilding rapidly developed the possibilities of trade, larger factories were built and machinery was increasingly introduced to speed up and multiply the production of goods.

The spread of machinery, railways and shipbuilding in turn provided a new demand for iron, steel and engineering. Without significant developments in the quality of iron production, mechanisation in other industries would have been greatly reduced. But as a result of technical improvements in mining, smelting and purifying steel, Britain soon outstripped all her rivals in iron and steel production.

The other important innovation was the introduction of steam-driven machinery which made it possible for manufacturers to have greater choice in where they put their factories and made them less dependent on water and 'human energy'. The development of steam engines and the increased demand for iron in turn affected the production of coal. Almost without exception new industries and the manufacturing towns which serviced them grew up near to plentiful supplies of coal. By 1850, therefore, Britain was without equal in terms of industrial production and trade. Her exports multiplied three and a half times between 1850 and 1870, when she was generally considered to be the 'workshop of the world'. In 1870 the total amount of British trade in manufactured goods was greater than Germany, Italy and France combined, though industrial developments in the USA and Germany were soon to challenge her supremacy.

The Organisation of Labour

Prosperity for the owners of factories and those who profited from trade was not without cost to those who provided the labour, however. Working conditions in the factories and heavy industries were notoriously bad. Women and children were exploited by the same insensitive greed as exploited men. Dangerous conditions, low wages and long hours were common, and in the days before trade unions were well established there was often little that workers could do but complain privately to each other. In the end appalling conditions and repressive measures designed to restrict workers' rights by the employers and government encouraged the development of trade union ideas. Small unions and working men's associations were established and in 1868 the TUC was formed.

Skilled workers were the first to get organised although many of the early craft unions were little more than 'friendly societies'. Unskilled workers in the docks, fishing and gas industries, for example, took longer to form trade unions. They lived on low wages with little protection from the law so far as their rights at work were concerned and they had no state benefits to rely on if they lost their jobs. Chronic unemployment, ill health and poor living conditions were permanent features of their lives in the late nineteenth century and not the most effective base from which to demand better working conditions and higher wages (see Chapter 9).

As profitability in the gas industry declined towards the end of the nineteenth century, employers tried to compensate for their losses by imposing longer hours and worse conditions on their workers. Their activities precipitated a strike in 1888 and did much to encourage the spread of trade union ideas and organisation. Led by Will Thorne, the gas workers' union (later the GMWU) confronted the employers with the demand for an eight-hour day and got it. Encouraged by their success, the London dockers marched through the streets of London with totem poles crowned with fish heads and rotting onions as an indication of the sort of food they were forced to live on. In 1889 they went on strike in an effort to achieve a minimum wage of 6*d* an hour and to put an end to the contract work which was the chief cause of their sweated labour. They got their 'dockers' tanner' but the end to casual labour in the docks and the achievement of some degree of job security took another fifty years to achieve.

Whilst the enthusiasm for the new unionism increased, trades councils, representing different unions and industries in a local area, began to be established and a new political party, the Independent Labour Party, was set up in close allegiance with the concerns of the emerging labour movement.

Industrial Change

Meanwhile, in the older industrial areas, those in which the Industrial Revolution had begun, the decline in the traditional economic base had already started. The repercussions of industrial change proceeded at different rates in different parts of Britain but the pattern of decline, redevelopment and diversification became a familiar one over the next three quarters of a century. A significant watershed was the First World War.

In 1914 Britain still controlled about one third of the world's trade and there seemed to be no shortage of ways in which money could be made, especially by investing abroad. Eighteen months after the war was over, however, the short-lived, post-war boom in industry collapsed. Between 1920 and 1940 there were never less than a million unemployed and those who suffered most were the workers in the long established industries of coalmining, steel production, heavy engineering, textiles and shipbuilding. Some areas like Saltley in Birmingham were able to avoid the worst effects of industrial decline for a while by the development of new industries like car production and the introduction of new manufacturing techniques. In other areas electrical goods, chemicals and artificial fibres were some of the new developments which helped to change the face of industrial Britain.

The problems of the older industrial areas were dismissed as 'regional problems' and were rarely analysed as the consequence of significant shifts in the growth and expansion of capitalism which might in time spread their effects to other areas. A major characteristic of the historical development of capitalism over the last two hundred years or so has been the decline of small independent capital and the growth, centralisation and concentration of capital in large national and now multinational organisations. Industrial changes in the North-East of England provide a useful illustration of this development in operation.

Industry and Capitalism in the North-East
before the Second World War

For two hundred years, successive waves of investment in the North-East have served to replace industrial enterprises which have in turn become obsolete or unprofitable to their owners. At each of their peaks—in the heyday of coal, heavy engineering and ship building, for example—surplus profits were used to buy into other emerging industries, to establish banks, to purchase large estates and extravagant mansions. By the beginning of the twentieth century, not only was industry, but also the schools, parks, houses and libraries used by the workers provided and controlled by those who employed them. Local politics, education and the press—in which the major issues of the day were debated and interpreted—all belonged to them and reflected their influence. Their sons went to the same public schools, successive generations of them became MPs, and for their political, social and economic services several were elevated to the peerage.

Surplus profits were not only consumed locally, to enhance the power of the local ruling class over its labour force, but in the fifty years leading up to the First World War, massive amounts of capital left areas like the North-East to be invested elsewhere. The prospect of higher returns, new markets and cheaper supplies of labour encouraged the owners of British capital to establish factories and new enterprises throughout the developing world. Between 1911 and 1913 twice as much money was invested abroad as was invested at home. This, of course, was happening at the same time as much needed local investment in coalmining, heavy engineering and shipbuilding could have provided new plant and new equipment to prevent the progressive decline in each of these industries.

By 1920 the entire economic wealth of the North-East was concentrated in the hands of about seventeen families—most of them interconnected by marriage, friendship and business and banking associations. Whilst their home base remained in the North-East, as local industry was allowed to decline, the personal and collective wealth of the owners was maintained by investments increasingly laid down elsewhere.

By the 1930s, when unemployment in Jarrow had reached 69 per cent, all the big industrialists and bankers had moved out of Newcastle to large estates and mansions in Northumberland and Durham. As the slump in world trade increased, all of the heavy engineering industries either laid off workers or closed down. As the team from the Benwell Community Development Project comment in *The Making of the Ruling Class*, the families which for at least one hundred and fifty years had profited from industrial development and change in the North-East 'retained a close involvement with declining companies, but their overall strategy was one of minimal reinvestment, so that the large amounts of capital which they had extracted from the industries could be redirected to more profitable sectors'.

Later generations of the same families were to put this capital into banking, building societies, stockbroking, the law, insurance, investment trusts, investment holding companies and property.

For those who laboured in the local industries the consequences of capitalist economies were not so beneficial. Since they had no say in the investment decisions made by their employers, and probably no knowledge of them, they could do nothing to influence the changing structure of local industry. The decision taken by the Ridley family, for example, in the middle of the nineteenth century to stop investing in glass manufacture, at a time when Tyneside was a major centre of glass production, effectively prevented its continued development. In the same way decisions to allow coalmining, heavy engineering and shipbuilding to run down left thousands of people in the North-East without work and without hope.

Industrial Decline—A Regional Problem?

The explanation most often advanced by governments to account for Britain's economic difficulties in the thirties were those which looked for problems 'in distressed areas' and offered solutions designed to revive local industry at a regional level and thus relieve regional problems. Of course the causes of the problems were much more complex than this and had more to do with old machinery and outdated plant, which had been deliberately run down, with the severe economic crisis which was also affecting most of the rest of the industrialised world at the time, and with the investment decisions made by local industrialists.

Industry and Capitalism in the North-East after the Second World War

The three main characteristics of industrial change in the North-East after the Second World War—as in Britain generally—were increasing State intervention in the management of the economy, the centralisation and concentration of industrial power and the growing importance of big financial institutions like building societies, insurance companies, banks and investment holding companies.

Their influence as MPs and as members of the House of Lords, and their official representation on government commissions and advisory bodies, enabled Newcastle's influential families to help national government arrive at its conclusions about the needs and problems of the North-East.

The decision to nationalise the coal industry immediately after the war, for example, was not the challenge to private ownership which many people imagine. At a stroke the owners were relieved of their moral responsibility for an ailing industry which had lacked investment for almost half a century and they received, by way of compensation, millions of pounds which they could immediately put into more lucrative undertakings elsewhere. A good deal of the money went into finance companies like the North Rock Building Society, which is now one of the largest in the region, and which in turn has made a fortune out of increasing owner-occupation and property development since the war.

Once the 'ownership of coal' passed to the state, as in other areas, the miners of the North-East soon learned who their 'new employers' were to be. Key positions in the National Coal Board were taken up by former owners. By the 1960s the chairmanships of a wide variety of state and state-financed agencies were also held in the North-East by members of the old establishment. The National Coal Board, the Northern Industrial Development Board and the Development Corporations of new towns like Newton Aycliffe, Peterlee and Washington were dominated in the period by the sons of men who once 'owned' Newcastle.

At each phase of its development, from being an area which in the middle and late nineteenth century helped establish Britain as the 'workshop of the world', West Newcastle today has come to exemplify all of the worst characteristics of an inner city area in decline. In the 1930s it was known as a 'depressed area'. In the 1970s it was more kindly referred to as a 'development area'. In 1980 it still had one of the largest unemployment rates in the country.

Industrial Decline—An Inner City Problem?

Concern about industrial decline in the 1960s and 1970s tended to focus on the problems of the inner cities. To some extent this was in line with parallel preoccupations about law and order, race, housing and education. It became fashionable to identify inner cities as 'areas of priority' or 'special need', requiring 'positive discrimination'. In focusing on local solutions to industrial decline and unemployment, however, it was possible to ignore the more fundamental weaknesses in the British economic structure at that time, weaknesses which have become more apparent in the face of fresh competition from abroad, the introduction of new technologies, rising oil prices and seemingly insoluble international monetary problems.

In their account of 'Jobs and the Inner City' in *The State and the Local Economy*, Cochrane and Dicker outline the three main explanations given to account for the employment problems of the inner cities:

1. Small firms have been forced out of the inner cities because of council redevelopment policies and because town planners have been too strict in applying their rules. There has been too much concern for the environment and housing in these areas and not enough concern for the associated unemployment.

2. There has been too great a concentration at national level on new towns policy, which has enticed employers away from the older urban areas. This is alleged to have been a particular problem in London, but also to have been of some importance elsewhere.

3. There is a concentration of unskilled workers among the population of the inner city areas. Because unemployment levels are higher among unskilled workers, therefore, an explanation is provided for the high levels of unemployment in them.

Cochrane and Dicker are not convinced by these explanations, however. They point out that whatever redundancies have come about as the consequence of action by small firms, by far the largest reduction in the labour force has been made by big manufacturing and industrial concerns. And restrictions imposed by town planners have had precious little to do with the process. 'More than 16,000 jobs have been lost in the Vickers factories in Newcastle, while the large shipbuilders on the Tyne, Tate and Lyle in Canning Town and Vauxhall (Liverpool) and the docks in London and Liverpool have dramatically reduced their workforces since the early sixties.' None of them did so as the consequence of disagreements with town planners.

On Merseyside 26,000 manufacturing jobs were lost in the two years between 1977 and 1979. Much of the factory space was created from converted ammunitions plants after the Second World War. Little was spent on modernisation or renovation, and once manufacturing industries were cut back, these were the first to go. The catalogue of closures and redundancies was not confined to small firms but included Courtaulds, Spillers, British Leyland, English Electric, Birds Eye, Plessey, Tate and Lyle and Lucas Aerospace.

The Class Factor

The Benwell CDP report, which traces the costs of industrial change to the working people of the North-East, attributes the cause of inner city decline to persisting class distinctions, based on economic divisions within capitalism which, they argue, can be applied to countless other areas of Britain. '. . . working-class families . . . consistently over the years . . . experiencing a pattern of poor housing and bad amenities, insecurity of work, high unemployment and low wages'. This contrasted to the industrialists, coal owners and financiers whose families have for generations, in one way or another, dominated the economy of the North-East. They underwent no such privation. 'Their fortunes prospered and their sphere of influence extended far beyond Tyneside.' Their relative independence at the turn of the century 'became integrated within an economy which is now nationally and internationally organised'. The influence of the old ruling families was 'central to this transition, through their active involvement in the state machinery which encouraged the process, and through their direct participation in companies which have become major multinational corporations and highly sophisticated central banking and financing institutions'.*

Capitalist Concentration

Part of what has been happening to British industry over the last thirty years or so can be accounted for by the intensification in the process of centralisation and concentration of capital. In 1950 the top 100 firms in Britain produced 20 per cent of the total manufacturing output. Twenty years later their share had risen to 50 per cent and was expected to increase to at least 66.5 per cent by 1985. Many of them in turn are now the subsidiaries of huge multinational corporations which may be administered locally or nationally but which are pursuing policies decided in the boardrooms of America, Europe and Japan. This process of centralisation and capitalist concentration may cause the inner cities and the older industrial areas to be most vulnerable in the short term but when the manufacturing power and profit from capital is concentrated elsewhere, all British industry becomes vulnerable. Take shipbuilding, for example. Britain is still the world's fifth largest producer of ships, but her share of the total world output

---

* *The Making of the Ruling Class*, CDP Report No. 6, 1978.

in 1979 was only 3.6 per cent: 17,325 shipbuilding jobs were lost in Tyne and Wear alone between 1965 and 1972, and today more than half of the world's shipping is produced in Japan.

The car industry presents an even clearer illustration of the likely effects on British industry when the centralisation of control passes to multinational organisations based outside Britain. In the fifties and sixties Britain's car towns like Coventry and Luton were widely regarded as 'boom towns' in which their workers had become so affluent that optimistic politicians and sociologists were predicting the end of class society as we know it. By 1980, however, the British car industry was reeling and experts were predicting that by the middle of the decade only six major car firms would be operating in Europe and none of them would be British. Successive governments have shown themselves virtually helpless when it comes to taking on the big multinationals and most of their energies have been directed towards subsidising ailing companies and attempting to encourage new investments.

Government Intervention

In general, the effects of new investments, attempts to halt the decline of local manufacturing industries, the special incentives paid to new employers and the attempts to increase productivity in various ways, have all been at the expense of preserving jobs.

By definition all new investments which provide capital-intensive, high-technology plant, imply more complex forms of automated production, and less demand for human labour. The vast majority of the extra million workers who joined the dole queues in the 1970s were those made redundant by the closure of manufacturing business or 'shaken out' of their old jobs as new production and manufacturing processes made their skills obsolete.

Because of better communication links and available land for redevelopment, a good deal of the available investment went to newer towns and to factories built on the outskirts of cities. In the event, they have proved only marginally more secure than similar initiatives in the inner cities. Corby—a new town built around new developments in the steel industry, and attracting workers from Scotland and other depressed areas—was in 1980 a one-industry town with its main industry on the brink of closure.

At the same time, in the older areas, traditional industries continued to decline. Many once-important centres of production became, in Ian Harford's words,* 'vast transit areas for the distribution of goods made elsewhere'. As factories closed and redundancy payments ran out, one-time skilled workers were forced into lower-paid production-

---

* *The State and the Local Economy*, Ian Harford, CDP PEC, 1979.

line jobs or to be the storemen in the warehouses which replaced their factories.

Some were accounted for by the shift in emphasis to the service industries which took place in the 1970s—to banking, insurance, retail, the leisure industry and to the public services of the welfare state. But the employment opportunities in the service industries were generally confined to what emerged as 'women's jobs' and they did little to offset the numbers of jobs lost to men in manufacturing and heavy industry.

An alternative strategy was to encourage small firms to take over existing factories and to put them to different use. In practice this has meant low-productivity, low-wage companies, without the money or the inclination to invest in modernising the premises they use. They have done little to bring prosperity to declining areas and are frequently characterised by the kind of working conditions in which 'sweated labour' is common and trade union organisation is weak or actively discouraged. Many employ low-paid women workers and immigrants in the production of clothing and food processing, for example. Indeed, many of them represent the kind of employers and the kind of working conditions which the labour movement has been struggling for over a century to defeat. In any event, they are unlikely significantly to reduce unemployment, although they may come to enjoy increasing respectability if the monetarist economic policies identified with the 1979 Conservative Government become established (see p. 244).

The Impact of Science and Technology

A key feature of the historical development of capitalism as an economic system has been the need to increase the productivity of the labour force. Once capitalism had reached the limits of expansion on the earlier basis of its organisation, that which relied on simple machinery and the lack of protective legislation and trade union organisation to protect the labour force, productivity could no longer be increased by merely lengthening the working day or by employing women and children at half rates. Increased productivity had to come through the application of science and technology.

Over the two hundred years or so this has meant the development of mechanisation, mass-production techniques and automation. (Although, as we have already seen, a major cause of Britain's inability to compete in today's market has been her reluctance to modernise quickly enough.)

Automation

Automation takes the process of mechanisation and mass production one step further by the addition of more complicated machinery and computers which are able to produce goods, control the rate of production, feed back information and coordinate different processes with very little help from human operators.

Automated industries need fewer workers because most of the machines 'work themselves'. They need different kinds of workers on the whole—those who can program the computers and understand the work process sufficiently to supervise its progress. They need maintenance staff and engineers whose responsibilities are greater than those of assembly line workers and whose status is consequently higher. But working in automated industries can also mean sitting by switches and panels in control rooms far away from where the work process is actually happening, and this can be as boring and unrewarding an occupation as the routine of an average assembly line.

Microelectronic Processors

The most startling development of the 1970s has been the invention and production of silicon chips. These small microelectronic processors have already revolutionised automation and made it possible for the most complicated of manufacturing production to be directed and carried out by ultra-efficient, robot-like machines, controlled by highly sophisticated computers.

Already in America and Japan, for example, increasing numbers of companies are using microprocessors to automate their industries and experts predict that this development has the potential to double production, increase profit and reduce manpower to a fraction of its present level within a few years.

And it is not only manual jobs that are threatened by this form of advanced automation. Already in America, computers relying on microprocessors are being used to store the information, knowledge and skills held by key professional workers and in the process reducing considerably the need for 'human' doctors, surgeons, teachers, bankers and lawyers.

It is only recently that the British government has acknowledged the potential of silicon-chip technology and during 1978–79, without much publicity or public debate about the issues involved, £400,000,000 was made available to produce microprocessors for use in British industry.

The long-term implications of this decision are, of course, enormous. Scientists predict that microprocessors could, if they were generally developed, make a whole generation unemployed by the turn of the century. Sixty thousand soft-ware engineers employed full-time to program computers could be all the labour force necessary to organise the whole industrial production of Britain. In the short term, since developments using microprocessors are already established in America and Japan, these will undoubtedly provide a competitive challenge which British industries will be incapable of meeting.

A New Industrial Revolution?

The invention and increasing use of microprocessors has led many contemporary commentators to view the new computer-based technologies as the dawn of a 'Second Industrial Revolution' in which not only the strength of men and women workers, but also their brains, may be superseded by the activities of machines. The extent to which Britain becomes a base for high-technology industries, owned and controlled by multinational companies and 'staffed by white-coated operatives in a sea of mass unemployment', remains to be seen. Green, Murray and Davis * argue that this oversimplifies the picture of what is likely to happen to industrial production over the next twenty years or so.

The monetarist philosophy of Milton Friedman, the American economist and Nobel prize winner, has had a good deal of influence on modern capitalist thinking. He points out, with a good deal of approval, the persistence of numerous small businesses and factories in America, which exist 'despite' protective legislation and government regulations about safety and hygiene. Their workers are paid less than the minimum legal wage and they work long hours in atrocious conditions. Although they may flout the law, and represent only a slight advance in terms of working conditions since the early days of the first Industrial Revolution, these 'slum factories', according to Friedman, provide work. Without them people wouldn't have jobs at all.

In the US this division of labour is already well advanced and goes 'respectably' by the name of 'economic dualism'. It means in practice that advanced high-technology industry and large multinational corporations exist side-by-side with extensive low-wage and highly exploitative 'sweated labour'.

Green, Murray and Davis suggest that a similar trend is already happening in Britain. The void left by the decline and closure of traditional industries has been filled to some extent, as we have seen, by a shift to warehousing and distribution and by capital-intensive, high-technology industry. Both developments have created vast surpluses of labour—not only of men and women made redundant, but of young workers leaving school with limited job prospects and immigrants and married women trying to find ways of supplementing an inadequate family income.

The availability of large and principally unorganised sources of cheap labour has attracted to the inner city a number of low-wage, labour-intensive firms, encouraged there by the recent Labour Government's 'small firms policy' and 'inner city strategies' (see

---

* *The State and the Local Economy*, CDP PEC, 1979.

below). In a worsening economic climate, in which the restructuring of British industry by the introduction of new technologies may bring prosperity in the long term, high unemployment in the short term represents to many—and not least to those who experience it—one of the least acceptable aspects of modern living.

Support for Small Businesses

Support for small businesses has long been a feature of both Conservative and Liberal philosophies but the Labour Party's conversion to the idea came in 1976 when Peter Shore, then Secretary of State for the Environment, proclaimed in Manchester, 'I see it as the job of central government to provide the framework and flexibility for local government to foster confidence in the inner cities, so that private investment is promoted.' And in 1977 Prime Minister Callaghan promised more help to smaller companies in the hope that 'big oaks from little acorns grow'. In 1978 Ernest Armstrong, the Junior Environment Minister, said in Newcastle, 'The Government's view is that the growth of employment that we desperately need . . . depends to a significant extent on the contribution to be made by medium and small firms. In this region especially we have been too dependent in the past on traditional large-scale heavy industry and . . . small firms are still under-represented in the region by national standards. It is all the more important that we should exploit to the utmost the potential of our inner city areas for the development and expansion of small businesses. . . . The government sees that there is an inter-relationship between the regeneration of our inner cities and the prosperity of the small firms there.'

Those inner cities designated 'industrial improvement areas' found their local authorities and local industries 'in partnership' with the government, and committed to policies of encouraging small businesses. But like previous offers of help from Urban Aid, positive discrimination for Educational Priority Areas and the Home Office sponsored Community Development Projects (see p. 240), no *new* money was available. The money redirected towards encouraging private industry came from cuts in other forms of public spending. The shift of resources came as a consequence of local authorities spending their government grants on encouraging private industry, rather than on local housing, social and welfare services and health. In addition, a government circular sent from the Department of the Environment in 1977 requested local authorities not to 'displace firms by slum clearance' and to 'relax their attitudes towards the non-conforming user'. Though if the relaxation of regulations relating to planning and health and safety provision continue to be eased in this way, the consequences in terms of declining working conditions are clearly obvious.

Not surprisingly, local authorities were responsive to these recommendations. At local level they had been the ones who had been forced to cope with the decline, dereliction and low morale which had taken place as private industry moved from their areas into more lucrative markets. And they had frequently been made to feel responsible for industrial decline by edging out small firms during the process of slum clearance and redevelopment. By taking positive steps to encourage small businesses to expand and to return it now appeared as if something useful was being done to resolve local problems.

The links between developments like these and the concentration of capital in the big multinational corporations is perhaps difficult to understand. But there has certainly been no shortage of financial aid from big companies like ICI, IBM, Shell, BP, Marks and Spencer and British Oxygen to boost small businesses in the inner city. A spokesman for Shell in 1978 explained why, at the same time as the major oil companies were closing down small unprofitable garages all over the country, they were also announcing increases in financial aid to small businesses in the inner cities: 'We believe that the best business environment for big companies includes a thriving small business sector.'

Milton Friedman has explained the logic in terms of providing incentives to reward enterprise, and to encourage both managers and workers alike to price themselves *into* the market by policies of cutting costs, skimping on facilities, using homeworkers and enforced overtime when necessary and side-stepping traditional labour organisations.

But there is another logic in it all. One of the main reasons which encouraged British capitalists to invest abroad in the past was that they could find other countries in which labour was cheaper than at home. *The Economist* noted as long ago as 1975 that Britain was fast becoming just such a 'cheap labour country'. It is possible that today's small firms with their poorly organised and low-paid workers will latch on to the spirit of 'free enterprise' enshrined in the free market philosophies of economists like Friedman and 'make good'. But it is perhaps more likely that the relaxation of government interference in private industry—and the removal of planning standards and protective legislation of various kinds—will continue to keep a ready supply of cheap, depressed labour 'in reserve', to attract the investments of foreign-based multinationals looking to 'use' British workers in just the same way as Britain once used those in a similar position.

The Pattern of Industrial Change—A Summary

It is important to remember that changes in industry do not just affect changes in jobs and conditions at work. Just as manufacturing towns at one time developed in response to new industries, so now are present-day communities affected by the kind of work which is available locally. Over the years it is possible to see how many areas have first thrived and then declined in direct relationship to the fact of their local industry. Table 8 summarises the relationship between industry and community through the three phases of industrial growth, maturity and decline described in this chapter.

Table 8. The Growth and Decline of Industrial Areas

Industry	*Community*
Growth	
Industries are set up in an area using capital which comes from profits made elsewhere. The industries expand and employment grows. All the available land is filled up.	A new population moves into the area in search of work. Houses are built for them. Many have come from other areas where industry/agriculture is in decline.
Maturity	
Local firms remain profitable. Few firms leave the area and new growth slows down. (Meanwhile a new generation of industrial investments is being laid down elsewhere, partly financed by the profits made here.)	Employment remains at a fairly stable level. The local population settles and amenities develop. Local employment and housing opportunities are still relatively good.
Decline	
Local industries begin to decline. There is little new investment in existing plant. Employment is cut.	The housing stock begins to deteriorate and many of the better-paid and more skilled workers move out to newer working-class areas.
The traditional manufacturing sector continues to decline and provides fewer and fewer jobs—especially skilled jobs. Several firms close altogether, leaving vacant sites.	The reduction in job opportunities locally also encourages them to move away. The rate of leaving the area increases as local industries continue to decline. Redundant workers remain unemployed or find work outside the area. The housing stock is now in a worse condition. The continued shift to a low-income population means that the deterioration of the housing is accelerated because residents are less able to afford improvements.
Vacant sites remain derelict or are developed for warehousing or offices. No new manufacturing businesses are attracted to the area because the sites are relatively expensive, in need of development and because there are now too few skilled workers living locally.	
But the easy availability of cheap, old premises, together with a pool of poorly paid workers, attracts a number of small-scale, low-wage, low-productivity industries which do nothing to increase the prosperity of the area.	The emigration of younger, more skilled workers continues, leaving behind an increasingly aging, unskilled, badly paid and insecurely employed or unemployed, badly housed population.

(Based on Community Development Project, *The Costs of Industrial Change*, p.10.)

Revision

1. Refresh Your Memory

Make sure you know the meaning of the terms: mechanisation, mass production, automation, microprocessors, multinational companies, nationalisation, redevelopment, redundancy.

2. Check Your Understanding

Be able to explain in your own words:

(a) Why Britain was once referred to as 'the workshop of the world'.

(b) The difference between 'mass production' and 'automation'.

(c) The difference between 'friendly societies' and the 'new unionism'.

(d) The difference between 'distressed areas' and 'inner cities'.

(e) What is currently meant by the term 'new technologies'.

(f) What is meant by 'capital-intensive high-technology plant'.

(g) What is meant by 'sweated labour'.

(h) What is meant by 'economic dualism'.

3. Essay Questions to Try

(a) 'Automation is the name given to industrial processes which use machinery and computers not only to make goods but also to control, by 'feedback' mechanisms, the rate of production, the input of raw materials and the co-ordination of separate processes. In automated factories less manpower is needed, but workers have to understand the whole process and their responsibility is much greater.' Why are sociologists interested in automation?

(b) 'It has been suggested that automation will bring a new golden age of leisure and plenty for everybody. It has also been suggested that automation poses the greatest threat to our standard of living and way of life since the Industrial Revolution.' (Adapted from E. Kristenson, *Automation and the Workers*.) What are the possible consequences of automation?

(c) What factors helped to make Britain one of the first industrial nations? Why did those areas which helped to pioneer the Industrial Revolution begin to suffer as soon as capitalism began to expand?

(d) How were the old ruling families of Newcastle able to flourish for more than 150 years in the North-East of England?

(e) In what ways has the state attempted to intervene in the economic problems caused by industrial change in Britain since the Second World War?

(f) 'No one should be surprised at the concentration of the unskilled in the inner city. It can be explained very simply. Most of the firms employing skilled labour have moved elsewhere, and those which remain no longer use traditional skills.' Discuss.

(g) To what extent does 'sweated labour' contradict the process of concentration and centralisation that has taken place in the development of capitalism during this century?

(h) Explain how, over the years, the social characteristics of local communities are directly related to the fortunes of their local industries.

(i) Why has there been a decline in Britain's manufacturing industries since the war?

Further Reading

The Costs of Industrial Change
The Making of the Ruling Class
The State and the Local Economy
Workers on the Scrapheap

(All of these are CDP publications and can be obtained from the Home Office, Urban Deprivation Unit, Horseferry House, Dean Ryle Street, London SW1P 2AW.)

8

WORKING LIVES

The Definition of Work

You may consider that four hours spent digging in the garden is an example of 'hard work'—or that a housewife who cleans the house, washes and irons the clothes and buys in the family's groceries for the week is engaged in 'work'. But neither of these activities is technically regarded as work. The modern definition of work is not something which demonstrates activity, effort or achievement in itself, but something related specifically to paid employment. Work is something that earns a wage or a salary and which involves being hired by an employer.

For many people work is the least rewarding part of their lives. The hours they spend each week at work are often hours of endurance rather than hours of pleasure. For them work is a 'necessary evil', something which has to be done to earn a living but which brings little personal satisfaction. In times of high unemployment many feel grateful to have jobs, even though they do not particularly enjoy the work they do.

Other people find their work interesting and rewarding, especially if it gives them the opportunity to make full use of their skills and abilities. If their wages and working conditions are good so much the better, but often the sense of 'job satisfaction' is an extra bonus which cannot always be measured in monetary terms. Most people spend their prime waking hours at work, base their identities on the jobs they do and are rated by others in relation to them. And yet the impact of work is often neglected compared to the brash, glossy, consumer-orientated view of society that so many people accept.

Studies of Work

The studies of 'work' referred to by sociologists are varied. Some have concentrated on the personal experiences of different kinds of jobs—for example, the case studies collected in the *New Left Review*'s two volumes on *Work: Twenty Personal Accounts*, edited by Ronald Fraser. Others have examined the impact of 'extremely dangerous' occupations like coalmining (*Coal is Our Life*, Dennis, Henriques and Slaughter) and trawler fishing (*The Fishermen*, Tunstall) as a way of understanding the wider family, social and community life of those

186

involved. In their studies of 'Affluent Workers' in the Luton car industry of the early sixties, John Goldethorpe and David Lockwood set out to investigate the embourgeoisement thesis of Abrams and Rose (*Must Labour Lose?*, 1960), Zweig (*The British Worker in an Affluent Society*, 1961), and Klein (*Samples From English Culture*, 1965)—in other words, to find a 'typically affluent' working-class population and to discover how middle-class it had become in terms of its political and social allegiances and general lifestyle. Huw Beynon's study, *Working For Ford*, is also about what it is like to work in a car plant, but reveals in a vivid and direct way the processes by which conflict is managed in large companies, and how shop floor workers and their shop stewards express their political and economic aspirations through their unions. Others have tried to identify the characteristics of work which provide 'job satisfaction'—sometimes in an attempt to advise about the improvement of working conditions or to make comments on the quality of industrial relations between different employers and their workers.*

Job Satisfaction

People attach different meanings to their work and derive different amounts of satisfaction from doing it. In trying to identify the factors which make for job satisfaction, sociologists have carried out a number of surveys. In general it is thought that people with professional jobs and skilled workers get more job satisfaction than others, especially if they enjoy a fair degree of independence and responsibility. Those jobs which involve a 'caring responsibility' for other people—like nursing, social work and teaching—are often referred to as 'vocations' and it is assumed that workers like these are more committed to the people they care for than arguing about wages and working conditions. This idea that certain people have 'a sense of vocation' has often been used to persuade workers in these jobs to be less trade-union-minded than other employees. In recent years, however, the low pay of nurses and social workers in particular has made many of them feel that their sense of responsibility to their patients and clients is being exploited by employers and they are now much more likely to consider using trade union tactics to improve their wages and working conditions.

Other kinds of jobs which seem to provide a fair amount of satisfaction are those done by skilled workers and craftsmen. Sociologists have found that when a worker is involved in making something himself—like a piece of furniture—which involves judgement and skill, he is much more likely to find that work satisfying than if he is con-

---

* *Job Satisfaction*, edited by Mary Weir, Fontana, London, 1976.

tinually pulling a lever or fixing a screw on an assembly line, without ever seeing the finished product he has helped to assemble.

Contact with others also seems to be a crucial factor. If relations at work are friendly and if the employers are considerate and fair, workers are likely to be much more content with their jobs than if they are treated unjustly or if they are working with people they do not like.

For many people, however, work is only a necessary evil which provides little personal satisfaction. They need to earn money to live. When working conditions are bad, wages are low and tasks are routine and boring, it is hard to develop enthusiasm and commitment to what you are doing. Lateness, absenteeism and 'skiving' of various kinds are typical responses to tedious and unrewarding jobs. For many, there is a sense of 'never really achieving anything' and a dreary sameness which makes work something to be endured rather than enjoyed.

Jobs which involve hard physical labour or dangerous and unpleasant conditions, like coalmining and deep-sea fishing are hardly likely to provide much job satisfaction either. But sociologists have noticed a special unity and sense of mutual support among workers in such jobs, that spreads over into their family life and leisure time, and is probably a response to the awfulness of the conditions and the frequent dangers they share at work. Although the British trawling industry is now virtually dead, the unemployed and aging fishermen in ports like Hull and Grimsby still talk with surprising emotion about their experiences at sea. And miners, for many years a badly paid labour force working in dangerous and unhealthy conditions, have turned their sense of mutual allegiance and shared experiences into a particularly effective and militant form of trade union organisation.

One of the consequences of automation, as we have already seen, has been the reduction in need for skilled labour and the increasing use of machines and computers to do the jobs once done by men. In terms of job satisfaction such developments have brought mixed blessings. Working conditions have become easier and the working week has become shorter, but many feel reduced to the role of machine minders. Others have experienced redundancy and unemployment for the first time in their lives.

Although work can be tedious, unemployment—in a society in which everyone is expected to work—can be a debilitating and depressing experience. Because the job people do affects so many other aspects of their lives, and influences the way in which they are regarded by others, to be without work can reduce a person's status, self-image and identity as a 'useful member of society'. The unemployed are so often either pitied or denounced as work-shy and neither stereotype provides a very attractive image to live on.

The Influence of Work on Leisure Activities

Ask most people about themselves and they will tell you what job they do. Whether they enjoy their work or not, it certainly is one of the main ways in which people establish their identities.

Work also has a tremendous influence on people's 'non-working' lives in a variety of obvious and less obvious ways. Since a person's job determines his income, it also determines where he can afford to live and how much money he has to spend on furnishing his home and financing leisure activities. Hobbies like skiing, yachting and scuba-diving, for example, are obviously reserved for the relatively affluent (and energetic!), whereas fishing, watching football, dancing and drinking can be enjoyed by more or less anyone.

For some workers their leisure time seems to be almost an extension of their work. It would be difficult for professional writers and cricketers to know when work stops and leisure begins, for example. For low-paid workers, on the other hand, leisure time is often a precious commodity. Much of it gets eaten up by the overtime and shift work that seem necessary to ensure a living wage.

Workers in routine and boring jobs are those most likely to make a clear distinction between their work and their leisure. Many may actually feel that they only really 'come alive as people' when they leave work.

Studies of workers in dangerous and demanding jobs like coalmining and trawling have shown how the comradeship of working relationships, in which people often have to depend on each other for their own safety, spills over into leisure time friendships. Although Hull trawlermen in the heyday of the fishing industry and on three-week trips to Iceland had only a day or two at home with their wives and children between trips, they spent a good deal of it in the local pubs and clubs with their shipmates. And in traditional coalmining communities, the men's world of the pubs and working men's clubs is still one that is only grudgingly shared with wives and girlfriends on certain days of the week.

For some, leisure time is an escape from the tedium of routine jobs, and most factory labour forces have a surprising number of active sportsmen, amateur gardeners, fly-fishermen and musicians. But for many, the monotony of work spills over into the monotony of leisure, and television viewing and tinkering with the car become the main demonstrations of activity.

Workers engaged in professional jobs and those who experience a good deal of job satisfaction are more likely to have an active and varied social life than manual workers. This is partly a matter of income and the ability to afford holidays and travel, for example. But workers in professional occupations are also more likely to have had satisfactory educational experiences in the past. Interests kindled at school or college in the arts, theatre, music or painting may well continue into adult life. Certainly the adults who continue with part-time study, evening classes of various kinds and 'educational' hobbies are more likely to be those who have already experienced a good deal of educational success.

For women workers leisure time is less likely to be something they call their own. Although more women work outside the home these days, and the roles of husbands and wives within the family have had to change as a result, women are still mainly responsible for housework and childcare. For full-time workers a good deal of their leisure time is eaten up by catching up with their other work as housewives and mothers. Compared to manual workers, professional women workers may be more fortunate. Their extra earning capacity often allows them to afford domestic help at home or to be able to pay for child-minders and for nursery provision for their children.

The Culture of Work

Paul Willis * stresses the importance of understanding the 'culture of work', precisely because it is so central to the cultural identity of individuals. By 'culture' he is not referring to 'artifice and manners, the preserve of Sunday best, rainy afternoons and concert halls' but to 'the very material of our daily lives, the bread and butter of our most common-place understandings, feelings and responses'—in other words to the whole of our way of life (see p. 111).

In one sense there are as many cultures as there are jobs and workers involved in them, but at the risk of oversimplification it is possible to distinguish between two main cultural responses to work: that of the working class and that of the middle class. The two are different from each other in most respects, and in many ways they are opposed to each other. They are certainly not of equal force when measured in terms of social power. So far as society is concerned, the middle-class culture of work is part of the dominant or mainstream culture of society and the working-class culture of work is subordinate to it.

Middle-class Culture of Work

The middle-class culture of work is described by Willis in 'ideal type' terms. It is not based on actual experiences of work but on the values, assumptions and framework within which various middle-class experiences of work are usually understood. It has three main character-istics:

1. It is 'dead straight'—that is, the 'private world' of the workers'

---

* 'Shop-floor Culture', in *Working-Class Culture*, J. Clarke, C. Critcher and R. Johnson, Hutchinson, London, 1979.

values, attitudes and aspirations are just the same as those of the 'public world' of the enterprise they're engaged in. The concepts of 'career', 'staff', 'job satisfaction', etc., all belong to the middle-class world in which work and non-work selves are in harmony. The possession of 'professional identity', 'intrinsic satisfactions' and even 'vocation' are central to this experience of work.

2. The second characteristic is based on a sense of rationality, the knowledge that future career prospects and promotion can be accurately plotted by 'careful assessment and the rational analysis of ability and opportunity ... set your target, aim at it, monitor your progress, correct course, achieve it'. This expectation of choice and control is, of course, quite different from the resignation with which most shop-floor workers accept that the same thing will happen to them, *whatever* they decide to do.

3. The third characteristic reflects the 'monopoly over definitions' which the members of dominant groups in our society have established in everything from the educational system to the mass media. Applied to work this monopoly is able to present itself as 'the way things are', the 'only sensible way' of looking at things, against which all other views are misguided, unreasonably subversive or just plain silly. You cannot beat the system; nor should you try since it represents the best of all possible worlds. This consensus view of society, in which all are engaged in a common enterprise concerned to 'increase the national cake', rarely asks itself the questions which might interest others like, 'How, and on what terms is the cake made? Who chose the ingredients? Why is the cake cut horizontally to give icing to some and sponge to others? and why do those who weren't even in the cookhouse get the biggest portions?' (Willis). If you ask any of these questions you are a trouble-maker.

Working-class Culture of Work

The extent to which people accept or subscribe to the middle-class culture of work is largely academic so far as Willis is concerned. Having recognised that, for good or ill, it is the one which reflects the values of ruling groups in our society, his concern is rather with the culture of the subordinate class. He concentrates his attention on the working-class culture of work for three reasons: because it relates in number terms to the experience of the vast majority of the people; because, he claims, it is systematically misrepresented by middle-class culture and the media; and because it is important to know the life experiences which go into the production of commodities in a consumer-orientated society.

Although the surface features of working-class labour may have changed since Marx first discussed the relationships of production in the nineteenth century (see p. 7), the essential characteristics of people working in conditions set by others—to make goods for the profit of others, in return for wages—still holds true. The major reason for this kind of employment is not to provide fulfilment and the satisfaction of a job well done—though this may result incidentally, depending on the work—but to create profit. If this means boring, repetitive or physically hazardous employment there is nothing in the moral code of capitalism to prevent it. One of the main themes repeated consistently in the personal accounts of manual work collected by editors like Fraser is the alienation described by workers in mindless, routine jobs, in which time hangs heavy on their hands, in which no intelligence or control over the work process is required and in which nothing, except wages, is expected from the drudgery of work. A job is not done out of interest but merely as a way of earning money.

An assembly line worker at Fords interviewed by Huw Beynon* sums up the view exactly:

'You don't achieve anything here. A robot could do it. The line here is made for morons. It doesn't need any thought. They tell you that. "We don't pay you for thinking," they say. Everyone comes to realise that they're not doing a worthwile job. They're just on the line. For the money. Nobody likes to think that they're a failure. It's bad when you *know* that you're just a little cog. You just look at your pay packet—you look at what it does for your wife and kids. That's the only answer.'

They all tell the story about the man who left Ford's to work in a sweet factory where he had to divide up the reds from the blues, but left because he could not take the decision-making. Another said, 'When I'm here my mind's a blank. I *make* it go blank.'

It is not surprising, therefore, that many such workers have little sense of loyalty to the work—a fear of redundancy maybe, but no sense of 'hard work and commitment' that permeates definitions of vocation and responsibility in middle-class jobs.

Shop-Floor Culture

A common fallacy of sociological accounts of alienated labour, though not Beynon's, which concentrate on 'the meaninglessness' of boring work, is the failure to recognise that, despite bad conditions, lack of control, and frequent exploitation, people do look for meaning, they do impose frameworks, they do seek enjoyment in activity, they do exercise their abilities. In practice this response occurs in spite of, rather than merely as a result of, the prevailing conditions of work. In many respects it is 'in opposition' to the prevailing ideas of work

---

* *Working for Ford's*, Huw Beynon, E.P. Publishing, Wakefield, 1975.

which characterise middle-class culture. Willis identifies two of its main strengths:

1. The strength of the sheer mental and physical power to survive in hostile conditions. Not much, you may say, if you have never had to face the prospect of hard physical labour, but it provides the basis of other forms of response and also the focus for a good deal of pride, self-esteem and the mystique of masculinity in working-class culture. It may be that new technologies are increasingly replacing the need for physical strength in many jobs, although such jobs do still exist in abundance. But even where mechanisation predominates, in the so-called light industries, considerable endurance is still required and images of physical strength persist to make factories very masculine institutions.

This association between self-esteem and masculinity based on strength is, as we have already seen (see p. 129), very much a part of traditional working-class culture. But it is a characteristic which helps perpetuate sexist attitudes to women in the home and divisive competition between male and female manual workers in the labour force.

2. The strength of profound confidence expressed in the culture of the shop floor, based partly on common sense, partly on ability and partly on cheek. In one way it is a means of 'regaining control' over a process which others *really* control, by joining with fellow workers in an informal resistance against a good deal of the formal organisation of the workplace. A bit like the counter-school culture of 'the lads' (see p. 124), shop-floor culture has a solidarity and sense of camaraderie which enables those involved to manage a good deal of their time at work 'on their own terms' and 'in opposition' to what is considered ideal by the formal management structure. This includes the distinctive language and humour of the shop floor. Willis estimates that up to half of the verbal exchanges on the shop floor are not serious or concerned with work activities. They are practical jokes, 'pisstakes' or 'kiddings'—some are sharp, others cruel and many are about disruption of production and the subversion of the bosses' authority and status.

Cultural Weaknesses

The culture Willis describes is vigorous and strong and like the counter-school culture of 'the lads' is full of political significance. But like their culture also, it is equally limited. Because it exists as a sub-culture in a context dominated by the decisions of others (about investment policy, the organisation of production, marketing and the extraction of profit, etc.) it is ultimately unable 'to challenge the middle-class culture of work which sits on top of it and obscures it'. The shop floor, like the school and the neighbourhood, is an arena for economic and cultural conflict, but it is very parochial in its vision: 'its riveting concern for the workplace—and specific work places at that—prevents the connecting up of work experiences, issues and social structure'. It is not political; even in its relationship to and representation by the trade union movement, shop-floor culture is largely unpolitical.

Just as the Labour Party 'in theory' represents the interests of the working class, but draws some of its support, and most of its personnel, from other groups, so too does the trade union movement act as a form of working-class political representation which is 'one remove' from the majority of those it represents. It presents the institutionalised form of the opposition culture of the shop floor, but although it is close to that culture, and has been born out of it, it is also distant from it. In becoming organised, in defining ends and means, and in entering into negotiations with management 'in a responsible way', the trade union movement has frequently become another kind of authority over the worker. It often intervenes to cut out 'time-wasting' practices—the seedbed of shop-floor resistance—and can even 'put over' the management's case to workers in order to abide by agreements it has already made with management negotiators. Frequently, therefore, trade unions, acting as a kind of cultural go-between, and in the process of 'responsible negotiation with management', concede a good deal of the strength held by the shop floor.

Clearly this tendency is greater the more elevated officers in the union structure become, and local organisers and shop stewards are likely to be closer to shop-floor culture. Willis sees this as the unions having 'lost touch with' and even as 'a betrayal' of the real radicalism of the shop floor. But recent history does not always support his interpretations.

Just as the mystique of masculinity also sustains the most reactionary of attitudes to women, so too can other aspects of shop-floor culture be seen as something short of radical. A significant number of shop-floor workers are dominated by or deferential to those who employ them. It is a well-known fact that Conservative governments which consistently represent social and economic interests not particularly in sympathy with the class interests of manual workers are repeatedly returned to power with the considerable support of working-class voters (see p. 270). A major reason for the Conservative electoral victory of 1979, for example, was that a vast number of shop floor workers among others blamed the Labour government for the behaviour of the unions, and resented the increasing power which they seemed to be appropriating 'on behalf of the workers' but which the workers did not agree with.

An undue tolerance of the media provides another challenge to Willis' romantic notion of shop-floor radicalism. Again it is well known that the media in general are owned and controlled by middle-class people with economic interests different from those of working-class interests. And yet the working class provide a huge and largely uncritical audience for reactionary and often disparaging media messages on television and in the popular press. Because those who create the television programmes and write the newscopy are with few exceptions middle class, their distance from the realities of working-class life means that they rely on stereotypes and prejudice for most of their assumptions. The irony is that the 'real cultural meanings are taken by the media, transformed and caricatured, and returned to the working class—the mass audience—in unrecognisable forms'. Indeed, the misrecognition is so great that despite what working-class people *know* of their *own* lives, they are prepared to accept contrary media images as a legitimate picture of how *other* people live. It is not difficult in these circumstances to persuade working-class people that on the one hand affluence is within their grasp, and on the other the destructive behaviour of trade unionists has to be prevented and opposed.

These are perhaps arguments for conceding that national unions 'have lost touch' with the shop floor but not for assuming that shop-floor culture is automatically a radical one.

'Enlightened' Management

The radical potential of shop-floor culture without a coherent or cohesive political identity has also been weakened by its discovery and colonisation by the 'human relations' school of management. Tony Topham * describes how psychologists in America in the twenties and thirties first discovered that the social bonds between small groups greatly influence their attitudes and help determine production levels, and that relationships in informal work groups are much more influential on worker behaviour than the physical conditions of work. Workers in small groups tend to have loyalties and allegiances and to make up their own rules in a way which is not always in the best interests of their employers. From this 'discovery' arose a 'human relations' breed of social investigators—academics and others—employed by management to find solutions to their problems of low productivity and lack of cooperation on the shop floor. Their advice to management—considerably extended and elaborated over the succeeding decades—has been to find ways of manipulating the social relationships of informal groups to achieve cooperation, improve morale and to encourage greater productivity. Willis describes this process as 'the colonisation of shop-floor culture' which, like other

---

* 'Approaches to Workplace Organisation in Industrial Studies', Tony Topham, *Industrial Studies, 1. The Key Skills*, Arrow, London, 1975.

colonisations, is based on the attempt to destroy the culture already existing. Thus innovations concerned with 'employee-centered supervision', 'worker participation' and 'job enrichment' have been employed to harness the strength and neutralise the opposition of shop-floor culture. The illusion of self-control given to the workers by these innovations has distracted many from the fact that the basic structures of power remain exactly the same as before and that much of the potential power of the shop-floor culture has been destroyed in the process.

The Professions

To talk of people 'having a profession' is to talk of those the Registrar General, sociologists and most members of the general public would agree are middle class. The definition of a profession is generally held to be an occupation which involves knowledge and a good deal of training with some kind of advanced education, but it is not a concept which is very precise. The professions have always presented sociologists with problems—what is their real character? How do they differ from each other and in relation to other occupations? And what is their significance in the class system and social structure? A major weakness of most sociological definitions is to take the profession's own definition of itself too seriously, without looking critically enough at what is being said. The result is that a number of traits or characteristics have been identified as those which the professions are believed to possess and which are then used as a yardstick when assessing the claims of other occupational groups to professional status.

The 'Old' and the 'New' Professions

The term profession is often associated with older and prestigious occupations like medicine, the law and the church, but there has been a steady increase during this century of 'newer professions' associated with science and technology, education and journalism, government and welfare services. The tendency is sometimes to lump them all together but in fact there are considerable differences between them in terms of status, influence and autonomy.

The old image of a profession was one based on independence and, the church and the army excepted, one in which a rare breed of experts sold their skills directly, in return for a fee. This characteristic still persists in some respects and helps to keep the legal, stockbroking and accountancy professions, for example, extremely lucrative and exclusive occupations. Many of those increasingly referred to as the 'newer professions' on the other hand—teachers, social workers, government officials and scientists, for example—earn salaries (as distinct from wages) like other paid employees and some of them, like teachers and nurses, make up quite large occupational groups in society.

Most professions, old and new, have some characteristics in common. To become a member of a profession usually requires a long period of specialised training in order to master a body of knowledge, like law or medicine, at the end of which a qualification is obtained. Most professionals are also bound by a code of conduct, either written or unwritten, which defines their relations with clients and also controls the conduct of the profession itself. The most exclusive professions have a good deal of control over who is allowed entry to their ranks and in maintaining standards of 'proper conduct' within them. The British Medical Council, for example, receives complaints about its members but makes its own private decisions about their culpability. Those guilty of outrageous personal or professional conduct may be 'struck off' the medical register, but in most cases a 'united front' is maintained in the interests of preserving 'the good name of the profession' from public censure.

Professions and Other Workers

Comparisons between members of the professions and other workers reveal differences in their work, market value and status. Membership of one of the older professions usually allows the most independence. They sell their skills to a client in return for a fee, and work individually or in partnership with others as they choose. The newer professions like teaching, journalism and social work are treated by the general public with less reverence. They too have a good deal more independence and flexibility in their working responsibilities and more job security than manual workers, but like other paid employees, they work for wages and can be hired and fired. Unlike wage labourers in manual or white collar jobs, the work of professional workers goes relatively unsupervised. They have more control over the day-to-day organisation and practice of their work and very often they are concerned with exerting influence over and making decisions about other people's lives.

Professional workers are likely to get more 'job satisfaction' from their work—which does not mean it is easier than other types of work. It can in fact be very consuming of time and energy outside the strict confines of the working day. It is often said that when manual workers or office workers go home they are able to put work out of mind until the next day, but that professional workers find it difficult to distinguish between their working selves and their private selves. Members of professions tend to be committed to what they are doing—for many and varied reasons, no doubt—but this means that there is often no clear demarcation between their work and non-work time. This takes different forms depending on the profession. A good deal of business is agreed 'over dinner' or 'at the club'; many teachers spend their own time in out-of-school activities with children, or in attending in-service courses and conferences; social workers with clients to be concerned about do not always forget about them as they leave the office. But if the demands are great, so are the rewards. Professional workers are much less likely than wage labourers to be bored by their work, they are allowed to exercise a good deal of personal judgement, and salaries, especially in the older professions and in science and engineering, for example, are high.

Professional Status and Social Respect

The status of different professions reflects the different values which society places on their skills. The more a society values a particular skill the higher the remuneration is likely to be and the greater the degree of independence and influence the profession can claim for itself. Doctors and lawyers provide two of the best examples of well entrenched professional occupations. They act independently, they decide who they will recognise as colleagues, they preserve a monopoly over the body of knowledge which identifies them as expert, and they control, as we have seen, the conduct and discipline of their members.

The extent to which the status and influence of key professions is the result of society's dispassionate recognition of their worth is a matter for debate, however. Some hold strongly to the view that 'almost anyone' can be a labourer but very few can be lawyers, architects or accountants. Others, whilst recognising the special expertise of professional workers, take the view that in a hierarchical society in which economic resources, power, influence and educational opportunities are unevenly distributed, the capacity of those in positions of influence to define as superior the resources which they have the monopoly of, and which they can in turn use to reinforce their superiority over others, acts as something of a self-fulfilling prophecy. It may be that there is no significant difference between the professions and other occupations which entitles them to special status and favourable financial rewards, merely that in the competition between different occupations in the past the professions have been more successful at persuading others of the legitimacy of their claims.

Sociological Disagreement

The disagreement between sociologists about the description and significance which is given to professional occupations depends to some extent on differing sociological perspectives. Functionalists (see p. 10) tend to explain professionalism as a way of organising those occupations which are socially most important in an appropriate way. Such work is said to involve the application of specialist knowledge only available through lengthy training and reflecting values which are considered to be unquestionably good and in the public interest. The high financial rewards of some professional workers are justified by reference to their qualifications. The independence and the right to control their own concerns represents a kind of 'deal made with society' in which freedom is allowed in return for high standards of service.

The functionalist description of the professions is challenged by all those who claim that what counts as 'socially important' is not always accepted as equally important by all sections of society. Also the claim that professional workers are concerned with the 'common good' is not always the view shared by their clients or by those who cannot afford their services.

An important comment has been made by Wilson in a study of professionalism in medicine and social work. If the professions are all involved so intimately in the pursuit of the 'public interest' and have philosophies and practices based upon commonly shared values, why is it that conflicts between different professions arise? (For example, between medicine and social work and between education and government.) The only explanation of such inter-professional rivalry is that different professions have different definitions of the common good or that they are trying to denigrate or usurp each other's knowledge.

Professionalisation

In a society in which there is competition between different occupational groups, one of the main ways of promoting the interests of one against the other is to gain the power to influence public policy decisions. A popular strategy available to occupations concerned to do this, apart from trade union organisation, is to increase the strength of their organisation by the process of professionalisation. One way of looking at this is to concede that professional workers will best be able to serve the interests of their clients if they constitute a strong, independent and well qualified group. Another way is to suggest that power and influence also serve the personal ends of their possessors.

Social Work

Let us take social work as an example of an occupation currently undergoing professionalisation.

Origins

The origins of social work lie in early voluntary and philanthrophic organisations which responded to the problems brought about by rapid industrialisation and urbanisation in the nineteenth century. Contemporary social work has grown out of increasing state intervention in those areas of family and community life which have presented problems to the state or which have persisted as a result of poverty and disadvantage in an unequal society. The majority of social work today is supported by state legislation and most social workers are the employees of local or central government and other official agencies. To achieve some kind of professional recognition for themselves social workers have sought to establish their credibility in terms of those criteria usually used to define a profession: specialist knowledge, a code of ethics, competence and autonomy.

Knowledge

The study of the theory and practice of social work is currently developing its own literature based on the social sciences and the application of these to social work practice. Most social workers in training also have 'fieldwork placements' in which they are supposed to learn the skills of 'group work' and 'case work'.

Ethics

The British Association of Social Workers' (BASW) code of ethics states:

'. . . basic to the profession of social work is the recognition of the value and dignity of every human being irrespective of origin, status, sex, age, belief or contribution to society. The profession accepts responsibility to encourage and facilitate the self-realisation of the individual person with due regard for the interest of others.'

The Central Council for Education and Training in Social Work claims that this is a very liberal value which is highly regarded in western society and is by no means the monopoly of social workers. However, western society frequently seems to be ambivalent about its importance and often allows it to be over-ridden by other considerations. Ferguson, in *Social Work: An Introduction*, comments:

'The belief that the individual is worthy of the social worker's concern and his best efforts stands in marked contrast to working assumptions in other fields, where differential treatment is given to individuals according to their intelligence, their "moral goodness" or their socio-economic status. The responsibility which this principle places on the social worker is that he must consider every individual, however ignorant or dirty or deviant, worthy of respect.'

Some of those who, as clients, have experienced the 'respect of social workers' frequently complain that many of them also pay only lip service to their ideals.

Part of the problem is that social workers are caught up in a fundamental contradiction. They are employed by, and accountable to, the state and must abide by certain legislation. Yet their declared concern is for the autonomy of their clients and the satisfaction of their needs. For those who hold a consensus view of society there may be no conflict in these two responsibilities, but for those who do not it may well be argued that the needs of the individual and the needs of the state do not always coincide. For example:

1. A main method of working so far as social work practice is concerned is to present the client with a full range of options, help him/her to explore each one fully and thus enable the client to arrive at an informed decision about what to do. However, for clients who are victims of multiple economic and social deprivations the illusions of choice between alternatives may be more apparent than real.

2. Equally, social workers have statutory responsibilities which mean that, despite the wishes of clients, they are often impelled to intervene and to implement the arbitrary decisions of social service departments.

3. In other circumstances, and domestic violence is a good example, because there are insufficient places in which battered women and their children can be housed, and because a major concern of social work is to enable 'families in trouble' to sort themselves out so that they can live together in harmony, few of the 'full range of options' available to battered women are ever seriously presented.

Competence and Autonomy

Only about 40 per cent of those presently employed as social workers are professionally trained and this undoubtedly handicaps the BASW in gaining professional recognition, status and autonomy for social workers. It cannot claim 'special expertise' so long as many of its members work alongside untrained personnel with identical responsibilities and tasks to perform. To speak with any real authority the association needs to increase the proportion of trained social workers and exercise some degree of quality control over the process of professional training. An additional strategy, and one which the BASW is campaigning for, is to make sure that only appropriately qualified personnel are appointed to new vacancies.

Because trained social workers are still in a minority, however, those who are trained tend to be promoted rapidly to senior posts, in which they no longer deal personally with clients, but in which they have major responsibilities for the supervision of less experienced and unqualified staff.

Moves to distinguish between untrained and qualified social workers and to identify the latter as an elite group within the profession, entitled to a greater degree of professional freedom, are matched by trends in some social service departments towards the establishment of 'career grades' which enable experienced and competent social workers to continue direct work with clients without sacrificing their promotion prospects. Trends like this seem to be indicative of moves within the profession to 'recognise training' and to 'create greater autonomy'—both of which are developments characteristic of attempts to strengthen professional credibility, organisation and identity.

Women in the Workforce

It is interesting that when most people, including sociologists, talk about work, it is generally assumed to be a predominantly male activity. We are so accustomed to thinking of 'manpower' as masculine that we ignore the fact that between 40 and 50 per cent of the labour force consists of female workers. Perhaps it is time to consider some of the special factors relating to the work done by women.

Out of a total workforce of 25.9 million in 1976, 10 million were women. In the 25 years between 1951 and 1976 the number of people working rose from 22.6 million to 25.9 million—an increase of 3.3 million. Of the increasing numbers of workers, 3 million were women and 0.3 million were men (see Fig. 9). Of the 10 million working women, 6.7 million were married.

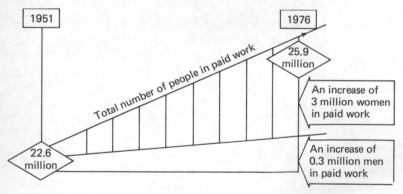

Fig. 9. Increase in the total workforce 1951–76.

Married Women

In 1951 less than 22 per cent of married women were in employment (either full-time or part-time). By 1971 the number had risen to 42 per cent of married women. By 1976 the proportion of married women under 60 who were doing or looking for paid work was over 50 per cent in each age group, and experts were predicting that the numbers would go on rising (see Table 9).

Table 9. Proportion of Married Women in Employment

Age	Actual percentages			Projected percentages
	1951	1971	1976	1986
16–19	38.1	41.6	51.9	51.9
20–24	36.5	45.7	54.6	55.7
25–44	25.1	46.4	56.3	62.8
45–59	21.5	53.4	61.3	70.5
60+	4.6	14.2	13.5	16.0
Total	21.7	42.2	49.0	54.9

Women's Jobs

'Most employed women in Britain are doing a job that provides a background against which other people can carry out what society believes are the more productive and important kinds of work. The woman employed outside her home is much more likely to be making biscuits than cars, serving coffee than building ships, doing the dry cleaning rather than the dock work.' (*Women at Work*, Mackie and Pattullo.)

Roughly four out of five women working in Britain today are to be found in one of four types of jobs: clerical and secretarial work, domestic and catering work, unskilled factory work and shop work.

Women in the Professions

'Anyone reading newspapers over the past five years would imagine that women, rather in the manner of astronauts, have done the impossible. The news of the first woman judge, the first woman to become Prime Minister, the first woman professor of brewing, the first woman rabbi, suggests that there is now very little for women to complain about in employment prospects. If one woman can do it so, the feeling goes, can they all. A useful counter to this list of firsts is trying to spot the tenth woman judge, a female majority in the Cabinet, the female vice-chancellors of British universities. Sightings here will be conspicuous by their absence.' (*Women at Work*, Mackie and Pattullo)

Despite the fact that women now make up almost 50 per cent of the labour force, the proportion of women in top professional jobs is low, as Table 10 shows.

Table 10. Women in the Professions

Profession	Number of women (%)
Architecture	4.3
Bar Council	8.0
Institute of Directors	1.0
Medicine	27.0
Law Society	4.0
Engineering and allied industries	2.0
Journalism	23.0
Universities: teaching and research	11.0

So far as the 'top professions' go there is nothing inevitable about women gaining more equality. There have always been a few women who have 'reached the top' and whilst they may have had to prove themselves almost 'better' than men to be 'equally' respected, they have not paved the way for the general acceptance of women on equal terms in the professions.

Teaching, nursing and social work are, of course, the exceptions. But they are also the less well paid and least socially powerful professions. And, of course, the hierarchy in each of them is male with women not promoted to key posts in proportion to their numbers in the lower grades.

Part-Time Work

Many women take part-time work because they need to earn money but still need time to look after children, do the housework, shopping and cooking and care for old or disabled relatives.

Because of these other demands on their time they have to be 'less choosy' than women without such responsibilities or men, and as a result often have to accept wages which would be unacceptable to full-time workers. Consequently, most part-time work is badly paid and unprotected by the legislation and conditions of employment which apply to full-time workers.

A report published in 1978 by the Low Pay Unit explained why women part-time workers are frequently used as a cheap alternative to full-time men by many employers. 'Their attachment to work, need for money and potential for workplace militancy is low compared with full-time male workers. It is thought that female part-time workers will accept not only low wages but less favourable conditions of service as well.' The worst examples of low pay are apparently in pubs and shops. The Report found that four out of five barmaids and half of part-time shopworkers earned less than 85p an hour. But low pay is not the only problem. Part-time workers have to put up with poor working conditions and they are often excluded from fringe benefit schemes. Part-time workers are less likely to belong to trade unions and more likely to be made redundant in times of economic crisis.

The Wages of Full-Time Workers

Women's wages in manufacturing industries tend to be higher than in the service industries. In industries in which women are the majority of the workforce, their wages tend to be lower. Textiles, clothing and footwear were the three lowest paid manufacturing industries in 1976.

In a report published in 1978 by the Equal Opportunities Commission (see p. 208) it was shown that despite equal pay legislation the gap between what men earn and women earn is still considerable. Although young men and women starting work in their teens earn about the same, the difference soon begins to show. In 1976 the highest paid male manual workers, aged between 21 and 24, were averaging £80.80 a week, while women of the same age were averaging £54 a week. Among the same group of non-manual workers, men were earning £74.60 per week compared with women's £59.10. The report showed clearly that the lowest paid section of the workforce comprised mainly women and in 1976, 43 per cent of full-time women workers earned less than £40 a week compared with only 5 per cent of men.

Muriel Turner of ASTMS (the Association of Scientific, Technical and Managerial Staff) commented at a recent TUC women's conference: 'Women are told so often that they are patient, conforming, modest, good at routine work and so on that in the end they come to believe it themselves: and a very useful belief it is for employers who want an uncomplaining workforce slaving away unambitiously at routine work on low pay, and for those men—and there are many of them—who are afraid of female competition. The problem with most women is not to make them work harder but to stop them breaking their backs for a pittance. . . .'

Equal Pay and Sex Discrimination

At midnight on December 28th, 1975, important legislation affecting women came into force in Britain. The Equal Pay Act, first introduced in 1970, finally became law and the Sex Discrimination Act made it illegal, in most circumstances, to differentiate between men and women in work, leisure and educational opportunities. A special Equal Opportunities Commission was set up to hear complaints about discrimination and to make recommendations to the government about future changes in the law.

In some ways the legislation has helped women. It has helped to create a social climate in which women increasingly expect to be treated equally with men and it has prevented some of the more obvious forms of social and legal discrimination. But many people feel that the legislation does not go far enough. Loopholes have appeared which make it possible in practice for employers to find ways of avoiding paying women equal wages, and the Equal Opportunities Commission has turned out to be a rather moderate, secretive body, reluctant to campaign actively on behalf of women or to speak out strongly against continuing discrimination.

Equal Pay in Practice

In circumstances in which employers do not give equal pay to women when they are doing 'the same or broadly similar work' to a man or when their jobs have been rated as being of 'equivalent value' to a man's in a job evaluation scheme, women can have their claims heard by an Industrial Tribunal.

Industrial Tribunals

Industrial Tribunals sit all over the country. Each has a lawyer as a chairperson and two lay members: one trade unionist and one nominated by management. Only 23 per cent of lay members are women but it is government policy to have one woman member on every tribunal dealing with sex discrimination or equal pay cases.

Application to Industrial Tribunals under the Equal Pay Act

The figures for applications to Industrial Tribunals concerning equal pay in the two years 1976 and 1978 are given in Table 11.

In the three years between 1975 and 1978 when the Equal Pay Act

Table 11.   Equal Pay Applications to Industrial Tribunals

	1976	1978
Total number of applications	894	343
Settlements reached by conciliation before the Tribunal hearing	81	29
Withdrawal of application before the Tribunal hearing either as a result of private settlements 'out of court' or for unknown reasons	499	234
Applications upheld by the Tribunal	83	24
Applications turned down by the Tribunal:		
(a) Not 'like' or 'equivalent' work	169	22
(b) Not 'same' employment	4	—
(c) Evidence of 'material differences' in the job	38	27
(d) Other reasons	20	7

first came into force only 2,836 people brought cases under the Act compared to more than 35,000 men and women who brought cases for unfair dismissal under the terms of the Employment Protection (Consolidation) Act, 1978. For those who did, the success rate was low. Some applications were withdrawn before reaching the Tribunal—not always because a satisfactory settlement was reached but because women were intimidated or unconfident about continuing with their case. Only about a third of the applications which have been made so far have been successful. In the early days especially, judgements by different Tribunals in different parts of the country often contradicted each other and women who won equal pay in one area were denied it another for no logical reason.

Has the Equal Pay Act given Women Equal Pay?

Despite some improvements in pay levels, women are still paid significantly less than men. A report published by the EOC in the summer of 1980 said the gap between men's pay and women's pay was wider than at any time during the previous 10 years. If overtime pay was included, the gap would be larger still as men generally work longer hours than women.

Table 12. **Average Gross Hourly Earnings (excluding Overtime)**

	1970	*1977*
Men	67.4p	177.4p
Women	42.5p	133.9p
Women's earnings as a percentage of men's	63.1%	75.5%

(*Source:* Equal Opportunities Commission, Second Annual Report, 1977)

The main reason for women's continuing lower pay is lack of equal job opportunities. Most women find themselves trapped in less-skilled and lower grade jobs which will continue to be less well paid regardless of legislation.

It was to deal with this problem of inequality of opportunity that the Sex Discrimination Act was passed.

The Sex Discrimination Act

The Sex Discrimination Act came into force on December 29th, 1975, at the same time as the Equal Pay Act. Under the Sex Discrimination Act it is now illegal to treat one person less favourably than another on grounds of sex in employment, training and education, and in the provision of housing, goods, facilities and services. The Act also applies to discriminatory advertising.

The Sex Discrimination Act in Practice

Compared with other employment laws, relatively few people have used the Sex Discrimination Act. In the first three years the Act was in force only 643 individuals took cases to Industrial Tribunals under the Sex Discrimination Act, compared to over 35,000 men and women using the Employment Protection (Consolidation) Act, 1978, to complain about unfair dismissal. For those who have tried to use the Act the success rate has been low: only about 16 per cent of cases brought before Tribunals have been successful.

Some changes which have come about as a result of the new Act being introduced are noticeable but very superficial. For example, advertisements used to recruit new employees are not allowed to encourage applications from one sex or the other but that does not mean that employers do not continue to discriminate once the applications have been received. Questions asked of women at interviews about their domestic responsibilities and the kind of prejudices which encourage employers to give preference to men rather than women are illegal but very difficult to prove. Like the Equal Pay Act, but *unlike all the other employment legislation* in the Sex Discrimination Act, the burden of proof is on the applicant and not the employer. The employer is presumed to be innocent until he is proven guilty.

Ignorance Reigns

Research done by Mandy Snell at the London School of Economics showed that ignorance of the sex discrimination legislation is widespread among managers, trade unions, and women. Knowledge of the law relating to equal opportunities is negligible. The small number of cases taken to Industrial Tribunals proves that ignorance can be paralysing. Equally serious is the fact that many managers and trade unionists do not recognise that they have a problem of a lack of equal opportunity. Nevertheless, a lot of women bitterly resent their low status and lack of opportunity to improve their skills.

Some sections of the Sex Discrimination Act are potentially quite useful here but are seldom used. *Sections 47 and 48* provide for special training programmes for jobs where women are under-represented. A company could, for example, decide to choose only female apprentices in an engineering trade because none of their engineers are women. This kind of positive discrimination is permissible and could be an important way of increasing the numbers of women entering skilled jobs previously monopolised by men.

The Equal Opportunities Commission

The Equal Opportunities Commission was set up under the Sex Discrimination Act in 1975 to help create a climate of opinion in which attitudes about equality between men and women in every aspect of social and economic life could be encouraged.

The Commission was given powers to undertake formal investigations into employment practices, the organisation of education, the provision of goods and services and any other areas in which discrimination against women is suspected. It has the power to serve non-discrimination notices on employers and other agencies to stop discriminating practices. In addition, it can take legal action in the courts on behalf of individuals. However, the Commission has been frequently criticised for taking too little advantage of the powers at its disposal. In 1978, for example, it took only three cases to courts under the 'goods, facilities and services' section of the Act. It carried out no formal investigations and issued no non-discrimination notices. Fear of failure has been a major deterrent.

In the area of employment and education from 1975 to 1979, the EOC launched only six formal investigations: one into the Thameside Education Authority, accused of withholding grammar school places from girls, which failed to prove discrimination; three into the recruitment and promotion policies of the Leeds Permanent Building Society, Gwent College of Further Education and the Sidney Stringer School and Community College in Coventry; one into the structure of SOGAT (Society of Graphic and Allied Trades); and one into Electrolux at Luton.

It took the Commission more than two and a half years to serve a non-discrimination notice on the Electrolux Company. Compared to the Commission for Racial Equality, set up in 1976, which has undertaken more than 60 formal investigations in three years, the EOC has simply not been very active. It has tended to rely on persuasion and to avoid confrontation as the best way of influencing practice. Many have argued that its reluctance to be more positive is a betrayal of its more vital role of propaganda, active campaigning and of encouraging women to make better use of the legislation intended to help them.

Unemployment

The period after the mid-1970s has seen a level of unemployment in Britain which has been higher than at any other time since the Depression of the 1930s (see p. 168). Automation and factory closures have been one cause of the problem, but the dramatic increase in the numbers of people unemployed (nearly 3 million in 1981) is not only the result of a fall in the numbers of those who are employed. The number of people in employment has decreased in the last three or four years, but at the same time the number of people in the labour force has increased. So unemployment has been added to by the fact that there are fewer jobs available and more people looking for work.

As unemployment has increased, as a result of redundancies in industry and cuts in public spending, the first workers to be laid off have been those who are most vulnerable—women, school-leavers, young workers and immigrants.

Women are vulnerable because they are often part-time, non-unionised and subject to the familiar prejudice that they only work for 'pin money'. The view is still common among employers and trade unionists alike, that men, as the 'breadwinners' in families, should have more job security than women. The fact that many women, as single parents, widows and divorcees, are frequently the sole breadwinners in families is often forgotten. The official figures show that unemployment among women increased dramatically during the 1970s but the real extent of the problem is disguised. Many women do not register as unemployed because they have not been encouraged in the past to pay full National Insurance contributions which would entitle them to unemployment benefits (see p. 231). The proportion of unemployed women in the country almost doubled between 1973 and 1975 but a survey published by *Woman's Own* in 1976 found that of the women seeking work, only three in ten were registered as unemployed. In other words, the numbers of unemployed women were much higher than the official statistics would lead you to believe.

Immigrant workers are also particularly hard hit by unemployment. Many work in the public services industries like the Health Service and public transport. These are some of the key industries in which jobs are being cut to reduce public spending costs. Others work in small businesses, restaurants and factories, many of which have been forced to close down because of the economic depression. Whatever the industry, immigrant workers are often the first to lose their jobs because the union has accepted a 'last in—first out agreement' with the employers. Young black workers leaving school know that unemployment is especially bad in some areas but that to be black is an additional disadvantage because of racial prejudice. In the eighteen-month period before May 1975 unemployment rose by an average of 65 per cent for all workers. But for West Indian, Asian and African Britons the increase was 156 per cent, and for young West Indians it was 182 per cent.

Most public attention has been focused on the plight of young people out of work. In 1972 the school-leaving age was raised to 16. Although the official reasons given at the time for raising the school-leaving age were educational ones, many people now believe that this was the first of many subsequent attempts to disguise the real extent of youth unemployment.

Youth unemployment, like unemployment generally, is currently an international problem. At a conference of world leaders held in London in May 1977 it was reported that 7 million young people in the rich countries of Western Europe, North America and Japan were out of work. In these countries the under-25s made up 22 per cent of the working population but 40 per cent of the unemployed.

A report from the Common Market at the beginning of 1976 confirmed that in the EEC one quarter of unemployed workers were under 25. By the end of that year the proportion had risen to one third and the level of unemployment among the under-25s was double the level for the workforce as a whole.

The British Government's response to youth unemployment has been to give financial subsidies to firms offering new jobs to unemployed young people, and to introduce a whole series of job creation schemes and training opportunities. The Job Creation Programme, for example, was intended to provide six months' temporary employment in jobs which would be 'useful to the community'. Schemes for environmental improvements and various sorts of community service have been created by local authorities and various charitable bodies to help keep the youngsters 'off the streets' for a while and to give them something useful to do. But schemes like these have only ever been seen as providing temporary employment: once a youngster's brief experience on a Job Creation Project was over he or she was returned to the dole queue. Work Experience Programmes, Community Industry and now Youth Opportunities Schemes were also sponsored by the government's Manpower Services Commission to provide other types of temporary employment and further training. The real problem with such initiatives is that although they are apparently designed to make youngsters 'more employable', the number of jobs needed significantly to reduce youth unemployment does not currently exist. And as indicated earlier, once the 'silicon-chip revolution' takes hold of British industry, the number will be even fewer.

When unemployment figures began to increase in the mid-1970s, most politicians and social commentators regarded it as a 'regrettable but temporary problem' caused by an economic crisis abroad, inflation and bad industrial relations at home. The view most commonly expressed today, however, is rather different. It is now believed that far from being a passing phenomenon, unemployment at the present level will increasingly become an established feature of industrial society.

Revision

1. Refresh Your Memory

Make sure you know the meaning of the terms: work, culture, 'ideal type', alienation, profession, self-fulfilling prophecy, client, industrial tribunal, job evaluation scheme, 'pin money'.

2. Check Your Understanding

Be able to explain in your own words the difference between:

(*a*) A person's working and non-working life.
(*b*) Heavy industry and light industry.
(*c*) The 'older professions' and the 'newer professions'.
(*d*) Industrial Tribunals and the Equal Opportunities Commission.

3. Essay Questions to Try

(*a*) What is meant by the term 'job satisfaction'? What factors tend to contribute towards and to detract from a worker's feeling of job satisfaction?

(*b*) 'Most people spend their prime waking hours at work, base their identities on the jobs they do and are rated by others in relation to them.' How accurate a comments is this and what does it tell you about the significance of work in our society?

(*c*) Discuss with the help of illustrations some of the main differences between the 'middle-class culture of work' and the 'working-class culture of work'.

(*d*) Discuss the ways in which the shop floor can be described as an arena in which social, political and cultural struggle takes place.

(*e*) What factors should sociologists take into account in the study of professions?

(*f*) Identify some of the key strategies available to occupational groups engaged in the process of professionalisation. Why have some occupational groups sought to increase their professional status?

(*g*) 'Women are told so often that they are patient, conforming, modest, good at routine work and so on that in the end they come to believe it themselves: and a very useful belief it is for the employers who want an uncomplaining workforce slaving away unambitiously at routine work on low pay, and for those men—and there are many of them—who are afraid of female competition. The problem with most women is not to make them work harder but to stop them breaking their backs for a pittance.' (Muriel Turner, ASTMS.) Discuss.

(*h*) To what extent has recent legislation about equal pay and sex discrimination helped to improve the pay and job opportunities of working women?

(*i*) Discuss the reasons which make women, immigrants and working-class youngsters most vulnerable in times of high unemployment.

Further Reading

Coal is our Life, N. Dennis, F. Henriques and C. Slaughter, Eyre and Spottiswoode, London, 1956.

Human Experience and Material Production: The Culture of the Shop Floor, Paul Willis, Centre for Contemporary Cultural Studies, Birmingham University, Birmingham, 1975.

Job Satisfaction, Mary Weir (Ed.), Fontana, London, 1976.

The Affluent Worker: Industrial Attitudes and Behaviour, J. Goldethorpe and D. Lockwood, Cambridge University Press, Cambridge and London, 1968.
Work: Twenty Personal Accounts (Vols. 1 and 2), Ronald Fraser (Ed.), Penguin, London, 1969.
Working for Ford, Huw Beynon, E. P. Publishing, Wakefield, 1975.

9

POVERTY AND WELFARE

State Intervention

In this chapter we shall consider poverty, welfare and the role of the state in the process of social control. It is usual to make a distinction between the state's benign intervention in things like education, health, housing, poor relief, social insurance and other social services—those areas which are usually considered the responsibility of the Welfare State—and the state's more repressive mechanisms exercised through the criminal law, the police force and the army.

In both respects it is hard to distance oneself and become a critical observer of these institutions because of the morass of ideological assumptions which surround the way we think about them. The dominant view in society promotes the idea of the state as a neutral organisation made up of, and representing the interests of, all classes, pursuing 'the common good' in 'the national interest'. This is especially true of the Welfare State, more so in the 1960s and 1970s than now perhaps. The slogans of that era about 'community development', 'participation', 'family-centred services', 'equality of opportunity' and 'positive discrimination' in favour of the 'socially disadvantaged'—all extended the philosophy of liberal democracy and led people to believe that humane, universal, egalitarian and non-stigmatising services could be developed within the context of the existing economic structure.

To consider these ideas now, after a period of significant cuts in public spending by both Labour and Conservative governments, presents a fairly different picture of the way in which the Welfare State is currently regarded by present governments. Frequent attacks on 'welfare scroungers' and 'waste' by both the politicians and the media reflect a disturbingly reactionary ideological response to the sentiments of the late sixties and early seventies and have begun to creep into more overt political strategies associated with monetarist economics.

Functionalist sociology associated with Durkheim, Parsons and others has traditionally explained the purpose of various state institutions as fulfilling necessary roles which enable society to continue. As societies become bigger, more complex, more dependent on advanced technologies and intricate divisions of labour and more urbanised, the simple tasks of education, caring for dependent members, containing antisocial behaviour and the like can no longer be left to the family or to the immediate community. The state must increasingly intervene to organise and rationalise those aspects of social life which in a complex society can hardly be left to chance.

Richard Titmuss in his famous *Essays on the Welfare State* (1963) was greatly influenced by this tradition. He suggested that the Welfare State's important role was to support complex divisions of labour and the social needs generated by an industrial society.

'All collectively provided services are deliberately designed to meet certain socially recognised "needs"; they are manifestations first of society's will to survive as an organic whole and secondly of the expressed wish of all people, to assist the survival of some people.'

More recently, sociologists critical of functionalist perspectives have taken a rather different view. They point to the coincidence between the interests of capitalism in general and the functioning of the Welfare State in particular and explain the expansion of the state as being in direct relationship to the needs of the prevailing economic system—in simple terms, the need to reproduce the social relations of production. But more of this later.

It is also important for sociologists to consider those views of state intervention which do not coincide with dominant ideology. Given that the Welfare State, for example, is often said to be administered in the interests of the working class, and is frequently portrayed as a major achievement won in historical struggles by the organised pressure of the labour movement, why is it that so many 'clients' of the social services and those 'dependent' upon the state for their income are so ambivalent, disillusioned and suspicious of its practices? For women especially, nowhere is their economic and ideological oppression by the state more clearly demonstrated than in the provision of social security. For many consumers of the Welfare State there is a real contradiction between the alleged benevolence, sexual and class neutrality and state institutions, subject apparently to democratic controls and people's individual and collective experiences of the very opposite.

The Discovery of Poverty

Of all the social problems faced by the Victorians, the increasing concern that society was being polarised into classes of people hostile to each other was summed up by Disraeli in his novel *Sybil*, in which he described the rich and poor as 'Two nations between whom there is no intercourse and no sympathy; who are ignorant of each other's habits, thoughts and feelings, as if they were dwellers in different zones, or inhabitants of different planets.'

Marx and Engels, although motivated by rather different concerns made the same point three years later in 1848: 'The modern bourgeois society that has sprouted from the ruins of feudal society has not done away with class antagonisms. It has but established new classes, new conditions or oppression, new forms of struggle in place of the old ones. Our epoch, the epoch of the bourgeoisie, poses however this distinctive feature: it has simplified the class antagonisms. Society is more and more splitting into two great hostile camps, two great classes directly facing each other: Bourgeoisie and Proletariat.' *

Marx and Engels viewed the increasing polarisation between classes as a crucial stage in the inevitable destruction of capitalism by class conflict. Disraeli's views were rather more in line with the thinking of other social reformers in Victorian England. He was concerned in some way to relieve poverty as a way of closing the gap between the lives of the rich and the poor. Unlike Marx and Engels, he did not use an historical and economic analysis to trace 'the logic' of social developments but like many other Victorians assumed that the social conditions which they were concerned about—although they did not really *know* very much about them—somehow emerged in a fairly haphazard and unrelated kind of way. Shocked by the possibilities of class hostilities, they remained confident that with appropriate social intervention, harmony could be preserved.

Whilst Disraeli speculated about transforming the country through a revitalised Tory party with relevant new ideas, other politicians, social reformers, statistical societies, Royal Commissions and philanthropists of various persuasions were busily gathering information needed to inform themselves about 'the real and actual condition' of the society in which they lived. These investigations had led to legislations like the Poor Law Amendment Act, 1834, the first Public Health Act, 1848, and the Factory Act of 1850 which introduced a 10½-hour day—all intended to check some of the worst abuses of industrial life.

The widespread and varied reform movements of the early and mid-Victorian period represented the first real attempts by governments to understand and come to terms with 'the strange society' they had inherited. Unlike Marx and Engels, none of these official and semi-official initiatives made explicit political links between the process of industrialisation, the development of capitalism and the social consequences of these people's lives. Rather, they took the view that if revolution, moral decline and human misery were to be prevented then information had to be gathered about the nature and the extent of poverty, and measures had to be introduced to alleviate its worst excesses.

It was in this historical context that Joseph Chamberlain, a leading Liberal of the time, advocated a state welfare programme (1885). He began with the question 'What ransom will property pay for the secu-

---

* Communist Manifesto, 1848 (Foreign Languages Publishing House, Moscow).

rity which it enjoys?' and later observed that 'the foundations of property are made more secure when no real grievance is felt by the poor against the rich'. In other words, the origins of the state's concern to 'help the poor', as with state intervention in education, was as much and perhaps more to do with protecting property interests by 'gentling' and 'controlling' the masses than any explicit commitment to social reform for its own sake.

By the end of the nineteenth century the principle of state intervention to relieve particular distress or to protect society from the consequences of unsavoury social problems which might get out of hand was well established.

Industrialisation and the Growth of Capitalism

One of the main consequences of industrialisation and the development of capitalism has been an increasing amount of state intervention in those aspects of social life which relate to and derive their characteristics from the social relations of production. Thus working conditions, housing, family life, health, education and welfare increasingly became the concern of state organisations as distinct from voluntary, religious, self-help and philanthropic organisations.

Since Britain was the first country to establish machine-based industrial production, she had unrivalled access to the world's markets for a significant period of time and the profits which were earned went to establish the vast wealth of the capitalist owners (see Chapter 7). But industrialisation did not only introduce new methods of working and new trading empires to conquer: it brought fundamental changes in the whole organisation and character of society. It necessitated shifts in population from the countryside to the towns which grew up around the factories, the main sources of energy, raw materials and trade routes. The population of cities like Liverpool and London mushroomed and new urban centres sprang up to house the workers and administer the business of expanding industry. All these developments brought about significant changes in the lives of working people. A large wage-earning class was created and concentrated in the growing urban areas. Industrial change also created a clear distinction between different groups in the relationship of production and reinforced the sexual division of labour between men and women in both production and reproduction. It created a clearer distinction between breadwinners and dependants than had been usual in pre-industrial family economies. And despite the visible affluence of the owners it brought poverty, hardship and living squalor to many of the workers and those who relied upon the vagaries of their wages.

By the end of the century legislation relating to elementary education, working conditions, housing and the prevention of diseases were all typical of the government's response to the changes in social conditions which were brought about by the Industrial Revolution. The significance of these developments has more to do with establishing the basis for future state interference than their effectiveness as reforms, however. Although parliament felt increasingly obliged to introduce social legislation on a scale hitherto unprecedented, neither the central nor local government institutions were equipped financially or administratively to enforce it.

At the same time, the concentration of large numbers of workers in workplaces and industrial towns provided the opportunity for class awareness to develop as workers learned from their common situation that their interests were not the same as those who employed them. By the middle of the nineteenth century the working class in Britain already had a history of political protest. At one time they had supported middle-class attempts to prevent the aristocracy retaining a monopoly over voting, but when the 1832 Reform Act failed to concede anything to the working-class people they turned to Chartism as an alternative. All kinds of popular politics, from the Corresponding Societies of the 1790s through Chartism and Owen's Co-operative Movement, contained a fairly lively and continuous educational tradition as well. This tradition was expressed in three main ways: a deep suspicion of all forms of provided and philanthropic education and benevolence, a wide range of alternative definitions of knowledge and alternative strategies for changing the world independent from bourgeois control, and a vigorous and varied educational and organisational practice which laid emphasis upon achieving a more just social order.

The growth of friendly societies and trade unions was a further indication of workers' concern to band together to protect their interests against the exploitation meted out by their employers (see p. 170).

Although the historical struggle of the working class has always been seen by their organisations as one of continually improving and securing their conditions of existence and standard of living, thus making the achievement of any social reform seem like a minor victory, historians tend to forget that workers have often been resistant and extremely suspicious of reforms provided by a capitalist state which are offered to forestall and control their potential for rebellion. Friendly societies are often viewed as essentially reactionary organisations concerned to prevent the emergence of social insurance and based on the internalisation of middle-class values about self-help. But 'self-help' can also be interpreted as 'independence' and there is no doubt that the members of friendly societies identified themselves as a class whose interests were contrary to those of other classes and they certainly identified in class terms with the poor who were not members of their societies.

So far as the middle class were concerned the philosophies of individualism, self-help and *laissez faire* which dominated social and political thought in the nineteenth century had to give way to new ideas in the face of increasing public concern about poverty and revolution. The gradual changes in ideas were influenced by other factors too.

In 1885 the working-class men had been given the vote and as a result the Liberal and Conservative parties had to take more interest in their needs and to ensure that they were educated to use their votes wisely.

Socialist thinkers and enlightened Liberals increasingly argued that competitive self-interest was an immoral foundation for a just society and that everyone would benefit if it were replaced by more collective cooperation. These ideas became the basis of a new movement—the Independent Labour Party—and by 1892 its first three MPs had been elected to parliament.

The enquiries and statistics published by social investigators like Charles and William Booth and Seebohm Rowntree presented evidence of extreme poverty which despite popular mythology was not confined to the weak, lazy and debased but was part of the regular condition of large proportions of decent hard-working families.

The Turn of the Century

In 1899 Seebohm Rowntree made his first historic survey of working-class poverty in York. He found 20,302 people, or almost half the working-class population, living in a state of poverty without enough food, fuel and clothing to keep them in good health. About one third of those living in poverty did not earn enough money each week to keep their families, the rest could only barely survive. He commented: 'The wages paid for unskilled labour in York are insufficient to provide food, shelter, and clothing adequate to maintain a family of moderate size in a state of bare physical efficiency.' This assessment was calculated on the assumption 'that the diet is even less generous than that allowed to able-bodied paupers in the York workhouse and that no allowance is made for any expenditure other than that absolutely required for the maintenance of merely physical efficiency'.

Ten years earlier Charles Booth, a Liverpool shipowner, had made a similar survey in London and found that roughly one third of its population earned less than £1 a week. The first volume of his *Life and Labour of the People in London* dealt only with the East End. The second volume, published in 1891, covered poverty in London as a whole. These two volumes were expanded to nine by 1897 and seventeen by 1902–3. Rowntree's study demonstrated that poverty was not a problem confined to London alone. Booth wrote to him in 1901: 'You know with what interest I have watched your investigation into the condition of life at York . . . and the comparison (with my findings) as you have shown is very close. At this I am not surprised. I have, indeed, long thought that other cities, if similarly tested, would show a percentage of poverty not differing greatly from that existing in London.' On the basis of his findings Rowntree was forced to conclude that 'if the proportion of poverty in London is practically equalled in what may be regarded as a typical provincial town, we are faced by the startling probability that from 25–30 per cent of the town populations of the United Kingdom are living in poverty'. And this at a time when 77 per cent of the country's population lived in towns.

By the end of the nineteenth century Britain was no longer omnipotent in world trade and had begun to feel the effects of German and American competition. The rivalry with Bismarck's Germany, the poor health of the Boer War recruits, the decline in the birth rate, high rates of infant and maternal mortality alongside working-class pressure pushed the newly returned Liberal government of 1906 into reforms providing old age pensions, school meals, school medical inspections, labour exchanges and health and unemployment benefits. The emphasis was on social insurance rather than services, however, and as with other earlier initiatives the labour movement was decidedly ambivalent about their implications. They particularly disliked the notion of national insurance for a whole variety of reasons, including the use of labour exchanges to recruit blacklegs and the threat to the cooperative and independent traditions of the friendly societies.

A good deal of public attention and ideological pressure was turned towards women as mothers, and the duty of women to fulfil their natural functions efficiently and effectively became the subject of countless contemporary speeches and publications. Since women were held somehow responsible for the prosperity and well-being of the nation they were all too readily blamed for the high rate of infant mortality. In 1913 Maud Pember Reeves and the Fabian Women's Group published their detailed account of what it was like for a working man's wife to bring up a family on only 20 shillings a week. The families in Lambeth whose daily budgets were scrutinised for four years between 1909 and 1913 were by no means the poorest of the poor. The men were 'respectable, in full work or at a more or less top wage, young, with families still increasing'. Their wives were described as 'quiet, decent, keeping themselves to themselves' kind of women, who were independent, resourceful, hardworking, respectable—but very poor. The conclusions of the Fabian women about the women of Lambeth was that 'the cause of infant mortality was not that mothers were ignorant or degenerate, but that they had too little money to provide for their own and their families' essential needs; that they lacked decent housing, domestic equipment, adequate food and clothing, and any facilities or opportunities for recreation.'* All this was to add more weight to the Fabian pressure for social reform and to encourage the intelligent and liberal middle classes that only the state could remedy such appalling injustices.

After the First World War a recession in world trade hit Britain earlier than other countries. The twenties and thirties were the period of the Depression during which time unemployment reached dramatic proportions and workers in the traditional industries of mining, iron and steel, shipbuilding and textile production found themselves out of work for months and years on end. Unemployment benefits were paltry and repeatedly cut back as economic conditions got worse. Apart from unemployment, housing was also a terrible problem and although in 1918 Lloyd George had promised 'a land fit for heroes to live in', for many people this was never to be.

Poverty and Unemployment Between the Wars

State provision for the unemployed in the period after the First World War still depended to a considerable extent on the Poor Law first introduced in the reign of Elizabeth I. It had been modified by the Poor Law Amendment Act of 1834 which established Boards of Guardians in each local area to administer relief. Enforcement of the Poor Law was very strict after 1834 although there were considerable local variations. Poor Law relief was only supposed to be granted to those who had no alternative but the workhouse. Those living at home could only receive relief in exceptional circumstances, it was means tested, and for those who were capable of work, labour yards were established at the workhouses where able-bodied claimants had to do menial work such as stone breaking in exchange for their out-relief (relief paid to those not resident in the workhouse). Norman Ginsburg† comments: 'Such attempts to keep the unemployed in readiness for work continued into the 1930s and have more recently appeared in the less punitive form of the Job Creation Programme.' (See p. 211.)

Towards the end of the nineteenth-century a number of riots and demonstrations urged the state to take more responsibility for the unemployed but initial responses were experimental and small-scale.

The Unemployed Workers Act of 1903 encouraged the setting up of Distress Committees in local authority areas using the combined resources of the local authorities, the Poor Law unions and the charities. Their main aim seems to have been to distinguish the 'worthy unemployed' from 'the loafers' and to reinforce old prejudices about the deserving and the undeserving poor.

In 1909 Labour Exchanges were set up by Beveridge at the Board

---

* *Round About a Pound a Week*, Maud Pember Reeves, Virgo, London, 1979.
† *Class, Capital and Social Policy*, Norman Ginsburg, Macmillan, London, 1979.

of Trade and a National Insurance Scheme, which provided un-employment and sickness benefits to workers in a fairly limited number of trades, was introduced in 1911. The trades covered by the Act were restricted to building construction, shipbuilding, mechanical engineering, iron-founding, vehicle construction, and sand-milling—including in all about 2½ million workers. In 1916 the government extended the scheme to include munitions workers and in 1920 to all manual workers and non-manual workers earning less than £250 a year. This brought the numbers of insured people up to about 12,000,000.

The scheme had various weaknesses, however. It only applied to workers who had paid sufficient contributions, it paid more to men than women workers, and made no provision for unemployed workers' spouses and children. And since it was designed as a fairly temporary measure to tide people over bouts of unemployment between jobs, the benefit soon ran out. Rather than make all unemployed workers de-pendent on the Poor Law, the government devised the notion of 'extended benefit'. The idea was that insured people could continue to draw benefit as a kind of 'privilege' because strictly speaking they were no longer entitled to it. The new measure was accompanied by a variety of administrative devices to make sure that additional benefits were not received too easily. Notions of deterrent, punishment and control were central to their administration, again to distinguish be-tween 'the genuinely unemployed' and 'the malingerer'. The two most important of these devices were 'the household means test' and the disqualification from benefit of those 'not genuinely seeking work' (NGSW). The household means test ensured that any earnings by any member of the family were taken into account when benefits were being calculated, which particularly discriminated against women, made other families totally dependent on the wife's earnings and caused the exodus of sons, daughters and even grandparents from the family homes, either to prevent their earnings being means tested or because the family members they depended upon could not afford to feed them.

A woman from St Helens describes the administration of the NGSW procedure:

'When you went in to see the clerk in the Labour Exchange, you had to tell him there was no work you could find. . . . They started a scheme of interviews during which you would be asked where you had looked for work. They made you go back for six days which was a week really. You were expected to name at least three places where you had looked for work in the morning and three places in the after-noon each day of the week. Most of the people who were called for interview didn't know of this unofficial rule and were knocked off the list wholesale. . . . At first you had to carry a notebook or a sheet of paper and get a signature from the manager at each works to say that there was no work. We soon put a stop to that. [She was a member of the Unemployed Workers' Movement founded in 1921.] We got two or three hundred men to queue at one place at the same time. The manager was soon ringing up the Labour Exchange telling them to stop. They altered it so you had to write it down yourself. Occasionally they asked to see it. If you failed to give the required number, you were sent before a court of referees and duly held to be "Not Genuinely Seeking Work".'*

There was an intense struggle over relief and benefits between the authorities and unemployed throughout this period and a fair amount of it became associated with the class struggle. Wal Hannington, born in North London in 1896, was a founder member of the National Unemployed Workers' Movement. In his book *Unemployed Struggles 1919–1936* he describes how masses of ex-servicemen returned home from the First World War to a land in which Lloyd George was still Prime Minister and after a war in which 'he had coined many trick phrases . . . to induce a war-weary nation to continue its sacrifices. The soldiers dying on the battlefield had been told that their sacrifices were not in vain, that they were "fighting for democracy", that they were "building a new heaven and a new earth" and that they were making "a land fit for heroes to live in", that it would be a land "flowing with milk and honey". The phrases lingered on after the war but . . . they rang like a bitter mockery in the ears of the men who had come from the bloody battlefield only to be cast on the industrial scrapheap of capitalism and to see increasing privation for themselves and their families.'

He describes how as unemployment rose in the winter of 1920, 'Local Unemployment Ex-Servicemen's Organisations' were formed. At first they had little sense of class solidarity and many of their members were too young to have experienced the organisation and political struggles of the labour movement before the war. They organised demonstrations to march the streets principally to collect money as charity from wealthy shoppers and others. Clearly this was a development which the authorities took little trouble to suppress because, as Hannington explains, 'charity-mongering was a safe outlet for the discontent of the unemployed, and was an effective means of keeping the unemployed divided amongst themselves and diverting their attention from the real problem of making the authorities face up to the task of providing adequately for them'.

As conditions got worse, however, social and political consciousness

---

* *Industrial Town*, Charles Forman, Paladin, London, 1979.

increased, demonstrations turned into confrontations and the police were used to disband both unemployed workers' marches and hunger marches with great ferocity.

For those not entitled to 'insurance-related benefits' or 'extended benefits' the only alternative was poor relief and attempts to influence the local Boards of Guardians became another important site of struggle between the unemployed and the authorities.

The Poor Law Boards of Guardians were locally elected bodies and by this time in some areas working-class and labour guardians were being elected. They were usually outnumbered but their influence could be considerable in areas in which they were supported by well organised unemployed workers' groups. The rallying cry adopted by the National Unemployed Workers' Movement was 'Work or Full Maintenance'. Technically 'out-relief' could still only be paid in exceptional circumstances, but with the slogan 'Go to the Guardians' huge demonstrations of unemployed workers marched on the offices of the Guardians, often occupying them, and refusing to leave until the Guardians agreed to relieve their distress. The agitation for poor relief became so strong that local Boards of Guardians had to provide out-relief irrespective of the law. At this point the government moved to prevent local labour guardians paying out relief at rates which threatened local wage levels by fixing the rates that local boards were allowed to pay. Relieving officers began to develop fixed scales of relief, varying according to family size and circumstances, and supervised increasingly by the means test. This is how a woman from St Helens describes it:

'They used to send the relieving officer to your home. If you had a piano, a gramophone, a good cupboard or any saleable article they would tell you to sell it before you got any relief. In some cases they looked to see how much was in the larder. I remember meeting a woman in Bolton with a son who was smaller than his next but two brother down, although he was 14. She said quite seriously, "We were on the means test when he was born. We couldn't afford to feed him properly." If you had any supplies at all, the amount was taken out of your parish relief. Sometimes, they didn't give you money at all, just food vouchers that you had to take to the grocer's shop. You weren't allowed to buy any luxury goods, no cigarettes, cakes or anything like that, only bread, bacon, tea, sugar and that sort of thing. They'd give you a cheque for ten bob or fourteen shillings, and that had to last.'*

Some Boards of Guardians continued to resist government pressures, however. Poplar and several other labour boards in East London, South Wales and the North of England continued to pay

---

* *Industrial Town*, Charles Forman, Paladin, London, 1979.

relief higher than government-recommended scales. In the years before the General Strike of 1926 about 200 boards, covering possibly half the population, were granting relief that in some way broke the regulations, though not always in the interests of the claimants. Before 1926 the 'Go to the Guardians' campaign had effectively established the principle of outdoor relief to able-bodied unemployed, and in many respects organised action by the unemployed, with the assistance of labour guardians, had succeeded in forcing the authorities to pay supplementary relief over and above what was being paid out at the labour exchanges. But such victories must be set in the context of continuing real distress. There was a very thin line between starvation and survival. And of course a good deal of class hostility and suspicion was generated then, as now, by the press. Wal Hannington comments: 'The capitalist press began to collect information about the amounts received by unemployed families and ran scare headlines about the "luxury of the unemployed at the expense of the ratepayers". They described this "generosity" as "a grave danger to the nation" and as "placing a premium on idleness".'

After the General Strike the government intervened again to reduce the local independence and resistance of labour guardians. Those boards which had been most sympathetic to the unemployed were by this time in serious debt and the government refused to allow them to borrow any money unless they abided by government instructions. 'Some of the principles of 1834 were implemented with a vigour reminiscent of the 1870s, which included rigorous investigation of suspected malingerers, stringent control of "out-relief" at uniform scale rates, labour tests and a more searching means test.' *

In 1929 the 635 Boards of Guardians were replaced by 146 Public Assistance Committees (PACs), direct election to them came to an end and poor relief became part of a more bureaucratic, more centralised and more remote system.

During the twenties the amounts of money spent on benefits to the unemployed and the numbers of people receiving benefit each year remained fairly constant, but in the first few months of 1930 both the numbers of people receiving benefits and the amounts of money paid out doubled and continued to increase. When the minority Labour Government of 1929 split in August 1931, Ramsay Macdonald formed a 'National Government' which quickly introduced measures to cut back on public spending, especially in relation to unemployment benefits. As a first step the level of National Insurance benefit was cut from 17 shillings to 15 shillings and 3 pence. Secondly, the contributory principle was reintroduced. Proper benefits could only be claimed for the first 26 weeks of unemployment and any 'extended

* Ginsburg, *op. cit.*

benefit' (renamed 'transitional benefit') was to be much more closely supervised by use of the means test. The means tests were to be controlled by the Public Assistance Committees rather than the labour exchanges and had the effect of removing thousands of unemployed claimants from insurance and transitional benefits onto poor relief. Because of the stringency of these reforms and the stigma attached to poor relief, and despite the record level of unemployment in 1933, a fall in the total expenditure on benefits and relief was achieved. The revisions created three distinct categories of unemployed: the short-term insured unemployed; the long-term ex-insured unemployed, receiving transitional benefits; and the long-term stigmatised unemployed, dependent on poor relief. None of the categories was without shame, however; they were socially divisive and by doing away with any sense of unemployment benefits being a 'democratic right' as distinct from 'an act of charity' or 'a punishment', they heightened tensions and bad feeling between conflicting class interests.

During 1932 and 1934 the National Unemployment Workers' Movement organised demonstrations and hunger marches to publicise their plight and to attempt to get the cuts made in unemployment benefits restored. The hunger marches of October 1932 and February 1934 were particularly brutally attacked by the police. In 1932 barricades were erected in the streets of Birkenhead and Belfast to protect unemployed workers from police raids whilst the press demanded special constables to protect ordinary decent citizens from the hordes of starving and unemployed workers who, they claimed, were being 'coerced by Moscow' to 'ferment hate'.

At the same time alarming reports from medical officers of local authorities, schoolteachers, and social workers drew attention to the serious deterioration in the health standards of the population. In 1934 Dr O'Hara, Medical Officer of the Durham County Society for the Prevention and Cure of Consumption, speaking at a meeting of the Society's governors, said: 'Most of our children are suffering not so much from tuberculosis as from starvation; 75 per cent of the cases admitted to the Society's sanatorium are definitely due to starvation.' A report written by the Medical Officer of Health for Gallygaer, issued in 1934, reported: 'The district has again had a continued epidemic of scarlet fever during the year, the majority of cases being of a severe type and complications were common. The general want of resistance to the attack and to the severity of the symptoms were in my opinion due to general malnutrition among the children, the result of the present unfortunate economic conditions prevalent in South Wales.' Sir George Newman, Chief Medical Officer of Health for England and Wales, reported in 1934: 'No fewer than 2 million homes in 1933 were striken by death or disease during the year. There was distress and privation, physical and mental in areas severely depressed by unemployment. Unemployment, undernourishment and preventable malady and accident seem to be the unavoidable concomitant of current civilisation in Western Europe today.' During 1933, 95,270 men and lads offered themselves as recruits to the army. Only 28,841 of them passed the eyesight and fitness tests.

After the 1932 hunger march the National Council for Social Services came into prominence in an effort to organise life among the unemployed. The Prince of Wales spoke in favour of social service centres 'to save the unemployed from demoralisation'. Mayors, councils, magistrates and clergy were urged to associate themselves with the provision of centres in which the unemployed could meet, play games, share out old clothes and possibly offer themselves for voluntary work. If this sounds familiar, so too were the objections to the idea voiced by the more politically conscious among the workers' leaders: 'We pointed out that whilst many of the persons responsible for these schemes might be doing so in the honest belief that they were helping the unemployed, nevertheless the sum total of their efforts amounted to keeping the unemployed quiet when they should be actively resisting their poverty conditions.' (Wal Hannington.) The National Unemployed Workers' Movement were perhaps justly suspicious. Nine government departments were represented on the National Council for Social Services, including the Ministry of Labour, the Ministry of Health and the Home Office. 'We could not believe that the Ministry of Labour which was operating the means test had any true interest in the welfare of the unemployed; or that the Ministry of Health would be any more sympathetic. Neither could we believe that the Home Office, which condones the clubbing down of unemployed workers in the streets when they march for bread, had suddenly become philanthropic towards the unemployed. . . . We saw social service schemes not merely as an effort to keep the unemployed quiet, but a clever move to prepare the way for a system of unpaid labour amongst the unemployed.'

The suspicions of men like Hannington were not altogether groundless and when in 1934 a new Unemployment Act was passed it was laid down that claimants who came under Part Two of the Act had to present themselves at residential or non-residential labour centres where they were to work in exchange for their benefit and pocket money. The significance of the 1934 Act was far greater than only this, however. It marked the end of the era in which locally organised pressure could be brought to bear on local employment committees, Boards of Guardians and even Public Assistance Committees. Now all authority was transferred to the central Ministry of Labour. Those who were uninsured had to apply for means-tested benefits at the new Unemployment Assistance Board, which was also administered by the Ministry of Labour, and which applied nationally uniform tests and rates of assistance. Despite local resistance, a centralised social security system had been created with an administration which was responsible to Parliament but immune from questioning on the day-to-day discretionary powers at its disposal. The local authority PACs were left with the sick, aged, disabled and women who were not compelled to register for employment but the Assistance Board took over responsibility for them as well during the Second World War. By 1948 all local political influence over out-relief was at an end and its administration was centralised in a huge and fairly anonymous bureaucracy called the National Assistance Board. So far as claimants were concerned, the loss of local control also meant an end to a much hated Poor Law structure and its replacement by a system of clear and uniform welfare rights centrally controlled and administered. But on the other hand, as Norman Ginsburg points out, 'State policy and administration had enhanced the divisions, within the working class and continued to ensure that at relatively low cost, the unemployed were kept in readiness for work at low wages.'* Since the 1930s there has been relatively little real change in the administration of social security, although the National Assistance Board is now known as the Supplementary Benefits Commission within the Department of Health and Social Security. One of the major effects of increasing centralisation has been to separate the issues relating to social security benefits and payments from the *general* class struggle and the concerns of the *organised* labour movement to a concentration on *individual* welfare rights and the take-up of discrete benefits.

A further step in the rationalisation of state intervention in social insurance and welfare provision was the famous Beveridge Report of 1942.

The Beveridge Report

In June 1941 the government ordered a special committee, under the chairmanship of Sir William Beveridge, to make a thorough investigation of all 'the existing national schemes of social insurance . . . and to make recommendations' about how they might be improved. The committee's report was published in 1942. It is generally thought that this report created the foundations of the modern social security system, but as we have already seen, so far as unemployment benefits and national assistance were concerned, the administrative procedures were implemented before the Second World War. It is more accurate to say that the reforms of the 1940s simply improved benefits and rationalised previous policies, but whilst Beveridge's recommendations became the basis of government policy after the war, his more progressive proposals about benefit levels and the unlimited extension of

---

*Ginsburg, *op. cit.*

the eligibility period for receiving unemployment benefits were in fact rejected by the post-war Labour government.

Beveridge's proposals were for a comprehensive system of social insurance to which all citizens over school age and below the age of retirement, and excluding students in full-time education, non-working wives and self-employed people earning less than a specified minimum, would contribute. Three guiding principles informed his recommendations:

'The first principle is that any proposals for the future, while they should use to the full the experience gathered in the past, should not be restricted by any consideration of sectional interests established in the obtaining of that experience. Now, when the war is abolishing landmarks of every kind, is the opportunity for using experience in a clear field. A revolutionary moment in the world's history is a time for revolutions, not for patching.

'The second principle is that the organisation of social insurance should be treated as one part only of a comprehensive policy of social progress. Social insurance fully developed may provide income security: it is an attack upon Want. But want is only one of the five giants on the road of reconstruction and in some ways the easiest to attack. The others are Disease, Ignorance, Squalor and Idleness.

'The third principle is that social security must be achieved by co-operation between the state and the individual. The state should offer security for service and contribution. The state in organising security should not stifle incentive, opportunity, responsibility; in establishing a national minimum, it should leave room and encouragement for voluntary action by each individual to provide more than that minimum for himself and his family.'

The plan was received with great enthusiasm by people generally—they queued up to buy copies and they read it. The TUC accepted almost every part of the report and despite the struggles over unemployment relief before the war their representatives declared themselves 'strongly in favour of contributory insurance ... contemptuous of "dodgers", and "of the type of person who will not join a Friendly Society" ... and favoured the withdrawal of public assistance from wives and children of workers who went on strike.' *

Interest in the Beveridge plan from the usually militant Clydeside Workers was also 'tremendous', according to a Ministry of Information document circulated in 1943. 'For a week or two war tended to take a back seat ... there has possibly been more discussion on this than on any other single event since the outbreak of war. ... Prac-

* Social Planning in Wartime: Some Aspects of the Beveridge Report, J. Harris, in *War and Economic Development*, J. Winter (ed.), Cambridge University Press, Cambridge and London, 1975.

tically everyone approved of the underlying principles and hopes ran high that the Plan would be put into operation as soon as possible.'

The wartime government and the ruling groups of the day were less enthusiastic. Churchill warned in 1943: 'A dangerous optimism is growing up about the conditions it will be possible to establish here after the war. Unemployment and low wages are to be abolished, education greatly improved and prolonged; great developments in health and housing will be undertaken; agriculture is to be maintained at its new high level. At the same time the cost of living is to be raised. The Beveridge Plan of social insurance, or something like it, is to abolish Want. . . . The question steals across my mind whether we are not committing our 45 million people to tasks beyond their compass, and laying on them burdens beyond their capacity to bear. While not disheartening our people by dwelling on the dark side of things, Ministers should, in my view, be careful not to raise false hopes, as was done last time about 'homes fit for heroes', etc. The broad masses of the people face the hardships of life undaunted, but they are liable to get angry if they feel they have been gulled or cheated.'

Labour spokesmen were more optimistic. James Griffiths, MP, said in the Commons debate of 1943: 'I suggest that the question which we ought to ask ourselves is not whether we can afford the Plan, but whether we can afford to face the post-war world without it. My view is that we cannot. . . . We have no right to ask our people to face readjustments without this Plan. We have made claims upon them and since the war began we have been increasing those claims all the time. We have called for sacrifices. . . . The response of our people has been wonderful, beyond praise, and I hope that we shall remember that we shall owe these people a debt that we must honour.'

Of course Churchill was right in his way: benefits and other Welfare State provisions would have to be paid for and they could not be bought lightly. Beveridge's scheme assumed a general consensus in society about 'the distribution of purchasing power' and the equal rights of everyone to welfare protection. A genuine Welfare State of the kind being advocated by Griffiths and socialists like Sydney Silverman within the Labour Party was not to be merely a palliative. It depended upon a rigidly managed economy. Such a situation existed during the war and for some time afterwards, and it helped to create a much more tightly-knit organic community than has existed either before or since. But these conditions did not last and when control relaxed and when personal affluence came to be regarded as socially acceptable again, a new basis for welfare had to be found. The Welfare State came to be judged in terms of its market value—and many felt that its true aim should be, as Charles Booth had suggested, the salvage merely of the casualties of society as it returned to an individualistic ethic.

Perhaps the greatest significance of the Beveridge Report lay in the way in which it was able to create support for a general philosophy of welfare despite opposition at the time from many in the wartime government and those in ruling groups. The enthusiasm for the report by the working class signified their acceptance of 'state welfare'— hopefully in exchange for full employment and in preference to private or trade union insurance, their only alternatives. But looked at critically, Beveridge's assumptions were not as 'revolutionary' as many people chose to believe. The report articulated more clearly than ever before in relation to social welfare a commitment to the ideology of citizenship, an unqualified support for the principle of contributory insurance and an implicit acceptance of women's subordinate position within the family.

Women Dependants

In the new Welfare State envisaged by Beveridge, women, especially married women, were allotted a very specific role. They were to be wives and mothers. The state would look after the breadwinner (the man), the breadwinner would look after his wife and his wife would look after the children.

The post-war Labour government helped to put this principle into operation by the National Insurance Act of 1946. Administrative costs were halved by this simple scheme: give the man the earnings, the tax allowances and the social security benefits, and allow him to look after his family in his own way. A married woman who did not work was provided for in her old age out of the married man's larger pension for which *he* had contributed. A married woman who did work could have a pension in her own right if she paid full National Insurance contributions but she was not encouraged to do so. In an attempt to strengthen women's economic dependency on their husbands and to emphasise their domestic and motherly 'duties', whilst at the same time 'keeping them in reserve' for low-paid labour when the economy needed them, married women workers were encouraged to opt out of most of the National Insurance scheme. Beveridge assumed that 'on marriage a woman gains a legal right to maintenance by her husband as a first line of defence against risks which fall directly on the solitary woman; she undertakes at the same time to perform vital unpaid service ... even if while living with her husband, she undertakes gainful occupation ... her earning is liable to interruption by childbirth. In the national interest it is important that the interruption by childbirth should be as complete as possible; the expectant mother should be under no economic pressure to continue at work as long as she can, and to return to it as soon as she can. ... To most married women earnings by a gainful occupation do not mean what such earnings mean to most solitary women [i.e. they represent 'pin money'—a term which Beveridge did not use but clearly meant]. . . . In sickness or unemployment the housewife does not need compensating benefits on the same scale as the solitary woman because, among other things, her home is provided for her either by her husband's earnings or benefit if his earning is interrupted.' Since married women's employment would be intermittent and low paid, National Insurance contributions would be a burden to both employees and those who employed them and if they were old, sick or unemployed they should surely be able to count on their husbands to support them! As a result, about three quarters of the married women in paid employment in the thirty years or so after the war were advised to pay reduced contributions, thereby excluding themselves from any independent right to unemployment and sickness benefits and National Insurance pensions (see p. 210). The minority who chose to pay the full stamp found that in relation to their wages the cost was high and the benefits minimal. Unemployment and sickness benefits were less than a man's and the pension rules were so complicated that very few married women were eligible anyway.

Peter Townsend's study of the Lancashire textile industry in 1951–52, which until its decline always employed predominantly women workers, found that official unemployment figures underestimated real unemployment by about 20 per cent, since most of the married women did not register as unemployed.* 'Having no entitlement to unemployment benefit and therefore not signing on at the labour exchange, these women returned to their families, where in several cases they had to support unemployed husbands and children out of savings and/or national assistance. Married women who had paid contributions received only 80 per cent of the benefit received by single people, while widows who had paid full contributions, received much lower benefit, because their widows pension was taken into account.' †

Since 1977 all women entering paid employment are obliged to pay a full National Insurance contribution. But those who were already 'opting out' before this date could continue to do so providing they stayed working for a further two years. This means that the new legislation could take as long as 30 or 40 years before it applies to all women.

Other Legislation

As we have seen, the National Insurance Act of 1946 implemented a modified version of Beveridge's proposals for universal benefits in return for contributory insurance. Other legislation passed by the postwar Labour government helped to cement the foundations of what is now considered to be the modern Welfare State.

---

* *The Social Minority*, Peter Townsend, Allen Lane, London, 1973.
† Ginsburg, *op. cit.*

In 1945 the Family Allowances Act was passed which gave an allowance of 5 shillings for each child after the first, up to the age of 16, or until he or she started work. The original amount, of course, has increased over the years. The cost of family allowances was not based on insurance contributions—the entire cost came out of taxation and any family could benefit regardless of its income.

In 1948 the National Assistance Act was passed to provide help for those who could not be expected to pay National Insurance contributions because they were blind, deaf, crippled, insane, disabled, unemployed widows or the wives and children of criminals. The Act established a National Assistance Board which, among other things, had to provide Reception and Re-establishment Centres for the homeless. In 1953 one quarter of the people living on retirement and widow's pensions could not manage without the additional help of the National Assistance Board. In 1966 the Board was merged with the Ministry of Pensions and National Insurance and it is known today as the Supplementary Benefits Commission within the Ministry of Health and Social Security. Unemployment benefits are still administered by the Department of Employment, however. Richard Titmuss argues that the Labour government wanted to maintain a distinction in the public image between 'social security as of right' and means-tested assistance. In other words, the 'image' of National Assistance was to be kept noticeably less attractive, and the rights relating to it were to continue to be hedged round with discretionary powers. Weightman, in an article in *New Society* (January 5th, 1978), claims that even today in DHSS offices there is a distinct difference in furnishings and atmosphere between the National Insurance section and the Supplementary Benefits section.

The National Health Service Act was passed in 1946 and came into force in 1948. From then on, the whole range of medical, dental, optical and hospital treatment was to be provided free to everyone. Those who wanted to continue paying for medical treatment could still go to doctors, dentists and opticians working in private practice but it was hoped that the state Health Service would be so good that everyone would want to make use of it.

All the teaching hospitals were nationalised and a national system of general practitioners was provided so that Health Service doctors could be available everywhere in the country. Local councils were to provide midwives and health visitors, ambulances and facilities for vaccination and immunisation. This was one of the government's most ambitious acts but it was not passed without a good deal of opposition, especially from the British Medical Association. Two months before it was due to come into effect, two out of every three doctors voted against joining the National Health Service. Some wanted to protect their private practices and others objected to state interference in their profession. The government refused to give way on any of the major points of the Act but they made sufficient compromises which, together with strong public support for the idea, forced more of the doctors to change their minds.

Despite increases in public funding over the years the National Health Service has proved a costly service to maintain. The original idea of a completely free service has proved impossible to achieve in practice. Patients are now paying varying charges for their prescriptions, glasses and dental treatment, although medical advice and hospital treatment are still free. Private medicine still flourishes for those who can afford it, operating not just in the context of private hospitals and clinics, but in the heart of the Health Service. Fee-paying patients can acquire beds in National Health hospitals for which their surgeons receive private remuneration and the hospital receives some payment 'for the bed'. But the services of nurses and ancillary workers and the cost of drugs are all provided from National Health resources, providing a significant 'hidden subsidy' in the treatment of private patients which is hard to justify during times of Health Service cuts and hospital closures.

The Appointed Day

July 5th, 1948, was 'the appointed day' on which the Welfare State in Britain was officially considered to be established. In explaining the new services to the nation, the Prime Minister, Clement Attlee, warned that the quality of the services would depend on the amount of money which the country could afford to spend on them. It was therefore important for everyone to work hard he said, because the 'general level of production settles our standard of material well-being'. This warning and its consequences have affected successive government policies in relation to public spending on social, welfare and education services ever since.

Post-War Developments

From the end of the Second World War until at least the mid-sixties the numbers of workers registered as unemployed remained small compared to the inter-war years, varying between 200,000 and half a million. In fact, there was a shortage of labour power in some areas and this was the period in which married women and immigrant workers were recruited into low-wage and low-status employment. Instead of dealing principally with the unemployed, the benefits system rationalised by Beveridge seemed to be mainly concerned with those not usually required to register for employment: widows, single mothers, pensioners and the sick and disabled.

Beveridge's assumptions that so far as women were concerned husbands would be 'their first line of defence' became increasingly debatable as women's lives experienced a number of profound changes in the sixties and seventies.

Increasingly women were having fewer children, they no longer left work when they married, some did not even leave work when they had children. Many had children without getting married and many others got divorced after having children. These alterations in living patterns forced changes to be made in the legislation relating to women in matters of social, welfare and economic rights but anomalies and discrimination continue despite recent reforms.

All of the reforms passed over the last few years—relating to property and divorce, maternity rights, the guardianship of children, social security benefits and pensions—will have little effect so long as women's economic dependence on men remains the cornerstone of state support for family and economic life. Despite the fact that between 1 in 6 and 1 in 5 families are totally dependent on the earning power of women, women are still not regarded by the state as primary wage earners. Even if a woman is paying full National Insurance contributions she is not entitled to related benefits for her dependants as a man in similar circumstances would be. She is still regarded by the state as dependent even if she is the breadwinner.

When a nuclear family arrangement is defined as the norm, women with children who are not part of such arrangements are heavily penalised. Ginsburg explains it as an attempt by the state 'to encourage if possible the renewal of dependence on men and to discourage the break-up of marriage by rendering single motherhood distinctly less eligible and attractive'. About three quarters of those adults dependent on Supplementary Benefit are women. As single parents they receive lower benefits and experience a worse standard of living than dependent married women in a two-parent family. In the last resort, the state takes over responsibility for women who are not dependent on men but only after attempts have been made to find a 'liable relative' who can be held economically responsible for them. The Supplementary Benefit Commission (SBC) encourages women to name the fathers of their illegitimate children and to take out maintenance orders against estranged husbands. The Commission employs Liable Relative Officers to investigate questions of paternity and the financial circumstances of other likely relatives who could be held economically responsible for single and deserted women. The DHSS also employs a considerable number of special investigators who are said to spend at least a third and probably more of their time attempting to find evidence of cohabitation. A single woman's independent right to benefits is immediately withdrawn if she is suspected of cohabiting with a man. The cohabitation rule is based on the evidence of two or three consecutive nights spent in the company of a man with whom a sexual relationship takes place. Not only does this policy deny single women

and their children the usual rights of benefits but investigation procedures encourage 'sex snooping', infringements of privacy and considerable harassment.

Mary McIntosh * argues that given the economic needs of capitalism
to reproduce and service the primary labour force, we should not be
surprised at the ways in which the capitalist state intervenes to support
and sustain systems like the family and to discourage alternative
arrangements (see p. 58). The administration of social security benefits acts to reinforce the needs of capital, 'on the one hand to establish
married women as dependant on their husbands (and therefore not
entirely reliant on wage labour) but on the other hand, by restricting
their direct eligibility for social security benefits, to make them more
vulnerable to use as cheap labour power when they do have to engage
in wage labour'. And so far as single mothers are concerned, since any
relaxation in the 'cohabitation' rules would leave cohabiting couples
better off than married couples, every attempt is made to shift the
dependence of unsupported women from the state, back onto men,
irrespective of the wishes of the women concerned.

Definitions of Poverty

In Rowntree's study of poverty in York in 1899 he divided people
living in poverty into two groups: those who did not earn enough to
meet their physical needs, and those who did earn enough to keep
their families, but who 'used' or 'wasted' some of their earnings on
other things. For Rowntree the important thing was to be able to
measure accurately which people were living in poverty and which
were not. He thought he could do this by drawing a 'poverty line'.
Those who fell below the line were poor, those who fell above the line
were assumed to be all right.

Absolute Poverty

He calculated where the absolute poverty line could be drawn by esti-
mating the minimum amount of money a family would need each
week to spend on rent, food, fuel and clothing. In 1899 he decided
that a family made up of a father, mother and three children needed a
minimum weekly amount of £1.08 to keep it above the poverty line.
But his calculations left no room for manoeuvre. Meat was considered
a 'luxury' and so it was not taken into account. Other 'luxuries' like a
cup of tea or a pint of beer or a ride on a bus were not taken into
account either. If people wanted to 'use' or 'waste' their money on
these things, they had to do it by going without food.

Rowntree's method of calculating the poverty line was adopted by

---

* 'The State and the Oppression of Women', Mary McIntosh, in *Feminism and Materialism*, A. Kohn and A.
Wolpe (eds.), Routledge & Kegan Paul, London, 1978.

Beveridge in his recommendations to the government in 1942. His calculations were based on figures for 1938 and on the strength of them he recommended that £1.60 was the basic amount necessary for a husband and wife to live on with an average of 35p for every additional child. It has been this method of measuring people's 'minimum needs' that has been the official way of deciding on National Assistance and Supplementary Benefits ever since.

Many people are critical of this official and arbitrary way of deciding where the poverty line should be drawn, however, and of the assumption that it represents the point at which poverty begins. It seems unfair to expect the poor to live on a carefully controlled budget which takes no account of the extras like holidays, leisure activities and household emergencies which others take for granted. Current supplementary benefit rates are not very generous either, despite press reports about 'Welfare scroungers living in the lap of luxury'. Over the years they have stayed fairly constant at about 29 per cent of average earnings. Also, the rates take very little account of real costs, and inflation over the last few years has made any increase worthless in practice.

Relative Poverty

The main problem with the poverty line and its absolute definition of where poverty begins and ends, is that it is based solely on ideas about minimum income and takes no account of other features of life. In Britain today the richest in the population earn 40 times as much as the poorest—those on supplementary benefits who receive less than one third of the national average wage. Some families on low wages would actually be 'better off' on state benefits! Given this kind of situation, critics feel that an absolute poverty line disguises the many facets and the real extent of poverty in Britain and fails to recognise the kind of impoverished lifestyle which many people are forced to endure compared to more advantaged groups. For in reality, poverty is also the lack of good schools, being without a decent house to live in, a noisy and depressing environment, inadequate play space, the lack of material possessions which other people take for granted and bad working conditions. Compared to the people who do not experience any of these things, those who do are poor. And so long as some individuals have very high incomes, vast amounts of wealth, countless possessions and a full range of opportunities in life, those who do not are relatively poorer by comparison. For these reasons many people prefer to describe poverty in relative and comparative terms rather than concentrate purely on measurements relating to an arbitrary poverty line.

Affluent Britain?

In 1959 a Conservative government was returned to power for the third time in succession with a large majority in Parliament. The election slogan chosen by the Conservatives was 'You've never had it so good'. The Prime Minister, Harold Macmillan, speaking in Manchester, confirmed that three million people a year were taking continental holidays, home ownership was rising and one family in three now had a motor car. So far as the politicians and many social commentators of the time were concerned, Britain was becoming an affluent middle-class country in which poverty was a thing of the past.

Housing

Despite claims to the contrary, the increases in home ownership only affected certain sections of society; for the majority of working-class people council lettings provided by the state and houses rented from private landlords were still the main forms of accommodation. The early philosophy of council housing was based on the notion that it was everyone's 'human right' to have a decent house to live in, and building 'homes fit for heroes' after the two world wars was claimed as a priority. But the supply of good housing has never been able to meet the needs of the people and this has been largely because financial considerations, rather than housing needs, have been the main influence on national and local government decisions.

During the thirteen years of Conservative rule between 1951 and 1964 the post-war vision of 'council housing for all' was replaced by a policy encouraging 'owner-occupation' for those who could afford it, and patching up old property or leaving the problem of housing the vast majority of working-class people to private landlords. The Labour government of 1964 also advocated 'owner-occupation' as a goal of 'a long-term social advance which should gradually pervade every region'. They returned to power committed to building half a million houses a year, at least half of which would be privately owned. So far as council housing went, the aim was to build fast and to build cheaply.

In practice this meant a considerable increase in 'factory-built' houses and high-rise accommodation. Between 1964 and 1972 over half of local authority building was in the form of flats. Some were four storeys high, which could be built without the added expense of lifts, but most were multi-storied. In addition, by 1968 the proportion of factory-built houses had doubled to 42 per cent. The large building firms benefited most and made huge profits out of contracts with various local authorities. Having developed methods of erecting houses in three or four days from pre-built sections, they sought contracts from local authorities committed to slum clearance and redevelopment for ongoing and massive building programmes.

Humanised planning, landscaping and adequate amenities were ignored in the 'overnight' construction of mammoth estates and high-rise 'concentration camps'. Not only were the socially bad effects of these soon to become apparent in the signs of depression, isolation and aggression displayed by the people consigned to them, but also the cheapness of the materials used and the shoddy construction methods soon showed evidence of damp, condensation, structural weaknesses and all the visible symptoms of newly created slums.

By 1968 the building boom was over. An economic crisis that year brought cuts in public spending which were soon to become very familiar, and as in more recent rounds of cuts, the housing programme was the first to suffer. Doctrinaire and fatal cuts were applied with special gusto by the Conservative councils returned to power in the 1967 local elections, who also capitalised on the familiar prejudice that 'council house tenants were enjoying the subsidy of hard-working rate payers'.

When the Conservatives were returned to government in 1970, private building was further encouraged while by 1973 local authority building had reached its lowest output since 1947. At the same time as the private property market was booming, largely to the advantage of the speculators, builders and estate agents, local councils were being encouraged to sell off their council houses to private buyers. No doubt this moved some more 'affluent workers' into the category of 'owner-occupiers', but it reduced the numbers of houses available for rent by the rest. The majority of working-class people still depend on renting and are in no position to contemplate buying their own house if insufficient council property is available.

As the economic problems of the seventies and early eighties got worse and public spending cuts increased, the provision of houses to satisfy housing needs were again subject to financial considerations. And as with other public spending cuts, those who were homeless or in the worst housing conditions had the most to lose from cuts and delays in building programmes.

Rediscovering Poverty

During the early sixties the government set up a number of commissions to investigate various aspects of life in Britain: for example, London housing (Milner-Holland), children and young people (Ingleby), primary education (Plowden), and the personal social services (Seebohm). One after the other the reports emphasised 'areas of bad housing', 'deprived neighbourhoods' and 'families in special need'. The picture that emerged was a challenge to the complacency of Britain's affluent image of itself in the sixties. Poverty obviously still existed and life for many families in Britain was a persistent struggle to make ends meet and a hopeless battle against appalling housing and terrible environments. And the figures suggested that the problems were much more widespread than the recent politicians had chosen to recognise.

The Government's Poverty Programme

In 1964 the Labour Party took over government and began a series of initiatives designed to reduce poverty. Its first move was to alter the rate support grant (money given by central government to add to the rates collected by local authorities and used to spend on local services). The change in policy meant that some local authorities with fewer resources were given more government aid than others. In 1968 the Urban Aid programme was launched to give grants of money to voluntary and statutory organisations working to improve the education, housing, health and welfare of groups living in areas of special need.

Educational Priority Areas were recognised as a direct consequence of the Plowden Report and schools in these areas were given extra staffing and special resources. In 1969 the Home Office set up the National Community Development Project (CDP) and placed small teams of community workers and researchers in twelve deprived areas of Britain like Benwell in Newcastle, Saltley in Birmingham and Canning Town in East London. Their brief was to organise 'a neighbourhood-based experiment aimed at finding new ways of meeting the needs of people in areas of high social deprivation', and they were given the promise of more government spending and expansion once their recommendations had been reported.

But all the initiatives were littered with the language of 'experiment' and 'project', emphasising the essentially temporary and token nature of their provision. And despite a good deal of public relations propaganda about 'positive discrimination' they operated on an incredibly small budget. The whole Urban Aid programme (of which the CDP formed only a small part) represented only one twentieth of one per cent of total public spending, and only one tenth of one per cent of total social service spending. Moreover, the Urban Aid programme did not receive additional money. It was deducted from the total rate support grant generally available for local authority spending. Together the various schemes never cost the government more than £10 million a year after 1968.

Because a lot of publicity had been given to them, many people were led to expect great achievements. The better coordination of local services was an important feature of the way in which they would operate. Seebohm had promoted the idea of a generic approach to provision in the personal social services. Better cooperation at local level between those of the various 'caring professions' and local authorities was seen as a good way of streamlining provision and concentrating resources. 'Participation' was another keyword, designed to challenge 'the latent apathy of the poor' and galvanise them into constructive self-help activities.

'Blaming the Victims'

In all of these initiatives there were related and important assumptions motivating the interventions. The final report of the Coventry Community Development Project identified them as:

1. Disadvantaged areas are a minor blot on the urban landscape.
2. The problem can be blamed partly on the apathy or abnormality of local residents and partly on the incompetence of local government.
3. The solutions lie in self-help and more active participation by local people and more sensitive services and better communication and coordination on the part of the local authority.
4. Solutions can be found at very little extra cost and that a carrot and stick approach by central government can spur the local authorities to do things better in the future.

The assumptions which underpinned strategies like CDPs, the EPAs and Urban Aid provide an important clue to their limitations. They were all based on notions of communities and people which attributed the causes of their disadvantage to deficiencies in their culture and character. The rediscovery of poverty and urban deprivation in the sixties led not to an examination of the structural relationship between capitalism and social class or between economic policies and social policies but to a concentration on the behavioural defects of the poor. Deprivation and disadvantage became two of the most overworked words in the English language and the effect of their overuse was that they became a kind of shorthand which lumped together a wide range of precariously related and generally denigratory tendencies into a common stereotype.

In 1972, Sir Keith Joseph, then Secretary of State for Social Services, voiced what in the circumstances was considered to be a logical appraisal of the poverty debate. He asked: 'Why is it, in spite of long periods of full employment and relative prosperity and the improvement of community services since the Second World War, deprivation and problems of maladjustment so conspicuously persist?' He was referring by deprivation to those 'circumstances which prevent people developing to nearer their potential—physically, emotionally and intellectually', which reveal themselves in 'poverty, in emotional impoverishment, in personality disorder, in poor education attainment, in depression and despair'. His conclusion was simple: in the majority of cases, the symptoms of the disease deprivation were endemic in the poor and were transmitted from one generation to the next in a 'cycle of deprivation' exacerbated by the feckless, apathetic and disorganised behaviour of those involved. He has of course gone on to clarify his association of deprivation with a form of personal pathology, transmitted from one generation to the next, and to recommend that every effort should be made to prevent those concerned from reproducing themselves in such irresponsibly large numbers.

Needless to say the logic and persuasion of Sir Keith Joseph's view of a 'cycle of transmitted deprivation' has come under strong fire, not only because of its reactionary nature, but because it seems to link poverty with maladjustment. Nonetheless, the insinuation that personally derived inadequacy is at the root of social and community problems has taken a long time to become discredited.

'Blaming the System'

When these assumptions were tested by those involved as workers in the government schemes, the result in most cases was that the workers came to reject the assumptions upon which their projects were established, and they began to redefine the problem of poverty in terms of the class structure and the exploitative nature of the capitalist economy. Explanation which turned attention away from the maladjustments and deficiencies of the poor and onto the concerns of capital to keep reserve armies of powerless cheap labour, disciplined by their struggle to compete with each other for scarce resources, and in conditions which act both as a deterrent and an incentive, was clearly not popular with funding authorities. The more this kind of analysis directed attention to the investment and employment policies of local firms and onto local and central government decisions about employment, social welfare, education and housing, the less enthusiastic the state became about the initiatives it had launched. One or two of the CDPs which got into conflict with local authorities were closed down prematurely before their 'action research' brief had been completed. Others completed their terms of office, submitted their reports, received official comments but were not asked to continue with their work. In a devastating critique of the government's 'poverty programme' of the late sixties and early seventies, *Gilding the Ghetto*, a report written by some of the CDP workers involved concludes:

'The state fight against urban deprivation has been exposed, like the "emperor's new clothes", as empty rhetoric. . . . The basic dilemma for the state remains the same—how best to respond to the needs of capitalism on the one hand and maintain the consent of the working class on the other. Now in the mid-seventies the problems we have described over the last decade have become more acute. The economy is in crisis and desperate measures are being called for. The profitability of British industry can only be restored by a reduction in wages and living standards. As the state responds to the needs of capital, the scope of the problem experienced by the working class can no longer be explained as a marginal problem of the inner city and the blame put upon the inadequacies of the people living there. The working class as a whole is being affected by reductions in real wages, by the threat of unemployment and by the fall in the value of the social wage, as public sector cuts affect services of all kinds. What kind of Welfare State is it which, at a time when economic recession is causing additional hardship, particularly among people living in "areas of special social need", cuts back the services on which people depend? Planned in the first place in order to partly protect working-class people from the harsher consequences of unfettered capitalism, its very structure is now being dismantled to help shore up an economic system that has patently failed to provide decent living standards for all. It is not surprising then that the "deprivation initiatives" were not about eradicating poverty at all, but about managing poor people.'

Cutting the Welfare State

The recent history of the seventies and early eighties has been one of serious economic difficulties in Britain. Unemployment has reached levels unheard of since the Depression and inflation has produced serious problems for successive governments to deal with. One of the main strategies which governments have chosen to try, besides encouraging industry to expand and workers to restrict their demands for higher wages, has been to spend less on social and welfare services.

The cuts began in 1973 under the Conservative government led by Edward Heath—but the same policies were continued when the Labour government came to power in 1974. In November 1973, for example, the Conservative government cut £111 million from the National Health Service budget. In 1975 the Labour government reduced it by a further £75 million and limited its future increases to 10 per cent a year. At a time when the yearly inflation rate was 25 per cent an increase of 10 per cent could not keep pace and proved, in real money terms, to be yet another cut in the money which the Health Service had to spend.

In housing it was the same story. The cost of building and maintaining council houses rises every year with increases in the value of land, higher interest rates on the money borrowed by local authorities, and the cost of materials and building. The fact that councils have to compete with private developers adds to the problem. The consequence is that fewer new houses than are needed get built. Their quality is reduced and their rents are higher. Add to this local government's need to economise and to cut public spending on, for example, repairs, maintenance and improvements, and you can see why council waiting lists grew in the mid-seventies and the quality of the housing they provided deteriorated considerably.

Money spent on education represents about 17 per cent of public spending each year. Some of it goes on capital expenditure (new schools, building improvements, furnishings, etc.), the rest on running costs (teachers' wages, heating and lighting, etc.). Between 1972 and 1975 capital spending on education fell by one third, plans to build new schools or develop nursery facilities were cancelled and many old schools were denied their promised improvements. The next thing to suffer was running costs. In 1975 the government issued a circular (No. 10/75) to all local authorities advising them about what had to be cut and where economies had to be made. Here were some of their instructions:

1. In large urban areas with falling populations, teaching staff were to be reduced.

2. In higher education steps were to be taken to alter staffing ratios.

3. In primary education those local authorities which had recently allowed 4-year-olds to be admitted full-time to ordinary infant classes had to review their policy in the interests of economy. Four-year-olds were not to be admitted unless they had no additional call on educational resources.

4. Maintenance was to be neglected, standards of material upkeep of premises had to remain below the level generally accepted as desirable in the recent past.

5. There was to be no scope for additional expenditure on the rest of the education service, including the youth, recreation and community services or in the library and museum services.

Although the cuts in public spending were bad under the Labour government, organised opposition by the labour movement was muted. Trade unions since the war have been much more concerned with issues relating to wages, redundancy and working conditions and less clear about policies relating to public spending, except in so far as jobs are concerned. But a change of government committed to public spending cuts on a much larger scale served to concentrate the energies of moderates and radicals alike.

The interpretation of economic policy which Margaret Thatcher brought to her task as Prime Minister in 1979 was unashamedly 'extreme'. Monetarist notions about 'controlling the money supply', 'letting the market find its own level' and 'increasing incentives' so that those who have the capacity to create wealth are encouraged to do so, also have their concomitants. Labour-intensive and non-productive public services can only be afforded if productivity and profits from economic production are high. Overmanning, waste and unprofitable enterprises cannot be subsidised out of government spending if it means 'printing more money' to pay the bills. Cuts in public spending, though regrettable, are not always as bad as people make out, especially in circumstances in which people have been cushioned by a too easy dependence on the state, rather than on their own resources. There is a sense in which too much subsidy of public services saps the initiative. Those people who choose to and who are able to pay for education and medical care should be encouraged to do so. Those who are clearly incapable of supporting themselves will of course not be jettisoned but there are many, the vast majority of the population in fact, who are well capable of paying a little more for the services they receive.

This kind of philosophy was rapidly transformed into expenditure cuts more decisive than any which had been contemplated in the seventies, in school meals charges and public transport costs and a rundown of education and social services at local level. Cuts in education have meant the virtual abolition of nursery provision, the dismantling of the school meals service, the lack of adequate funds to spend on new textbooks and resources and increasing restrictions placed on curriculum diversity, examination classes and remedial teaching. In the social services, increases in the charges made for home helps and 'meals on wheels' have been only part of a debilitating round of cuts which have closed special day centres, homes for the elderly and sheltered workshops up and down the country. The allegations made by those who are opposed to the cuts are unanimous in their condemnation of measures which seem to have been directed most pointedly at the least powerful members of the community and those least able to protect their own interests by organised resistance.

Jobs Threatened

Ancillary and part-time workers were also casualties of cuts in the seventies but since many of them were women who were poorly organised in trade union terms, their experience of redundancy was little different from that continually faced by cheap female labour in times of economic recession. Concern about unemployment in the seventies was largely a concern expressed by male trade unionists about redundancies affecting men. The gloomy prospects for unemployed school-leavers also caused a fair amount of public consternation and stimulated a number of temporary holding operations like Job Creation Schemes and the Youth Opportunities Programme (see p. 211). But women, without independent rights to unemployment benefits or redundancy payments, disappeared once more into the home. The threat to jobs in the eighties has been of a different order. The most vulnerable again have been women ancillary workers, especially part-time dinner ladies and clerical staff. But with professional vacancies frozen and further cuts in education and social service spending being demanded, the security of teaching and local government jobs at officer level are obviously in danger.

With inflation still in double figures and unemployment reaching its highest level since the 1930s, the monetarist solution to Britain's economic ills still has to be demonstrated.

State Care or State Control?

In 1973, Robert Carr, Home Secretary in the Heath Government, said in Parliament:

'The urban problem is fundamental to the problem of our society. . . . The level of crime is only the visible top of the iceberg of social ferment lying beneath.'

His anxieties were not new. Almost a hundred years earlier Sir John Gorst, a Tory MP of the period, warned:

'Modern civilisation has crowded the destitute classes together in the cities making their existence more conspicuous and more dangerous. They already form a substantial part of the population, and possess even now, though they are still ignorant of their full power, great political importance. . . . Almost every winter in London there is a panic lest the condition of the poor should become intolerable. . . . The annual alarm may some day prove a reality, and the destitute classes may swell to such a proportion as to render continuance of our existent social order imposible.'

State concern about poverty and welfare during the last hundred years or so has clearly been influenced by a number of considerations. We have noted the desire to satisfy the needs of capital and at the same time to retain the support of the working class despite being governed in ways which are inconsistent with their class interests. We have seen how policies affecting women have served to reinforce their traditional domestic and dependent roles within the family. A further concern has been the fear of political unrest. It was this fear which enticed the state into social and educational reforms in the first place.

The anxiety has always been that poverty, inequality and injustice might serve to politicise those who experience their worst effects, and that economic deprivation, expressed in social class terms, could lead to organised political resistance.

At no time has this fear been more evident than in the period immediately following the First World War, when police and troops were used to crush hunger marches and demonstrations of unemployed workers in Glasgow, Liverpool and London, although the confrontations in 1981 between the police and the poor—especially the young—have similar implications.

Since the Second World War the organised labour movement has tended to confine its political struggles to the workplace but discrepancies in social conditions highlighted by the administration and experience of the Welfare State have not been without political potential.

The effectiveness of the 'poverty lobby', made up of welfare rights and claimants' organisations and national pressure groups like the Child Poverty Action Group and Shelter, have done a good deal to publicise and to expose the failure of the Welfare State to meet the real needs of those who are dependent on its services. They have helped to increase awareness about welfare rights and have achieved some valuable reforms.

The main significance of the CDPs and their activities was not their brief and speedy demise once they began to question and challenge their employers, but the legacy of active consciousness raising and published reports which they left behind. The experience of CDP workers in areas of industrial decline very quickly led them to ask searching questions about the distribution of resources and wealth in the areas in which they were working and to encourage the tenants in those areas to do the same. And despite allegations about incitement, they found no need to induce feelings of polarisation between 'them' and 'us'. A strong and independent sense of class identity has existed historically in traditional working-class neighbourhoods and has provided a rich source of resistance to dominant values and formal institutions, though it has not always taken political forms.

The task of the state has always been to prevent this resistance turning into organised opposition—to win the consent of the governed and to establish 'the official versions of reality' as the only accurate explanations of events. So far as poverty is concerned, the working class have had to be repeatedly convinced, against all the evidence of their own experience, that their poverty has nothing to do with their position in the class structure. The lack of any serious political challenge to the organisation and ideology of capitalism in Britain is some measure of the state's success over the years in engineering this consent (see Chapter 10).

Ginsburg explains the arrangement as a 'quid pro quo or a "bribe" offered to the working class in exchange for political quiescence and industrial peace. . . . It is a "piece of cake" sacrificed by capital to secure wider cooperation. The Welfare State exerts an important cushioning effect on working-class experience, actively diverting attention from the real relations of appropriation and the structure of class inequality . . . but the "piece of cake" is not offered without important strings and it is certainly not allowed to threaten capitalist social relations.'

The relationship between capitalism and the Welfare State is full of contradictions. From the working-class point of view it can be seen in part as a victory in the continued struggle to improve and secure their standard of living. From a capitalist point of view, state welfare has helped in the business of accumulating capital both by assisting in the reproduction of the labour force and by containing its revolutionary potential. And although the Welfare State is both a direct consequence of the presence and the pressures created by the working class, and obviously goes some way to meeting their needs and expanding their opportunities, capitalism has been strengthened rather than weakened by its development over the years.

To assume that the Welfare State 'merely' serves the need of capital is to ignore that social institutions are dynamic arrangements which can be sustained or changed by human action, however. Paul Corrigan in *The Welfare State as an Arena of Class Struggle* points out that 'if we accept that welfare is controlled by capital and acts against the welfare of working people, then why should we fight the cuts? We should welcome them ... as a direct cut in the power of the ruling class over the working class'. And yet recent cuts in public spending have precipitated a marked reduction in the security, living standards and social wage of working people and need to be resisted. Mary McIntosh * describes 'working-class struggle' and 'capitalist power' as two sides of the same coin. 'If school dinners or a National Health Service help to keep the working class healthy, they fulfil aspirations of the class as well as merely help to reproduce it; or if welfare payments are used to damp down the fires of working-class protests, they can also be seen as an achievement of that protest.'

Such contradictions mean that there are always a number of conflicting forces at work and the policies of the state are like attempts to keep a variety of different balls in the air at once. In such circumstances there is always room for manoeuvre and there is always room for change.

Revision

1. Refresh Your Memory

Make sure you know the meaning of the terms: philanthropic, means test, workhouse, out-relief, malnutrition, consumption, maintenance order, cohabitation rule, poverty line, inflation.

2. Check Your Understanding

Be able to explain in your own words the difference between:

(*a*) Infant and maternal mortality.
(*b*) Boards of Guardians and Public Assistance Committees.
(*c*) Poor relief and unemployment benefit.
(*d*) National insurance and taxation.
(*e*) The poverty line and 'average earnings'.
(*f*) Multi-storey and factory-built houses.
(*g*) The Rate Support Grant and Urban Aid.
(*h*) Structural and pathological definitions of poverty.

---

* Mary McIntosh, *op. cit.*

3. Essay Questions to Try

(*a*) Suggest some of the main reasons why the state has taken an increasing interest in the social conditions of its citizens during the last hundred years or so.

(*b*) To what extent have notions of punishment and deterrent influenced the changing provision of state benefits?

(*c*) Assess the aims and achievements of the Beveridge Report.

(*d*) To what extent has the growth and development of the Welfare State contributed to the increasing emancipation of women?

(*e*) Discuss the difference between 'absolute' and 'relative' definitions of poverty. What problems are involved in finding a satisfactory definition of poverty?

(*f*) Why do we talk of the 1960s as the period in which 'poverty was rediscovered'? How have different governments responded to this discovery?

(*g*) Assess the work of the National Community Development Project in the fight against social deprivation.

(*h*) In what way does monetarist economic philosophy justify public spending cuts?

(*i*) 'The Welfare State exerts an important cushioning effect on working-class experience, actively directing attention from the real relations of appropriation and the structure of class inequality . . . but the piece of cake is not offered without important strings and it is certainly not allowed to threaten capitalist social relations.' (Ginsburg) Discuss.

Further Reading

A Hoxton Childhood, A. S. Jasper, Centerprise, 1972.
Class Capital and Social Policy, Norman Ginsburg, Macmillan, London, 1979.
Into Unknown England, Peter Keating (Ed.), Fontana, London, 1976.
Round About a Pound a Week, Maud Pember Reeves, Virago, London, 1979.
Unemployed Struggles 1919–1936, Wal Hannington, Lawrence & Wishart, London, 1977.

10

POLITICS AND POWER

The distribution of power in British society is another feature of social organisation which elicits conflicting explanations from sociologists and political scientists. Their concern is to explain what power entails, how it is distributed and what the relationship is between the ownership of power and the process of government. Does a change of government in Britain make any real difference to the distribution of power and does it have any major effects on the kind of policy decisions which are made?

The disagreements between different theorists arise as a result of ideological differences about the kind of society we live in and the role of the state (i.e. government) within that society.

Power

Power can be defined in a number of ways. At the most simple level it can imply the ability of an individual or a group to bring about immediate and visible change in the behaviour of other people. At a more complex level it is concerned with the process by which social consent is obtained in society generally.

C. Wright Mills* defines power as the ability of individuals and especially elite groups to realise certain aims or objectives against the wishes of others. For Mills power means quite simply power over others. Talcott Parsons, on the other hand, is concerned with the process by which societies ensure their own continuation, and how elements within a society—like various social, economic and political institutions—fulfil specific functions which enable that society to operate effectively over time. He is critical of Mills for not understanding the role of power in ensuring that social institutions function to fulfil the needs of society. But his argument is weak in that in describing power as the relationship *between* social institutions and society he fails to make clear that this relationship is *the result of* power having been *exercised*. He ignores Mills' point that power is, in fact, power over others.

One aspect of Parsons' argument is important, however. In describing the relationship between society as a whole and its constituent parts he emphasises the extent to which power must be examined in a

---

* *The Power Elite*, C. Wright Mills, Oxford University Press, 1956.

structural context, i.e. that power is not merely a relationship between individuals at an interpersonal level. Many sociologists, especially those influenced by Weber, have chosen to concentrate on the exercise of power by individuals over individuals, without paying sufficient attention to the way in which large-scale institutions accumulate and use power.

Once the power of institutions is recognised, it then becomes of interest to consider the extent to which power and the exercise of power is distributed between different institutions. Peter Worsley*, writing in 1964, argued that the exercise of power is not simply the prerogative of government and political parties but that other organisations—e.g. trade unions, armies, public relations firms and churches—also dispose of power. So far as Worsley is concerned power can only really be understood in terms of what it is used for. Its use has effects. It doesn't exist 'in itself'—it flows between people. 'Everybody has some of it—some area of choice, of ability to effect things his way. It may only be the power to be negative, to "vote with ones feet".... But some people have overwhelming and decisive power. Power is not randomly distributed but institutionalised.' And some institutions are considerably more powerful than others.

Thus another feature of the debate—especially in relation to the state—is about how power is exercised. Does power rely upon force or upon the dissemination of ideas, values and norms which help to make its nature and its effects seem perfectly legitimate? In this respect John Urry † has distinguished between three types of power: economic power based on the control of economic resources; political power based on the control of the resources of force; and cultural power based on the control of resources which create, transform and interpret society's norms. Power, therefore, has both economic and arbitrary dimensions as well as significant ideological substance in terms of the 'mental environment' of society.

Some of these issues will be examined in more detail in this chapter.

The Distribution of Power

In analysing the distribution of power in society sociologists tend to base their assumptions on one or another of three main explanations of the power structure: 'ruling class', 'elitism', or 'pluralism'.

Ruling Class

The ruling class model derives from the writings and social theory of Karl Marx. The key elements of his analysis of social class will probably by now be quite familiar to you (see p. 40).

---

* Sociological Review Monograph No. 8.
† *Power in Britain*, John Urry and John Wakeford (eds.), Heinemann, London, 1973.

The economic dominance of the ruling class is its principal source of power in the class struggle, but economic dominance alone is insufficient to maintain the class's absolute control. The ruling class must also use its economic dominance to determine and win control of key political and cultural forces in society. By control over the government, the military, the police force and those social institutions concerned with the production and dissemination of ideas and values (e.g. education, religion, law and the media), the power of the ruling class is deployed to ensure that the major policies and decisions which are made in a given society serve the interests and reinforce the power of ruling groups.

In terms of Marx' analysis, social classes are cohesive groups which have economic interests in common. The opposed economic interests of different classes mean that not only are they in fundamental conflict with each other to defend their own interests, but out of this conflict arises shared awareness and consciousness of the need for collective defence of class interests. A major task of the ruling class is to prevent the subject classes developing a coherent sense of class solidarity which might lead to collective action against the interests of the ruling class. In this respect the 'ideological state apparatuses'—or those social institutions that deal in ideas and values—are used to 'engineer' social consent and to persuade subject groups to accept the legitimacy, or the inevitability, of their inferior economic position in the class structure.

Others have developed and refined Marx' analysis. He did not specifically concern himself with the relationship between class power and political decision-making, although his writings leave the reader in no doubt that he viewed the state (i.e. government) as the coercive instrument of the ruling class. 'The executive of the modern state is but a committee for managing the common affairs of the whole bourgeoisie.' Subsequent writers influenced by Marx' social theories have taken this assumption for granted.

Applied to the contemporary discussion about the distribution and exercise of power, the ruling class model begins with the premise that an economically dominant and cohesive social group, which owns the main instruments of economic production, which controls the key political instruments of resource allocation and policy-making, and which exercises ideological and cultural dominance by virtue of its control of the state's ideological systems, is the starting point for any analysis.

Elitism

Elitism also takes the view that effective power in society is concentrated in relatively few hands but unlike the ruling class model rejects the notion of a society characterised *principally* by economically determined social classes which are in fundamental conflict with each other. Elitism views society as an essentially organised minority confronting an essentially disorganised mass. This minority of leaders dominates the various decision-making processes in society and either deliberately or by default serves to exclude or restrict participation and interference by the rest of the population.

Elitist models of society sometimes depict elites as benign and socially motivated groups who, on the basis of professional expertise and merit, operate to meet the needs of those whose lives they organise and make decisions about. Others describe elites as privileged groups who consistently exercise power in ways which further their own ends and which consequently disadvantage the masses who are excluded from their deliberations.

Both the ruling class and the elitist models assume that in the distribution of power and in the process of decision-making there is a distinctive and recognisable structure in society by which a specific class or number of elite groups consistently wields power and influence. Elitist models do not assume that members of governing elites necessarily monopolise power as a consequence of their social class background. The assumption is that they hold their positions by merit and appointment.

Elitist models also assume that there is no necessary relationship between elites in different institutions. It is possible to distinguish between educational elites, administrative elites and financial elites, for example. They exercise power in relation to different aspects of decision-making, they have different expertise and different responsibilities. They should not necessarily be seen as a mutually cohesive group.

But sometimes elitist and ruling class models do overlap. Miliband, for example, argues in *The State in Capitalist Society* that there are identifiable elites of top decision-makers in Britain, including cabinet ministers, military chiefs, higher civil servants, business leaders, 'the great and the good', and so on, who exercise power and control over everyone else. But whilst identifying a number of apparently different 'governing elites', he also recognises that these elites have a single, fundamental social characteristic in common. They are all, with rare exceptions, members of the same discrete upper and upper middle class. And their 'shared understanding' and 'common frame of reference' binds them together as a cohesive group with specific, social, economic and political interests to defend.

Pluralism

Pluralism, like elitism, rejects the notion of a class-ridden society characterised by irreconcilable differences, but unlike elitism is unconvinced about the notion of power being concentrated exclusively in the hands of a small elite, or even a number of different small elites. Pluralism depicts society as an arena in which there is a variety of competing, conflicting and cooperating groups of various sizes which are variously organised. In fact, society is characterised by an infinite number of competing interests with different power bases and different political concerns to defend and to promote. In such a fluid system there are numerous opportunities for individuals and groups to participate in the process of political, social and economic decision-making, in a variety of ways and at a variety of levels. No single group is able to monopolise power and influence at the expense of others because the activity of other groups check and balance the undesirable concentration of authority in too few hands. Those who make gains and win power one day will do less well the next.

A further assumption underpinning the pluralist view of society is that whilst individuals and groups may disagree and compete with each other, these disagreements are within clearly defined limits. In a broad sense, all members of the same society accept the same range of possibilities within broadly similar categories. There is, in short, a general consensus about values, objectives and ideas which might be called 'the national interest' or 'the common good'. The extent to which the notion of social consensus represents an essentially conservative view of society, and fails to question the origins of this so-called consensus or indeed the social basis of it, are two of the major criticisms levelled against pluralist models of powers.

Power and the Ruling Class

Kautsky, writing in 1902, commented that 'the capitalist class rules but does not govern . . . it contents itself with ruling the government'.

In defining the ruling class in contemporary Britain we first need to be clear about whom we are talking. In an industrial society like ours the ruling class has long ceased to be a purely aristocratic, land-owning minority, although the origins of its power and influence lie in the possession of landed wealth and titles. But it has had to adapt to an industrial society and a capitalist economy. This means that members of the ruling class have had to win control of business and industrial production, they have had to move into the boardrooms of industry and also to win the support of non-ruling class entrepreneurs for the ruling-class way of life.

Wealth and Income

Few commentators are in any doubt that the concentration of economic wealth and power is in the hands of a relatively small minority of the population. The knowledge that wealth in Britain continues to be concentrated in a few hands is fairly indisputable but difficulties persist in attempts to discover just how wealthy the rich really are.

One attempt to establish more reputable figures has been undertaken in recent years by the Diamond Commission. Its terms of reference were to 'collect data with a view to helping to secure a fairer distribution of income and wealth in the community', but it was dissolved by the Conservative government which was returned to power in 1979.

The reports published by the Commission before it was disbanded examined the distribution of income and wealth in 1976–7 and related it to the distribution in the past. They found that the share of income received by the different sections of the population was still grossly unequal and showed 'a remarkable stability from year to year'. The overall share of income by the top 1 per cent of income earners has been falling but there has been no significant redistribution among people generally. The drop in the share of income of the top 1 per cent has been balanced by an increase in the share of income of the people immediately below them. The share of income of the bottom 50 per cent has stayed virtually unchanged and has increased by only 0.8 per cent in the last 28 years (see p. 33).

In terms of overall wealth, the Commission identified land, houses and company shares as the most important constituents of wealth. In this area there has been some redistribution of wealth from the top 10 per cent to other sections of society. But the ownership of wealth so far as the top 1 per cent is concerned has been increasing since 1974. The simple explanation for this apparent redistribution in recent years is the ownership of houses. Roughly 50 per cent of the population in Britain own their own houses or are buying them on a mortgage, but clearly there are enormous differences between the houses of the very wealthy and those of new owner-occupiers at the bottom end of the market. The other major assets of land and shares are still highly concentrated in the hands of the rich.

The Diamond Commission reports are helpful but still do not adequately detail the real and the hidden wealth of the rich. The Commission was closed down before it had made any attempt to estimate the amount of control and power which is bestowed upon the rich.

Shareholdings

The most important kind of wealth is that derived from shares. Not only does the value of shares make those who own large quantities of them very wealthy but shareholdings also give control over the means of production, from which all other wealth ultimately comes. Those who own and control the means of production are in a position to decide what goods will be produced, who will be employed to produce those goods, what they will receive in wages and what the price of the produced goods shall be. The value of privately owned shares quoted on the stock exchange is about £17,000 million. Only 7 per cent of the adult population own any of these and within the small group which does, 1 per cent control 80 per cent of privately owned shares and 5 per cent 98 per cent of private shareholdings.

The Controllers of British Industry

The hundred largest companies in Britain today produce a half of all manufactured goods. They are controlled by boards of directors who own sufficient shares to enable them to have a controlling interest in the companies concerned.

Writing in 1968, Michael Barratt Brown* estimated that a significant number of top British companies were controlled either by tycoons or individual families. A current illustration of this concentration of shareholding power is Cadbury-Schweppes, a food-producing company with an annual turnover of £1,000 million. It is still controlled by Sir Adrian Cadbury and another director, N. D. Cadbury, who between them own 20 per cent of the company's share capital. The same picture is true for Lyons, Tate and Lyle and Lloyds Bank.

Lord Pilkington, who runs Pilkington Brothers, was worth £1½ million ten years ago and was a major shareholder in the company. Most of the rest of the shares in the firm are owned by other members of his family. Not only are millions of pounds held in trust for the family but all of those who own shares receive regular dividends. Record profits announced in 1978–79 increased share values and almost immediately added a further £2 million to the family fortunes.

Sir Arnold Weinstock owns £10 million worth of the shares in GEC, the company he has managed for the last 16 years. He is one of Britain's biggest employers and retains as consultants people like Angus Ogilvy (Princess Alexandra's husband), Lord Aldington (former Conservative Minister), Lord Catto (merchant banker), Sir Richard Powell (a former Chief at the Board of Trade) and Henry Kissinger.

The argument is frequently made that nowadays, because of the size of industries and the development of multinational corporations, those who own shares no longer control industry as they once did. This view was expounded by Anthony Crosland in 1956 and again in 1974. The substance of his argument, and that of others sharing his views, was that control in industry has passed into the hands of managers who do not own the assets which they manage. A 'managerial revolution' has removed control and decision-making from the capitalist class into the hands of those whose motives are more concerned with productivity than the accumulation of personal profit. This may be true so far as day-to-day decisions are concerned but the overwhelming evidence—so far as shareholdings and directorships go—is that little has changed. Crucial strategic financial decisions

---

* *The Controllers of British Industry*, Michael Barrett Brown.

about, for example, investment funding, the allocation of profit, mergers and takeovers are still made by the companies' chief executives and boards of directors.

An examination of the boards of directors of top companies and of the principal banks, insurance companies, nationalised industries, quasi-independent government advisory committees and regional development boards all reveal similarities in their composition.

Michael Barrett Brown suggests that 'the larger the company, the greater proportion of directors there will tend to be on the board with outside connections'. They also sit on the boards of other industrial corporations, banks and insurance companies, trade associations and government committees. Not only are directors of boards linked by commercial interests like these but also by interconnecting webs of kinship and marriage, public schooling, Oxbridge and the membership of certain clubs.

Business and Government

The other important link which joins those who are the owners and directors of industry and commerce is politics, and especially the Conservative Party. Just as the older public schools and Oxbridge are the route to power for something like three quarters of all Tory MPs and cabinet ministers, so too is Conservative government, and especially cabinet office, a significant and speedy way into the boardrooms of Britain. Lord Carrington, for example, Foreign Secretary in the 1979 Conservative government, was a director of Barclays Bank and Barclays International, Cadbury-Schweppes, Rio Tinto Zinc, Hambros Bank and the Amalgamated Metal Corporation. Geoffrey Howe, Chancellor of the Exchequer in the same government, was a director of Alliance Assurance, Associated Business Programmes, EMI, The London Assurance, Sun Alliance and London Assurance, and Sun Insurance. Jim Prior, Employment Secretary in the same government, directed United Biscuits, Avon Products, the IDC Group and the Norwich Union Insurance Company.

Of course many politicians are also businessmen in their own right. One third of the members of British cabinets between 1886 and 1950, including three prime ministers, have been businessmen and this trend has tended to increase rather than diminish over the years. As Labour representation in Parliament has grown the percentage of MPs with working-class backgrounds has progressively declined, and the two major political parties are now becoming increasingly similar in terms of middle-class background and career patterns.

Westerguard argues in *Sociology: The Myth of Classlessness* that 'The dominant grouping [in society] is that of a small homogeneous elite of wealth and private property—politically entrenched in the leadership of the Conservative party; strongly represented in, or linked with, a variety of public and private bodies; assured of the general support of the press; its members sharing for a large part a common, exclusive educational background, and united by fairly close ties of kinship and everyday association. . . . It is an elite which, while its economic base is that of financial and industrial capital, yet has its own uniquely British features, in part inherited from the agrarian mercantile nobility and gentry of the pre-industrial era.'

Others argue that despite the interlocking activities of businessmen in government, industry and commerce, they represent a relatively small minority compared to the state elite as a whole. For example, top civil servants, academics, lawyers, army officers and the like are hardly businessmen. Miliband argues that the significance of any 'relative distance of businessmen from the state system is markedly reduced by the social composition of the state elite proper. For businessmen belong in economic and social terms to the upper and middle classes and it is also from these classes that other members of the state elite are predominantly, not to say overwhelmingly, drawn. . . . There is also the matter of connection . . . such membership affords links of kinship and a sense of shared values.' It has been estimated by Otley*, for example, that 40 per cent of the top three ranks in the British Army are connected by birth or marriage to those who are major financiers, company directors, peers, cabinet ministers, senior diplomats and senior civil servants.

Miliband concludes, 'What the evidence conclusively suggests is that in terms of social origins, education and class situation, the men who have manned *all* command positions in the state system have largely and in many cases overwhelmingly, been drawn from the world of business or from the professional middle classes. . . . In an epoch when so much is made of democracy, equality, social mobility, classlessness and the rest, it has remained a basic fact of life in advanced capitalist societies that the vast majority of men and women in these countries have been governed, represented, administered, judged and commanded in war by people drawn from other economically and socially superior and relatively distant classes'.†

Elitism and Power

Vilfredo Pareto and Gaetano Mosca are two early theorists who helped develop the model of elitism to analyse power in society. Pareto (1864–1923) based his theories on the simple assumption that there are those—the elite—who exhibit excellence, and others—the non-elite—who do not. The governing elite was quite simply those with the best developed skills of ruling others, whether by force or fraud.

---

* *Social Affiliations of the British Army Elite*, Otley.
† *The State in Capitalist Society*, Ralph Miliband.

The masses, in comparison, were disorganised and incompetent. According to Pareto any kind of mass or majority rule was inconceivable. Changes in régime or changes in government did not fundamentally alter anything, they reflected merely the periodic transfer from one elite to another. For Pareto the origins of power and the business of ruling were based on individualistic qualities—not on any analysis of class structure. The economic and political dominance of elites was seen more as a consequence of their personal characteristics than of any shared social and economic interests.

Mosca also believed that some people perform tasks more effectively than others in ways which are not dependent upon social origins. He described how in a changing society, new people are continually recruited into the various elites and that whilst the political elite is the most powerful of all the elites, all are characterised by essentially open structures in which those with skill, application and merit can find a place.

Hewitt * distinguishes between three kinds of groups: political elites, social elites and non-elites. He uses the term elite to refer to 'those who occupy the leading positions in organisations or institutions'. Political elites are those who occupy such positions in the state, i.e. elected political representatives and top civil servants. Social elites are those who control 'non-political organisations that either embody sectional interests like business, labour and the professions, or represent attitudes and opinions like the media, law and the Church'. Non-elites are those who make up the ordinary rank and file members of organisations as well as the unorganised masses.

Tom Bottomore† neatly explains the difference between the elite model and the ruling class model like this. 'The concept of the governing elite contrasts the organised, ruling minority with the unorganised majority or masses, while the concept of a ruling class contrasts the dominant class with subject classes, which may themselves be organised or creating organisations.' From these different perspectives there follow different ways of describing the relationships between rulers and ruled. In the ruling class model, as we have seen, the conflict between classes is considered to be the driving force which produces changes in the social structure; whereas the elite model describes the relationship between the organised minority and the disorganised as essentially more passive, in which non-elites are not necessarily ruled against their own self-interests.

The other main difference between the two theories lies in the extent to which they refer to the social cohesion of the ruling minority. Elitist theoreticians take for granted the assumption that political and social

---

* *Elites and the Distribution of Power in Britain*, Hewitt.
† *Elites and Society*, Tom Bottomore, Penguin, London, 1970.

elites, i.e. those who occupy positions of command in society, may have quite a lot in common, based on common backgrounds and experience. But they attach no particular significance to this communality of interests. Theoreticians who define the ruling class as an observable class which owns the major means of economic production, whose members have definite economic interests in common, and who are supremely class-conscious of their shared interests as a group, attach much more significance to the class composition of ruling groups. As Bottomore points out, 'the [ruling class] concept states in a precise form what is the basis of the minority's ruling position, namely its economic domination; while the concept of governing elite says little about the bases of power which the elite possesses'.

C. Wright Mills* has described the essentially organisational function of elites. He distinguished between three major elites and attempted to explain why they were able to wield power: business executives because of the growth and size in business corporations; military chiefs because of increasingly technological weaponry and warfare; and national political leaders because of the increasing centralisation of politics at the expense of parochial and participatory democracy. Mills saw these elites as separate but socially interconnected.

So far as Max Weber was concerned in his writings about bureaucracy, the possession of the means of administration and not the possession of the means of economic production was seen as the main source of elite power. The extent to which bureaucratic and administrative elites actually receive their positions of power as a consequence of their social class origins has been largely ignored by elite theorists, however. Clearly there are enormous difficulties in measuring whether individuals attain positions of power because of their social origins, independent of their abilities, and whether they actually personally exercise power in a way which promotes identifiable class interests. The social, economic and kinship links between different members of different elites could be incidental, or at any rate insignificant, when it comes to decision-making and the organisation of the masses.

Elite theorists also talk in terms of 'the circulation of elites' and more recently 'social mobility'. Both concepts cast doubt on the notion of there being a distinctive ruling class. Bottomore explains: 'Since the power of a ruling class arises from its ownership of property, and since the property can easily be transferred from generation to generation, the class has an unending character. It is constituted by a group of families which remain as its component elements over long periods of time through the transmission of family property. . . . If, however, we were to find in a particular society or type of society, that the movement of individuals and families between the different social

* Mills, *op. cit.*

levels was so continuous and so extensive that no group of families was able to maintain itself for any length of time in a situation of economic and political pre-eminence, then we would have to say that in such a society there was no ruling class.' Elite theorists pointing to the achievement of universal suffrage in industrial societies and also increasing mobility, opportunity and openness, suggest that in such circumstances it becomes inaccurate to talk in terms of a ruling class. Karl Mannheim used these arguments to suggest that the development of industrial societies can best be seen as a movement from a class system to a system of elites, from a social hierarchy based on the inheritance of property to one based upon merit and achievement.

Pluralism and Power

The major characteristic of pluralist notions of power in society is the denial of a ruling or capitalist class. Pluralists argue that economic power, like all power, is diffuse, fragmented, competitive and subject to so many countervailing checks and balances that it becomes impossible to establish any one minority's absolute power and control over others. Even elites, because they are in competition with each other, and because they share no cohesion or common purpose, are incapable, according to pluralist analysis, of establishing any enduring cooperation of any kind.

Pluralism is closely associated with an expressed belief in democracy (see below p. 266). Baran and Sweezy * comment that 'except in times of crisis, the normal political system of capitalism, whether competitive or monopolistic, is bourgeois democracy'. Votes are the nominal source of political power and money is the real source; the system, in other words, is democratic in form and plutocratic in content.

Brian Smith † neatly summarises the pluralist model of power and applies it to the British political system. He identifies nine main characteristics:

1. Political equality and individualism are protected by the right to vote, to free speech and to association for political ends. Inequalities may result from the way the electoral system works but these are random in their effects and do not favour one social class rather than another.

2. Representative institutions and the rights of opposition protect individuals and sectional interests from unfair and arbitrary discrimination. There is balance between the political parties in terms of power and influence and regular elections, lobbying and the existence of pressure groups ensure open access to government.

3. The weakness of the individual in a modern democracy like Bri-

---

* *Monopoly Capital and Government*, P. Baran and P. Sweezy, Penguin, London, 1968.
† *Policy-Making in British Government*, Brian Smith, Martin Robertson, Oxford, 1976.

tain is compensated for by the right to join with others in collective action for political ends. The organisation of political parties and pressure groups ensures that different interests are represented. In a plural society power is diffused between all such groups. Their general equality of power induces balanced competition in any attempts to influence the decision-making process. 'Equilibrium is maintained by the countervailing power of different groups with different groups with different power bases.'

4. The state in a plural society can be regarded as a set of neutral institutions which serve to adjudicate between social and economic interests. The state serves to protect *all* economic interests by accommodating and reconciling them. It does not defend the interests of one class at the expense of another.

5. No class, interest or organisation is consistently successful in obtaining its objectives across the whole range of public policies. Most public policies, in the end, express the preference of the majority.

6. The pre-war power of the capitalist class over economic concerns has been progressively dismantled by the transference of economic power to the state itself (nationalisation) and to the trade union movement.

7. Although every state has its elites, including a political elite, a plural state is characterised by a plurality of elites. Clearly, in a complex society with large-scale organisations, power cannot be exercised by the direct participation of the masses in the decision-making process. Inevitably political representatives and leaders have to take on that task on behalf of the electorate. But this process is not elitist or anti-democratic because the composition of leadership groups is open to people from varied class backgrounds according to merit. Competition for power between elites and between political parties ensures that no single group will be dominant.

8. In Britain different economic, social, political, professional, administrative and other elites lack the cohesion necessary to turn them into a ruling class.

9. Since the Second World War there has been a marked decline in class-based and ideological politics in Britain. Samuel Beer* has described how the political system now reflects a general consensus between the different interests based on the acceptance of the welfare state and the mixed economy (see Chapter 9).

Playford in *The Myth of Pluralism* explains how the belief in pluralism is also given as the reason why democracy works in America. 'It is assumed that power in America is distributed in such a manner as to guarantee that no one group can dominate any particular segment

---

* *Modern British Politics*, Samuel Beer, Faber & Faber, London, 1965.

of society.' Pluralism guarantees freedom, diversity, the limitation of power and protection against extremist mass movements. Kariel in *The Promise of Politics* describes how 'virtually all the academic studies of American politics undertaken today seem to confirm this soothing vision of American politics, as an interminable process which gives every interest its due'. Playford does not accept this vision. Rather he demonstrates how 'liberal rhetoric' is used to uphold 'a most conservative ideology'. He quotes Schattschneider, who shows how pluralist policies ignore the diffuse, the unorganised and the inarticulate, how pluralism has a very pronounced business or upper-class bias and is loaded and unbalanced in favour of a fraction of a minority of the American people: 'The flaw in the pluralist heaven is that the heavenly chorus sings with a strong upper-class accent. Probably about 90 per cent of the people cannot get into the system.' The institutions which are said to sustain the rights of the individual against a unified ruling class are themselves 'oligarchically governed hierarchies' which actually seek to limit constitutional democracy.

In American pluralism does not extend its tolerance for diversity to those groups which might threaten the perpetuation of the social order. Those operating outside the consensus of shared values are discussed as 'dangerous extremists', 'irrational crackpots' or 'foreign agents'. According to Perrow in *The Sociological Perspective of Political Pluralism*, one of the major defects of pluralism is the view that 'conflict on the part of the least privileged is automatically disruptive, while the harmony of interests exists for those who have interests worth harmonising'.

So far as the 'neutral state' is concerned, Kariel suggests that the government in America systematically favours the interests of the stronger against the weaker and by acting to strengthen the power of those who already hold it, the government plays a conservative rather than a neutral role in American society.

Miliband, in *The State in Capitalist Society*, applies similar criticisms in his analysis of the relationship between capital, labour and the state in Britain. Although labour might be deemed to represent the majority of the population, its power in comparison to the power of capital is much less. The classic pluralist fallacy is that all groups have equal resources. In fact, producer groups are much more powerful than consumer groups. Sectional interests are generally more powerful than promotional interests. Some 'interests' are poorly organised and others are not organised at all. So far as capital and labour are concerned, it is capital that enjoys more influence with government because, quite simply, it controls economic resources. Just as labour, however well organised, cannot make the kind of economic decisions which the owners of capital can make because they own the production process, so neither can they exert the kind of influence which affects the economic decisions made by the state. Labour has no foreign support, 'there are no labour equivalents of the "gnomes" of Zurich, no labour equivalents of the World Bank, or the OECD, to ensure that governments desist from taking measures detrimental to wage earners and favourable to business; or to press for policies which are of advantage to "lower income groups" and which are opposed to the interests of economic elites'.

Labour's biggest weapon, the strike, is vulnerable, its leadership is less representative of the rank and file of its membership than is the case with business organisations. Labour is more often internally divided than in business organisations. Labour leaders have less access than business leaders to senior politicians and to officials in the administration of government, simply because business leaders share the same social, educational and ideological values as top politicians and civil servants. Common values, a 'spiritual rapport' and close economic connections all give much greater advantage to capital than labour when it comes to winning the ear of the executive. And just as less privileged groups and groups posing potential threats to the status quo are vilified in America, in Britain it is always easier to define labour demands as 'sectional', 'detrimental', 'selfish', 'unrealistic', or 'unsound'. The demands of capital, on the other hand, are always claimed to be 'in the national interest' and more important, capital, because of its control over economic resources, can act to promote its own definition of the 'public interest' by refusing to cooperate with the state in the implementation of economic policies of which it does not approve. Capital can also bring more resources to bear when it comes to influencing opinion. Much more than labour, it can count on 'free' propaganda from the supposedly 'neutral' mass media (see p. 143) and when necessary can supply funds for lobbying and propaganda purposes.

A further defect of pluralist theory is the extent to which it ignores the consequences of having, or not having, money in relation to other aspects of social life. Economic resources are closely linked to personal security, educational opportunities, the scope for travel and recreation, diet, health and countless other considerations which comprise the general quality of life. For those who lack economic resources and whose general conditions of life and standard of living are inferior as a consequence, it is unrealistic to talk in terms of political, social and economic power being fairly and evenly distributed, with no single group exercising undue control.

In this respect the process by which the exercise of unequal power is 'made legitimate' is interesting to theorists of all persuasions.

Legitimacy

Legitimacy is usually defined as 'the justification of power by reference to accepted values'. When power is made legitimate, it is imbued with authority. By means of legitimation, popular consent is gained for the exercise of power and the business of governing is freed from the need to rely on 'brute force'. The concern to establish legitimacy for the exercise of power is universal, but its forms and principles vary. Different societies justify 'the legitimate use of power' in different ways according to their different values. This quote from *The Ruling Class* written by Mosca and published in 1939 illustrates some of the different principles which have made power acceptable in specific groups:

'. . . Ruling classes do not justify their power exclusively by *de facto* possession of it, but try to find a moral and legal base for it, representing it as the logical and necessary consequence of doctrines and beliefs that are generally recognised and accepted. So if a society is deeply imbued with the Christian spirit the political class will govern by the will of the sovereign, who, in turn, will reign because he is God's anointed. So too in Mohammedan societies political authority is exercised directly in the name of the caliph, or vicar, or the Prophet; or in the name of someone who has received investiture, tacit or explicit, from the caliph. Chinese mandarins ruled the state because they were supposed to be interpreters of the will of the Son of Heaven, who had received from heaven the mandate to govern paternally, and in accordance with the rules of the Confucian ethic, "the people of the hundred families". . . . The powers of all lawmakers, magistrates and government officials in the United States emanate directly or indirectly from the vote of the voters, which is held to be the expression of the sovereign will of the whole of the American people'.

Legitimacy is thus a way of registering the acceptance in society that some will rule and others must obey. In most societies legitimate power tends to be restrained power, in that power holders are not entitled to do exactly as they please. For example, if the principle of legitimacy is based on popular elections, then the governing group cannot appoint its own successors but must hold elections to justify its continued power.

But not all forms of legitimacy are responsive to popular approval. Democracies require their rulers to be publicly accountable for what they do. Those who misuse power in a democratic society, or who lose the confidence of those they govern, can be replaced. But dictatorships also strive for legitimacy. Hitler justified his regime by claiming to represent the historic spirit of the German *Volk*. Others have appealed to tradition or religion as the basis of authority.

Different societies are characterised by different principles and values which are used to justify the exercise of power in a way which is legitimate. But this is not to say that the values and principles which ensure legitimacy are beyond critical examination. Pluralists and Marxists, for example, would interpret the process of legitimation in Britain quite differently.

The Pluralist Interpretation of Legitimation

Brian Smith* outlines the system of power and decision-making which dominant values in our society make legitimate. He likens the policy-making process to a game, in that it is 'rule-bound'. The relevant rules controlling the exercise of power are to be found partly in the constitution and partly in the political, social and cultural values which prescribe how political activity should be carried on. Constitutional rules set down how those in positions of authority should be recruited and how they should perform their tasks—for example, the procedure for electing MPs or appointing top civil servants. These 'rules' are made up of laws, customs and conventions which enable others to recognise offices and office holders and to recognise the related authority of their actions. The 'authority' bestowed on the actions of office holders depends on legitimacy having been achieved and on popular acceptance and respect for their position. Such respect is based on 'fundamental values and beliefs' about how relationships between government and the governed should be organised and about what is 'moral' and 'proper'. This set of beliefs, values, perceptions and emotions is generally known as the 'political culture'. Whilst the political culture of Britain reflects a broad, general consensus about the exercise of power, there are variations within it. According to pluralists, political culture is a dynamic force. Shifts in opinions and competing values effect changes in the scope of government policies, and governments are highly susceptible to the variety and balance of public opinion on different issues. Smith outlines his theory of legitimate power in Britain in terms of six main elements.

1. Democracy

The British system of government is democratic. Governments are elected and their decisions are expected to reflect the wishes of the people.

2. Representation

Because participatory democracy (i.e. everyone participating *directly* in the process of government) is impossible, representative democracy is the most acceptable alternative. In Britain the election of representatives who then act on behalf of their electors is not automatic. In practice MPs are 'not expected to act as delegates or as agents of their constituents'. Once in parliament they can vote according to their conscience—which in practice usually means according to their party line.

However, the fact that politicians have to be periodically elected ensures that they will be responsive to their electorate, otherwise they

---

* Smith, *op. cit.*

risk losing office. In this sense, argues Smith, the people can be said to be 'in charge' because they transmit their wishes to government and begin the process of legislation and policy making by voting for certain candidates rather than others.

3. Majority Government

Given that there are disagreements between parties and within government, conflict is resolved democratically by action being taken on the basis of majority decisions. It is not a question of the majority being 'right' and the minority being 'wrong'. According to Benn and Peters,* 'the majority is a shifting aggregate of interests and its only claim to prevail is that it is more numerous, not that it is more virtuous'.

Despite majority rule, the rights of minorities are preserved in notions of free speech and the right to organise for political ends. Majority rule is also based on the notion that those in power shall abide by the same laws as those who are not. A 'neutral' and 'impartial' judiciary has been set up to ensure that justice free from political bias is preserved.

4. Responsible Government

Office holders have a responsibility to fulfil their tasks properly and they are accountable to the elected representatives of the people. Governments have to 'answer to parliament' for their actions and resign if their actions prove to be unacceptable. Ministers are responsible for their own behaviour and for the conduct of those in their ministries. Again, if they are 'found wanting' in any serious way, they must resign their office. The paid officials who support government in the process of legislation and decision-making are supposed to be 'anonymous and loyal servants of the government, neutral in their political outlook, and recruited on the basis of merit, a qualification which excludes ideological predispositions and therefore patronage'.

5. Local Democracy

The administration of many decisions at a local level is in the hands of locally elected councils and not—in theory—local officials. Local councils have been created by parliament and have responsibility for administering certain local services. This decentralisation of authority, argue the pluralists, allows for a good deal of local participation in politics and enables the decision-making process to be responsive to different and peculiar local circumstances.

---

* *Social Principles and the Democratic State*, S. I. Benn and R. S. Peters, Allen & Unwin, London, 1971.

6. Consensus

The last element in Smith's theory of legitimate power is based on the level of consensus which is thought to exist to support the values outlined above. 'The British political system is thought to be one of the most stable in the world . . . a lack of profound ideological disputes about the nature of society and the economy and the existence of a relatively high level of confidence in and respect for British political arrangements has led to both substantive and procedural consensus. Neither religion, nationalism nor class threatens this consensus.' (Marxists also note the strength of this apparent consensus, but attribute rather different qualities to it as we shall discover in a moment.)

The pluralist explanation of consensus is expressed in terms of 'trust in the political elite', the feeling that despite individual likes and dislikes, the majority of politicians and office holders 'can be relied on' to do as good a job as anyone else. So long as government decisions appear to be fair and just, and not obviously discriminatory, then the system will be respected.

The Process of Legitimation—A Marxist Analysis

The specific characteristic of Marxist analysis is the way in which it regards the political system in relation to the economic system. Unlike pluralist analysis, political institutions are not thought to be autonomous and independent institutions legitimated by the general principles and values of democracy. Power resides with the ruling class who derive their power from their ownership of wealth, property and the production process. The ruling class uses the political system—as it uses all the complementary systems—to maintain its own dominance over subject classes.

According to Marxists, therefore, the political sector is controlled by the economically dominant class, who either hold the positions of power themselves (e.g. cabinet ministers, senior civil servants, diplomats and judges), or whose control of big business, the army, the church, academia and the mass media, is used to 'mould' and maintain the political system in a way which suits ruling class interests. The extent to which the ruling class has been able to make its own class interests *appear to be* the interests of the whole society means that it does not really matter whether it wields power directly or not.

Its class rule does not depend on force, although during times of crisis in British political and social history, the army and the police have been used, and are used, to quell opposition (e.g. during the general strike, in Northern Ireland and at major left-wing demonstrations). Much more effective than coercive power is the capacity to 'engineer consent' and to persuade those who are not members of the ruling class that they none the less share common values and common interests with those who are.

Thus Marxist analysis points to the ways in which religion, education, the mass media, party politics and the legal system all combine to present a particular 'view of the world' as if it were the *only* view of the world—and certainly the only one which represents the national interest.

The theoretical origins of the analysis come not only from Marx but from other Marxist theorists like Gramsci and Althusser. In *The German Ideology* Marx offered the now famous formulation that 'the ideas of the ruling class in every epoch are the ruling ideas' because 'the class which is the ruling material [economic] force in society is at the same time its ruling intellectual force. The class which has the means of material production at its disposal, has control, at the same time, over the means of mental production, so that, generally speaking, the ideas of those who lack the means of mental production are subject to it.'

Hegemony

Gramsci referred to the achievement by which the dominant class has been able to establish its ideological and cultural control over others as hegemony. Pluralists argue that increasing industrialisation, education and the spread of representative democracy have all served to erode the hegemony of the ruling class. Marxists argue that it has not been eroded so much as modified and adapted to suit changing social circumstances. Miliband points out that 'hegemony is not simply something which happens, as a mere superstructural (see p. 42) derivative of economic and social predominance. It is, in very large part, the result of permanent and pervasive effort, conducted through a multitude of agencies, and deliberately intended to create 'social consensus at both national and interpersonal levels of communication. The achievement of hegemony in terms of attitudes, values and beliefs—the whole realm of ideas—is the result of systematic socialisation, not to say "a process of massive indoctrination".'

Gramsci and Althusser attributed the major task of socialisation and the maintenance of ideological hegemony to the ruling class operating through the 'non-political' institutions of law, mass communications, religion, family life, education, etc., and assumed that the state (i.e. the political system) would merely maintain the necessary balance between coercion and consent. In many respects this is still an accurate analysis—political socialisation does come directly from the political system—but during the last hundred years or so the state has come to play a much more important part in it. The state now intervenes much more directly in economic life, in the organisation of education and in welfare provisions than it once did and all of these interventions can be explained (in Marxist terms anyway) as the introduction of policies which confirm the interests of the ruling class rather than those of subject groups (see Chapters 4, 7 and 9).

In his book *The State in Capitalist Society*, Ralph Miliband provides one of the clearest contemporary accounts of the process of legitimation based on Marxist social theories. He examines a number of key institutions:

1. Political Parties

As in all advanced capitalist countries there is at least one political party which most directly represents the interests of business and capital. In Britain it is the Conservative Party. Whilst the Conservative Party is predominantly the party of the ruling class, to appear legitimate it has had to attract popular membership. Thus lower middle-class and working-class people have been encouraged to join the Conservative Party and Conservative governments rely on the votes of considerable numbers of working-class voters to achieve electoral success. But whilst the Conservative Party can count on the support of a wide cross-section of the population, its leading figures, at both national and local level, are drawn from the upper and upper middle classes and include a substantial number of businessmen. When it comes to disseminating conservative ideas about free enterprise and competitive initiative, for example, the Conservative Party is obviously a major channel of pro-Conservative and anti-Socialist ideas. Of course, all political parties attempt to influence public opinion, but because of substantial donations from industry and from private benefactors the Conservative party has always got more to spend on general propaganda, local organisation and national campaigns than other political parties. The financial contribution that the trade union movement makes to the Labour Party has never been able to match that which is given to the Conservative Party by business interests.

Clearly it is much easier for the ruling class to work through a political party which explicitly represents its interests, but to maintain its hegemony over other classes, it must also be able to ensure that other parties do not present too radical an alternative. Miliband notes how the first Labour Prime Minister, Ramsay MacDonald, ended up by heading a coalition 'National Government' in which the Conservative Party had 556 seats out of 615.

John Rex * describes how Hugh Gaitskell and his intellectual mentor Anthony Crosland had established by 1953 that the Labour Party was no longer concerned about 'changing the system', but with getting fairer shares within it. Harold Wilson and James Callaghan continued the trend of trying to appeal not to the traditional working class with

---

* Rex, *op. cit.*

a programme of radical socialist policies, but to the aspiring working class and the middle class with moderate policies only marginally different from those endorsed by the Conservative Party. And as the Labour Party has become more established, its representatives in Parliament have become increasingly drawn from the educated professions and the business world rather than the labour movement.

To challenge and transform capitalism—if it were to be attempted— would require a massive transformation in popular consciousness, based on a clear understanding of socialist principles. Labour leaders have never attempted this, nor is it to be expected that they would, if the abolition of capitalism is not considered to be part of their purpose.

2. Religion

It used to be said that the Church of England was the Conservative Party at prayer and certainly throughout the nineteenth century the Church of England clergy visibly supported the Tory party. The position of the churches is more discreet today. With increasing secularisation they do not have as much influence and power as they once did and they have chosen, like top civil servants, judges and military men, to claim a neutrality which puts them 'above politics'. Their influence is nonetheless conservative, however. Even Methodism and other nonconformist churches, which at one time were associated with more radical ideas, are now more concerned with preaching an acceptance of the social and political order rather than opposition to it. Practising Christians are likely to express concern for the poor and the underprivileged both in this country and in the Third World—but this is more an extension of the churches' traditional concern about 'Christian charity' than any analysis which would lead to an attack on the economics of capitalism.

In the same way loyalty to the state, to the monarchy and to the nation in times of war, all help to express support for and confirm existing power structures rather than challenge them. And even though the churches may no longer count on direct influence over large congregations, the habits of obedience and the definitions of morality which religion teaches are voiced continually by church leaders in the ritual and ceremonial life of the country.

3. Nationalism

Nationalism among the Scots and the Welsh in recent years, and historically among the Irish, may be seen as a threat to the prevailing social order. But nationalism is most often a conservative ideology in advanced capitalist countries like Britain. Miliband comments: 'From the point of view of dominant classes, nothing could be so obviously advantageous as the assertion which forms one of the basic themes of nationalism, namely that all citizens, whoever they may be, owe a supreme allegiance to a "national interest", which requires that men (and women) should be ready to subdue all other interests, particularly class interests, for the sake of a larger, more comprehensive concern which unites in a supreme allegiance rich and poor, the comfortable and the deprived, the givers of orders and their recipients.' The denunciation as 'detrimental to the national interest' is frequently made about actions such as strikes and 'inflationary' wage demands. These are rarely denounced as being detrimental to employers but always as being injurious to the nation. 'National unity' is a theme to which both Labour and Conservative politicians repeatedly return in an attempt to mobilise electoral support. Shared memories of past struggles and contemporary victories are celebrated in a way which emphasis national solidarity. The monarchy plays a crucial symbolic and unifying role in this respect and even 'the dead are called into service once again' to help legitimise the regimes for which they died.

4. Advertising

Of course business interests are not above promoting themselves through organisations like the CBI, Aims of Industry and the Economic League. But one of the most effective ways of propagating a way of life, which also serves the interests of industry, is by advertising. By means of advertising, and the sophisticated propaganda of public relations, business interests do not only sell products, they also sell business 'as an activity wholly beneficial not only to those who own it, but to those who work for it, to those who buy from it and to society at large'.

Even more pervasive is the extent to which business interests and free enterprise generally are associated with socially approved values and aspirations. Products and the companies which make them can be 'relied upon' to 'serve the consumers', 'enhance family life' and bring 'happiness and comfort' to countless millions. It is not just that advertising helps business by stimulating demand for products in an acquisitive society, but also it helps to distract public attention from the fulfilment of other genuine and real human needs. It helps, in the Marxist phrase, to create 'false consciousness' so that personal acquisition is offered as the way of achieving success, happiness and fulfilment rather than the elimination of materialism and exploitation in social relationships. The concern of advertising then, is not merely to sell goods, its more important purpose is to sell a particular way of life.

5. The Mass Media

The ownership and control of the media by big business is discussed in Chapter 6. One or two additional points can be made here to illustrate the ways in which the media also serve to legitimate the prevailing distribution of power in society, despite claims to independence and impartiality.

Merton and Lazerfield in *Mass Communication, Popular Taste and Organised Social Action* argue that, so far as socialisation and indoctrination go, the media in advanced capitalist societies have assumed the task of 'rendering mass publics conformative to the social and political system'.

Not only are the majority of newspapers owned for economic gain and partisan in their support of the Conservative Party (see p. 156) but also alternative (i.e. oppositional) groups are given very little sympathy—e.g. strikers, communists, blacks, gays, foreign revolutionary movements, etc. In claiming the freedom of the press to be a 'public watchdog on behalf of the community', more often than not it is the activities of minority groups and left-wing movements which are most consistently 'watched'.

Television and radio claim to be more objective and more impartial than newspapers. Both sides of an argument are put in discussions and the main political parties are given identical air-time to promote and defend their ideas. But this 'impartiality' exists within very narrow limits. By denying, for example, equal air-time to the Communist Party, or the Anti-Nazi League, or even the National Front, media impartiality stops at the point at which political consensus stops. The more radical the dissent, the less impartial and objective the media are likely to be.

A good deal of sociological evidence about the effects of television on political opinion and public attitudes seems to conclude that news and comment, entertainment and advertising, political propaganda and moral rhetoric are more concerned with, and more likely to confirm and reinforce, existing beliefs, than to challenge them. But in situations in which consumers of the media are relatively inexperienced— either because they are children or because their personal experience is limited—the media can become the major source of information and interpretation (see p. 147).

There are those who argue that the media are really only concerned about entertainment and to accuse them of conservative indoctrination is unfounded. Certainly monopoly control in the entertainment industry (see p. 143) suggests a preoccupation with making profit out of recreation rather than anything else, but whilst the *purpose* of the entertainment industry may be profit, its *content* is rarely free from ideological connotations of one kind or another. In recent years newspapers, magazines, television and the cinema have all been criticised for explicit sexism and racism in their treatment of women and ethnic minority groups. Both trends reinforce stereotyped opinions which are more likely to confirm existing social and economic structures than to challenge them. And it is certainly difficult to think of popular television heroes, for example, who, however innocuously, present radical, left-wing or revolutionary views as an alternative to the overwhelming concentration on 'canned American values' and trivial 'situation comedies'.

Some have called television the new 'opiate of the masses'. Given the economic and political context in which television and the rest of the media operate, 'they cannot fail to be predominantly agencies for the dissemination of ideas and values which affirm rather than challenge existing patterns of power and privilege' and as a result play an important part in the process of legitimation.

6. Education

Despite the commonly held view that politics has no place in education, sociologists of all ideological persuasions have consistently challenged this assumption. It is possible to distinguish between political indoctrination of a narrow party-political nature and more hidden, less explicit political socialisation. Whilst party-political bias is not present to any significant extent in most education provision, Miliband argues that nonetheless 'educational institutions at all levels generally fulfil an important conservative role and act, with greater or lesser effectiveness, as legitimation agencies in and for their societies'. We have noted in Chapter 4 the social, political, economic and control functions fulfilled by schooling. Miliband explains the same process in terms of three levels of legitimation. The first level is the 'class-confirming' role of education, in which the education system serves to socialise young recruits into their future adult roles. In this respect there is a marked difference between the educational experience of ruling-class children in public and independent schools, for example, and working-class children in the lower streams of comprehensive schools. For some working-class children, schooling does provide the possibility of social mobility but the majority are confirmed in their social position, rather than 'educated out of it'.

The second level of legitimation is to make it appear as though working-class children do less well than middle-class children in school as a consequence of their own personal inadequacy and cultural deficiency (see p. 97). This is compounded by the imposition of middle-class cultural values which are alien to the cultural experiences of working-class children. The aim is to attempt 'to integrate the working-class child into the *given* society; those who are bright are helped to prepare their escape from their working class condition; the rest are helped to accept their subordination'.

That help at the third level of legitimation assumes a fairly clear ideological and political form. Durkheim, writing about education and society, described the need to ensure that children are socialised into accepting 'fundamental values' and 'essential principles'. The point is, of course, that the definitions of 'fundamental' and 'essential' are unlikely to be neutral and more likely to reflect the values of dominant forces in society.

As we have seen (see p. 124), schools may not always succeed in ensuring the acceptance of the prevailing power structure in society— but they certainly set out to try. Moreover, if Bowles and Gintis are right (see p. 103), education is little more than a 'training ground' in which the relationships of production, essential to the survival of a capitalist economy, are instilled.

What happens in schools is considerably influenced not only by the economic and political structures of society but also by the selection, control and management of knowledge in the curriculum and through the examination system. In this respect the universities continue to play a determining role. Despite the claims about 'academic freedom' and the 'neutrality of knowledge', universities also contribute to a rather one-sided view of things.

The universities are very dependent on the state for finance, but can accrue additional funds from the sponsorship of wealthy patrons and industrialists. It is unlikely, therefore, that university policies would ever seriously challenge prevailing economic interests or the integrity of the political system. And just as schools have boards of governors and managers, so too do universities receive similar guidance and sanction from the local 'leaders of the community' who sit on their governing bodies. In practice, these are the representatives of local industry, financiers of various kinds, politicians and 'respected' members of the older professions.

In *The German Ideology* Marx refers to intellectuals as 'the thinkers of the [ruling] class (its active, conceptive ideologists, who make the perfecting of illusion of the class about itself their chief source of livelihood)'. Despite the activities of radical intellectuals and radical students, those who can be described as conservative always outnumber radical minorities. And more than this, it is the conservatives who hold power in the university structure. In 1967 it was estimated that 49.3 per cent of the heads of colleges and professors at Oxford and Cambridge (i.e. almost half) and 32.5 per cent (almost one third) of the vice chancellors, heads of colleges and professors at English and Welsh universities had been to public school. Either by origin, education or achievement they and the majority of their fellows are more likely to identify socially with ruling groups than any others and in this respect can be seen as part of the same social elite which exercises general control in all major institutions.

Gramsci also depicts intellectuals as 'experts in legitimation'. They contribute to the stability of the prevailing social system not merely by actively promoting it but also by helping to prevent the intellectual and practical development of a counter-consciousness. The knowledge and ideas used to educate and train future economists, lawyers, businessmen, teachers and social workers, for example, may encourage controversy and debate about such issues as educational failure, deviance and poverty, but the controversy most often flourishes within manageable limits. Rarely does criticism of the economic basis of the social order occur, and students are most often encouraged to seek 'solutions' to 'problems' within the constraints of the system, rather than attempt to transform social and economic relationships. Such educational experience produces cohorts of liberal-minded and generally well-intentioned social workers, teachers, probation officers and community workers, prepared to act as 'professional go-betweens', to administer and control the poor on behalf of the state. If the Marxist analysis is correct and the state functions to endorse the economic interests of the ruling class, then the actions of the 'caring professions', as employees of the state, might also be said to satisfy and to legitimate those same interests.

Political Acquiescence

The outcome of the legitimation process, according to Marxist analysis, can be measured by the extent to which the ruling class has been able to 'engineer consent' and create 'false consciousness' among subject classes. As we have seen, the main institutions of 'mental production' are either in the hands of the ruling class or their representatives and are used to create and sustain a broad consensus among the masses generally, which enables those with privileged economic interests to defend to do so in line with what appears to be the 'national interest'. But part of the responsibility for the lack of opposition to ruling ideas must be sought in the condition of subject classes themselves. Marx was aware that a class *for* itself is very different in its degree of consciousness to a class *in* itself (see p. 41) and the economic relations of production, whilst creating the possibility of social change through class conflict, also 'develops a working class which by education, tradition and habit looks upon the condition of that mode of production as the self-evident law of nature'. This kind of fatalism induces enormous mental barriers when it comes to opposition and, as George Orwell describes in *The Road to Wigan Pier*, the 'business of petty inconvenience and indignity, of being kept waiting about, of having to do everything at other people's convenience, is inherent in working-class life. A thousand influences constantly press a working man down into a passive role'.

Working-class parents who have themselves learned deference and accepted subordination are likely to pass on the same behaviour to their children, and even those who actively seek improvement in their social conditions are more likely to encourage their children to aspire to the acquisitions, values and prejudices of the middle class, rather than to denounce them. In short, as Miliband also concludes, 'the condition of the working class itself is a major element in its political socialisation, and provides fertile ground for all the other forces which seek to enhance that position'.

Politics and Power

If this kind of analysis of the process of legitimation is correct, we should not be surprised to find that despite their 'real' class interests, considerable numbers of working-class voters can regularly be relied upon to endorse policies, to take on board values and to accept arguments which are not really in their best interests.

Similarly, since a general consensus based on notions of democracy, national unity and freedom of choice has been effectively established, even though many of the contestants may be 'nobbled' from the start they all run in what appears to be the same race, they rarely stop to ask who devised the rules, they accept their handicaps with equanimity and they respect those who have defeated them. Occasional disappointments (on average once every five years) can lead to a change of umpire and timekeepers, but in most cases the new officials know who their real sponsors are and have little or no intention of risking their displeasure, or seriously trying to rewrite their rules.

If the pluralist analysis is correct, the 'rules of the game' are there to ensure fair play. All the contestants have as great or as little chance of winning as everyone else and a bit of competition helps to keep them all on their toes.

Without taking the sporting analogy any further, pluralists would point to the regular changes in the composition of parliament as evidence that shifts in public loyalties and policy expectations are being democratically reflected. Marxists would question whether a 'mere' change of government from one party to another, in a system which is already heavily committed to a particular distribution of power and influence, really makes very much difference.

Those electors 'bored with politics' and 'tired of politicians who all sound the same' are usually criticised for their apathy and lack of knowledge. But maybe it is worth considering whether, in one sense at least, they have hit the nail precisely on the head.

Revision

1. Refresh Your Memory

Make sure you know the meaning of the terms: consensus, ruling class, elite, plural society, pressure group, mixed economy, propaganda, dictatorship, coercive power, hegemony, secularisation.

2. Check Your Understanding

Be able to explain in your own words the difference between:

(*a*) Mills' and Parsons' definitions of power.
(*b*) Promotional interests and sectional interests.
(*c*) Representative and participatory democracy.
(*d*) Political parties and political pressure groups.
(*e*) The Labour Party and the labour movement.
(*f*) Legitimate and non-legitimate power.
(*g*) Political culture and political socialisation.
(*h*) National government and local government.

3. Essay Questions to Try

(*a*) Compare and contrast the three main explanations of the power structure: ruling class, elitism and pluralism.

(*b*) Is there any difference between the ruling class and 'the establishment' in Britain?

(*c*) To what extent can the development of industrial societies be seen as a movement from a class system of elites, from a social hierarchy based on the inheritance of property to one based upon merit and achievement?

(*d*) To what extent can Britain be described as a pluralist society?

(*e*) How effective are the checks and controls which operate in a democracy when it comes to preventing the abuse of power?

(*f*) 'The extent to which the ruling class has been able to make its own class interests appear to be the interests of the whole society means that it does not really matter whether it wields power or not.' How far do you agree with this interpretation?

(*g*) To what extent is the general consensus about politics in Britain the consequence of 'shared values' or 'massive indoctrination'?

Further Reading

Decisions, Organisations and Society, edited by F. G. Castles *et al.*, Penguin, London, Second Edition, 1976.

Introduction to British Politics, P. J. Madgewick, Hutchinson, London, Second Edition, 1976.

Policy Making in British Government, Brian Smith, Martin Robertson, Oxford, 1976.

Power in Britain, John Urry and John Wakeford (eds.), Heinemann, London, 1973.

The State in Capitalist Society, Ralph Miliband, Quartet, London, 1973.

Glossary

Action research. Research carried out in order to improve a social situation, to 'change for the better' an individual, social group or organisation.

Alienation. An individual or group feels separated from some aspect of their lives, leading to, for example, a feeling of powerlessness. Usually used in connection with a person's work situation.

Altruism. The belief that the well-being of others is more important than one's own.

Anomie. Normlessness. It is said to occur during a period of rapid social change where the rules and norms governing behaviour are disrupted, so members of society are no longer sure what these rules are.

Anthropology. The study of man, involving a comparative approach to primitive societies.

Association. A number of individuals who come together for a specific purpose and whose interaction is limited.

Automation. The process whereby men are replaced by machines which are usually computer-controlled.

Behaviourism. A school of psychology which believes that all human behaviour is learned. The term sometimes describes an approach in sociology which stresses the individual and his/her interaction with others.

Bourgeoisie. The group who developed between the nobles and the peasants in the early stages of urbanisation. In the Marxian sense the bourgeoisie are the group in industrial societies who own wealth or capital.

Bureaucracy. A particular type of organisation most frequently found in modern societies. Max Weber drew up an ideal type of bureaucracy based on the rational-legal principle of authority, and saw this type of organisation as being the most efficient for modern industrial societies.

Capital. Wealth which can be used to produce more wealth e.g. money, stocks and shares, factory equipment.

Caste. A closed form of stratification where individuals are born into a particular caste or social group, and stay there for life. Found in Hindu society in India.

Charisma. 'Personal magnetism' enabling its owner to lead and influence people without the backing of a formal organisation such as an army or political party.

Community. Can be used geographically, but usually refers to a group of people who are bound quite closely together by the ties of kinship, neighbourliness, etc.

Concept. A word or words expressing a particular notion or idea.

Conjugal. To do with marriage: a conjugal family is one based on marriage rather than kin.

279

Consanguine. To do with blood-relationships: a consanguine family is one based on kinship rather than marriage.

Counter-culture. A group of people within society whose values and norms are different from and go against those held in the wider society.

Culture. The way of life of a society, consisting of norms and values. Involves behaviour which is learned and passed on from generation to generation.

Deference. Willingness to conform to the will of someone else purely on the basis of that person's superior wisdom, social standing, etc., as in 'deference voter'—one who votes Conservative because the belief that they are the natural leaders of society.

Delinquency. Socially disapproved behaviour, usually used in connection with juvenile crime.

Demography. Vital statistics of a society; the study of population.

Determinism. The belief that man is not free to think and act but is determined by forces outside his own will.

Deviance. Behaviour which does not fit the expectations of a social group, i.e. an act has to be seen to be deviant in order to be deviant.

Division of labour. Specialisation of roles, usually within a factory or other work situation, but also in society as a whole.

Dysfunction. An action which has the consequence of instability and mal-integration for a social system.

Elite. A group of people at the top of a social hierarchy who have considerable power over the other members of the hierarchy.

Empirical. Based on observed evidence of real events rather than on speculation about supposed events.

Empiricism. The belief or doctrine that all knowledge and thought is a product of sensuous experience—the formulation of scientific laws through observation and experiment.

Endogamy. Marriage within one's own kinship network or social group.

Epistemology. The theory or science of the methods of the grounds of knowledge.

Ethnic group. A group which has cultural characteristics in common, such as religion or dress.

Ethnocentrism. A term used by W. Sumner: a view of things in which one's own group is the centre of everything and all others are scaled and rated with reference to it.

Ethnomethodology. The study of the methods used by members of society to order and make mutual sense of activities in their everyday interaction.

Exogamy. Marriage outside one's own kinship network or social group.

Folkways. Customs, e.g. passing on a craft from father to son, type of dress, etc.

Function. A sociological concept that stresses the interdependence of the parts of society. It is concerned with the consequences or effects of social behaviour for the rest of society rather than the motives or causes of that behaviour. Functionalists believe that if something exists in society it is necessary to that society, i.e. it is functional.

Genetic. Inherited from our parents by means of the genes in the chromosomes in our cells.

Hierarchy. Concept of a ladder structure usually involving groups of people in a ranked order according to the amount of power they have over others.
Hypothesis. A supposition which is put forward for testing.

Industrialisation. The process whereby an increasing proportion of the population is employed in industry as opposed to agriculture.
Innate. Behaviour which has been inherited, not learnt.
Institutions. Social institutions refer to the organisation of established patterns of behaviour that are widespread, generally accepted as normal, and considered important within a given society, e.g. the family.

Kinship. The set of social relationships which are based on 'blood' or marriage ties.

Mechanisation. The process by which jobs, usually skilled crafts, are replaced by machinery.
Mechanistic. Like machines: used to describe explanations which treat human beings as if they were pieces of machinery.
Methodology. The philosophy of science; the study of the methods used in arriving at knowledge.
Milieu. Environment or surroundings.
Mobility. The ability to move—used in the geographical and the social sense.
Mores. The more salient or important norms within a society. Breaking them involves social sanction.

Norm. The standard of behaviour expected of individuals by their social group.

Objectivity. Emotional and moral detachment from the subject under investigation.

Paradigm. A preliminary model consisting of ideas and propositions, etc., which guide research.
Peer group. Usually used in relation to adolescence: a group of individuals of a similar age or social status with whom people identify.
Phenomenology. Essentially the study of the ways in which human reason orders human experience.
Positivism. The belief that the methods used by the natural sciences are the only legitimate ones for social scientists to use.
Power. The capacity to influence the behaviour of others.
Pragmatism. A philosophy based on the conception that the truth of a doctrine should be judged on its practical consequences.
Primary group. A group where the members have face-to-face interaction—they have a variety of shared interests, e.g. families, neighbours in a small community.
Proletariat. Marx used the term to refer to industrial workers and agricultural

labourers who had to work for wages because they owned no capital, though it can mean low-class people anywhere.

Reductionism. The branch of theory which reduces the important influences on society to one, e.g. technology.

Reference group. The group to which we refer for a model of our values, beliefs and behaviour. We do not have to be a member of the group ourselves, but may wish to be.

Role. The part a person plays in a social group—it is the product of interaction with others where their expectations of the person's behaviour are taken into account.

Sanction. Punishment or reward designed to control behaviour.

Secondary group. A group whose members share a common activity, but the activity only involves part of them, e.g. membership of a town or college.

Social class. A supposedly open form of stratification, usually found in industrial societies and related to a person's occupation, income and wealth.

Social control. Refers to the ways in which members of society or social groups are influenced to comply and conform with the established patterns of behaviour. Can be formal or informal.

Social stratification. The ranking of social groups in a hierarchical order, e.g. caste is the social stratification system found in Hindu India.

Social structure. The sum total of social organisations and social relationships within society.

Socialisation. The transmission of norms and values which results in individuals having a set of socially standardised ways of looking at the world.

Society. A general term covering the total collection of relationships of a population.

Status. A person's social position as defined by other members of the community. It has been said that role is the 'acting out' of status.

Tautology. Repeating something in different words intending to make the meaning clearer; unnecessary repeating of the same idea in different words.

Teleology. The belief that all things and events were specifically planned to fulfil a purpose.

Urbanisation. The process whereby an increasing proportion of the population live in towns; the spread of the urban way of life.

Values. Those principles which a community or society use as guides for conduct; the fundamental beliefs of a group.

Index